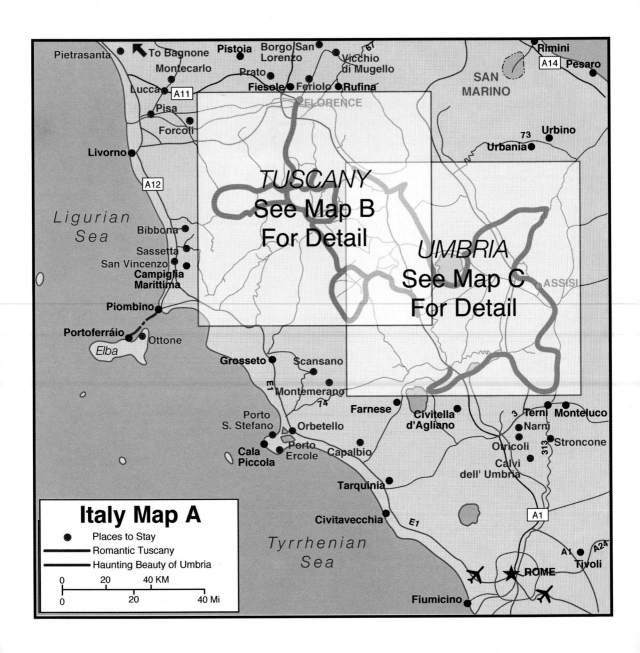

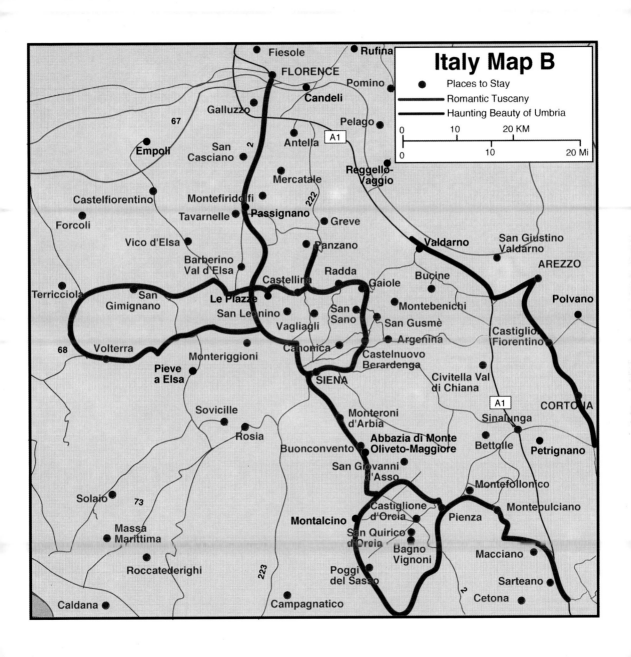

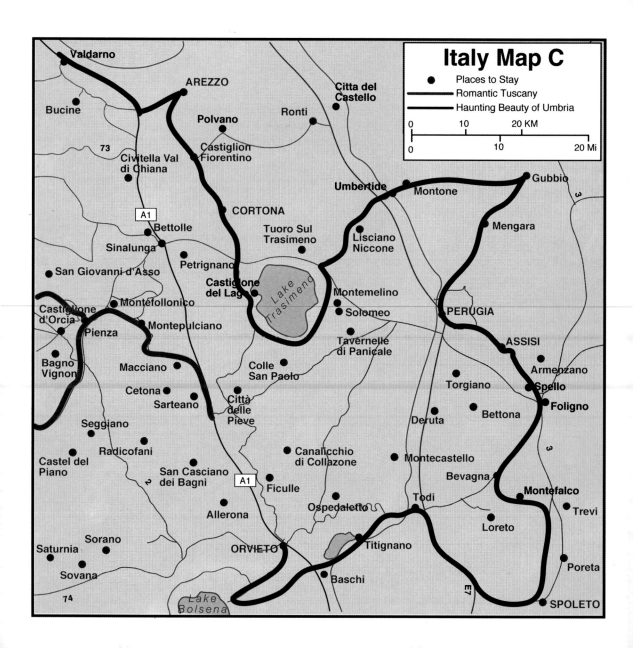

Italy Map C

- ● Places to Stay
- ── Romantic Tuscany
- ── Haunting Beauty of Umbria

0 ———— 10 ———— 20 KM
0 ———— 10 ———— 20 Mi

Valdarno

AREZZO

Citta del Castello

Bucine

Polvano

Ronti

73

Castiglion Fiorentino

Civitella Val di Chiana

Umbertide

Montone

Gubbio

3

A1

Bettolle

CORTONA

Tuoro Sul Trasimeno

Lisciano Niccone

Mengara

Sinalunga

Petrignano

Lake Trasimeno

PERUGIA

San Giovanni d'Asso

Castiglione del Lago

Montemelino

Solomeo

Montefollonico

Castiglione d'Orcia

Montepulciano

Pienza

Tavernelle di Panicale

ASSISI

Bagno Vignoni

Macciano

Colle San Paolo

Armenzano

Spello

Foligno

Cetona

Sarteano

Città delle Pieve

Torgiano

Bettona

Seggiano

Radicofani

Deruta

Castel del Piano

San Casciano dei Bagni

Canalicchio di Collazone

Montecastello

Bevagna

Montefalco

Trevi

A1

Ficulle

Allerona

Todi

Loreto

Sorano

Ospedaletto

Saturnia

ORVIETO

Titignano

Poreta

Sovana

Baschi

E7

SPOLETO

74

Lake Bolsena

Karen Brown's
TUSCANY & UMBRIA
2006

Contents

Tony
Thanks for 37 Exciting Years
June

Cover painting 2006: La Locanda, Radda in Chianti

Authors: Clare Brown, June Eveleigh Brown and Nicole Franchini.

Editors: Anthony Brown, Clare Brown, Karen Brown, Courtney Gaviorno, Debbie Tokumoto.

Illustrations: Elisabetta Franchini and Barbara Maclurcan Tapp.

Cover painting: Jann Pollard.

Photo front: Abbey Sant' Antimo

Maps: Michael Fiegel.

Technical support: Michael Fiegel, Gary Meisner.

Distributed by National Book Network, 15200 NBN Way, Blue Ridge Summit, PA 17214, USA. Tel: 717-794-3800 or 1-800-462-6420, Fax: 1-800-338-4500, Email: custserv@nbnbooks.com

A catalog record for this book is available from the British Library.

ISSN 1557 3702

Tuscany & Umbria

Tuscany and Umbria are two of our favorite destinations. The two itineraries included in this book are among the most popular of those featured in our other guides to Italy. We thought it would be a good idea to marry all of our recommended places to stay (hotels as well as bed & breakfasts) to our selected sightseeing and driving instructions. The result is our first truly regional guidebook. We hope you will find it an invaluable companion in planning your own vacation to this wonderful part of the world with its architectural treasures, historical cities, medieval hill towns, vineyards and enchanting countryside.

About Tuscany

Tuscany has become synonymous with Italy. Travelers flock to its famous cities and well-preserved countryside not only to view the breathtaking art found here, but also to be swept away by the magic of its enchanting landscapes. Florence is a highlight with its rich display of Renaissance masterpieces all concentrated within the historical center of 3 square kilometers. One must also visit the Piazza del Campo in Siena, one of Italy's most stunning squares, hosting the world-famous Palio horse races in July and August. The charming medieval hill towns of Montepulciano, Montalcino, and San Gimignano are home to some of the region's finest wines. The small historic cities of Lucca, Pisa, Arezzo, and Cortona, each with its own individual architectural characteristics, are also well worth visiting. Tuscany is also home to the famous Chianti area, with its endless vineyards and monumental castles. Maremma, in the southern, lesser-known reaches of the region touching the sea, is rich in Etruscan history and dotted with numerous stone villages to explore.

About Umbria

Enchanting Umbria, bordering Tuscany, is located in the lush heart of Italy. A circular road in the center of the region touches the well-known cities of Perugia, Assisi, Spello, Spoleto, Todi, and Deruta. The two most spectacular towns outside of the loop are Gubbio and Orvieto. Highlights include the town of Perugia, a modern-day town with the stunning Palazzo Dei Priori where the majority of the finest Umbrian paintings are exhibited in the Galleria Nazionale dell'Umbria. Assisi is another highlight with its many beautiful churches, including the mystical Basilica di San Francesco. The northern reaches of Umbria offer remote countryside and unspoiled landscapes. Umbria is home to world-famous ceramic centers, first and foremost, Deruta, and then Gubbio, producing hand-painted pieces for the past 600 years. Umbria also boasts the famous Orvieto Classico wine: varieties can be tasted at enotecas in Orvieto with its monumental cathedral and astounding façade.

About Driving Itineraries

The Tuscany and Umbria itineraries can be easily tailored to fit your exact time frame and suit your own particular interests. If your time is limited, you can certainly follow just a segment of an itinerary. In the itineraries we have not specified the number of nights at each destination, since to do so seemed much too confining. Some travelers like to see as much as possible in a short period of time. For others, just the thought of packing and unpacking each night makes them shudder in horror and they would never stop for less than three or four nights at any destination. A third type of tourist doesn't like to travel at all—the destination is the focus and he uses this guide to find the perfect place from which he never wanders except for daytime excursions. So, use this guide as a reference to plan your personalized trip.

Our advice is not to rush. Part of the joy of traveling is to settle in at a place to stay that you like and use it as a hub from which to take side trips to explore the countryside. When you dash too quickly from place to place, you never have the opportunity to get to know the owners and to become friends with other guests. Read about the places to stay and decide which are most suited to your taste and budget.

Handy Information

The following pointers are given in alphabetical order, not in order of importance.

AFFILIATIONS

A number of properties recommended in our guides belong to other private membership organizations. These associations impose their own criteria for selection and membership standards and have established a reputation for the particular type of property they include. The Abitare La Storia is an affiliation of outstanding hotels and bed & breakfasts that includes some of the finest places to stay in Italy. Two other affiliations that are very well recognized throughout Europe are the Romantik Hotels group and Relais & Châteaux. A number of properties that we recommend are members of these prestigious organizations. If a property that we recommend is also a member of Arbitare La Storia or Relais & Châteaux we note that in the bottom details of their description.

AIRFARE

Karen Brown's Guides have long recommended Auto Europe for their excellent car rental services. Their air travel division, Destination Europe, an airline broker working with major American and European carriers, offers deeply discounted coach- and business-class fares to over 200 European gateway cities. It also gives Karen Brown travelers an additional 5% discount off its already highly competitive prices (cannot be combined with any other offers or promotions). You can make reservations online via our website, *www.karenbrown.com*, or by phone at (800) 223-5555. When phoning, be sure to use the Karen Brown ID number 99006187 to secure your discount.

BANKS–CURRENCY

Normal banking hours are Monday through Friday from 8:30 am to 1:30 pm and 3 to 4 pm, with some city banks now opening on Saturday mornings. Cash machines accepting U.S. bank cash cards and credit cards are now widely distributed throughout Italy. An increasingly popular and convenient way to obtain foreign currency is simply to use your bankcard at an ATM machine. You pay a fixed fee for this but, depending on the amount you withdraw, it is usually less than the percentage-based fee charged to exchange currency or traveler's checks. *Cambio* signs outside and inside a bank indicate that it will exchange traveler's checks or give you cash from certain credit cards. Also privately run exchange offices are available in cities with more convenient hours and comparable rates. The euro (€) is now the official currency of most European Union countries, including Italy, and has completely replaced European national currencies. Visit our website (*www.karenbrown.com*) for an easy-to-use online currency converter.

CAR RENTAL

An international driver's permit is not necessary for renting a car as a tourist: a foreign driver's license is valid for driving throughout Italy. Readers frequently ask our advice on car rental companies. We always use Auto Europe—a car rental broker that works with the major car rental companies to find the lowest possible price. They also offer motor homes and chauffeur services. Auto Europe's toll-free phone service, from every European country, connects you to their U.S.-based, 24-hour reservation center (ask for the Europe Phone Numbers Card to be mailed to you). Auto Europe offers our readers a 5% discount (cannot be combined with any other offers or promotions) and, occasionally, free upgrades. Be sure to use the Karen Brown ID number 99006187 to receive your discount and any special offers. You can make your own reservations online via our website, *www.karenbrown.com* (select *Auto Europe* from the home page), or by phone (800-223-5555).

CREDIT CARDS

Whether or not an establishment accepts credit cards is indicated in the list of icons at the bottom of each description by the symbol [CREDIT]. We have also specified in the accommodation description which cards are accepted as follows: AX–American Express, MC–MasterCard, VS–Visa, or simply, all major.

DISTANCES

Distances are indicated in kilometers (one kilometer equals 0.621 miles), calculated roughly into miles by cutting the kilometer distance in half. Distances between towns are also indicated in orange alongside the roads on the Touring Club Italiano maps. Italy is a compact country and distances are relatively short, yet you will be amazed at how dramatically the scenery can change in an hour's drive.

DRIVING

A car is a must for this type of travel—many places are inaccessible by any other means of transportation. Italy is not quite the "vehicular-free-for-all" you may have heard about, at least not outside major cities. Italians have a different relationship with the basic rules of the road: common maneuvers include running stop lights and stop signs, triple-parking, driving at 100 mph on the highways, passing on the right, and backing up at missed highway exits. But once out of the city, you will find it relatively easy to reach your destination. Road directions are quite good in Italy and people are very willing to help.

ENGLISH SPOKEN

At most hotels there is usually someone who speaks good English. This is not always the case with bed & breakfasts and self catering accommodation. We have indicated the degree of English spoken (fluent, good, some, very little, and none) at bed and breakfasts and self catering listings as well as other languages spoken. We would like to note, however, that this is just an indication, as the person who speaks English may or may not be there during your stay. In any case, it is helpful (not to mention rewarding) to have a few basic Italian phrases on hand. A phrase book or dictionary is indispensable. And when all else fails, the art of communicating with gestures is still very much alive in Italy!

FINDING YOUR ACCOMMODATION

At the front of the book is a key map of the whole of Italy plus maps showing each recommended place to stay's location. The pertinent regional map number is given at the right on the *top line* of each bed and breakfast's description. Directions to help you find your destination are given following the description. However, they are only guidelines, as it would be impossible to find the space to give more details, and to know from which direction the traveler is arriving. The beauty of many of these lodgings is that they are off the beaten track, but that characteristic may also make them very tricky to find. If you get lost, a common occurrence, first keep your sense of humor, then call the proprietors and/or ask locals at bars or gas stations for directions. It is important to know that addresses in the countryside often have no specific street name. *A common address consists of the farm name, sometimes a localita' (an unincorporated area, or vicinity, frequently not found on a map and outside the actual town named), and the town name followed by the province abbreviated in parentheses. (The accommodation is not necessarily **in** that town, but it serves as a post office reference.)* The *localita'* can also be the name of the road where the bed and breakfast is located, to make things more confusing. We state the *localita'* in the third line of the details and many times that name is the map reference name as well. Ask to be faxed a detailed map upon confirmation. Detailed maps for the area in which you will be traveling are essential and we recommend purchasing them in advance of your trip, both to aid in the planning of your journey and to avoid spending vacation time searching for the appropriate maps.

GASOLINE

Gas prices in Italy are the highest in Europe, and Americans often suspect a mistake when their first fill up comes to between $55 and $100 (most of it in taxes). Most stations now accept Visa credit cards, and the ERG stations accept American Express. Besides the AGIP stations on the autostrade which are almost always open, gas stations observe the same hours as merchants, closing in the afternoon from 12:30 to 4 and in the evening at 7:30. Be careful not to get caught running on empty in the afternoon! Many stations have a self-service pump that operates on off hours (€10 or €20 accepted).

HOLIDAYS

It is very important to know Italian holidays because most museums, shops, and offices are closed. National holidays are:

New Year's Day (January 1)   Assumption Day (August 15)
Epiphany (January 6)   All Saints' Day (November 1)
Easter (and the following Monday)   Christmas (December 25)
Liberation Day (April 25)   Santo Stefano (December 26)
Labor Day (May 1)

ICONS

We have introduced these icons in the guidebooks and more on our website, *www.karenbrown.com*. ❄ Air conditioning in rooms, ☕ Breakfast included in room rate, ❧ Children welcome (age given on website), ♨ Cooking classes offered, [CREDIT] Credit cards accepted, ☎ Direct-dial telephone in room, ⚠ Dinner served upon request, 🐕 Dogs by special request, ⏫ Elevator, 🏋 Exercise room, 🚭 Some non-smoking rooms, P Parking available, 🍴 Restaurant, 🛎 Room Service, ☘ Spa, 🏊 Swimming pool, ⚲ Tennis, 📺 TV in bedrooms, ⚭ Wedding facilities, ♿ Wheelchair accessible, ⚓ Beach nearby, 🏌 Golf course nearby, 🚶 Hiking trails nearby, 🏇 Horseback riding nearby, ⛷ Skiing nearby, 🏄 Water sports nearby.

Icons allow us to provide additional information about our recommended properties. When using our website to supplement the guides, positioning the cursor over an icon will in many cases give you further details.

INFORMATION

Italian Government Travel Offices (ENIT) can offer general information on various regions and their cultural attractions. They cannot offer specific information on restaurants and accommodations. If you have access to the Internet, visit the Italian Tourist Board's websites: *www.italiantourism.com* or *www.enit.it*. Offices are located in:

Chicago: Italian Government Travel Office, 500 N. Michigan Ave., Suite 2240, Chicago, IL 60611 USA; email: *enitch@italiantourism.com*, tel: (312) 644-0996, fax: (312) 644-3019.

Los Angeles: Italian Government Travel Office, 12400 Wilshire Blvd., Suite 550, Los Angeles, CA 90025, USA; email: *enitla@italiantourism.com*, tel: (310) 820-1898, fax: (310) 820-6357.

New York: Italian Government Travel Office, 630 5th Ave., Suite 1565, New York, NY 10111, USA; email: *enitny@italiantourism.com*, tel: (212) 245-4822, fax: (212) 586-9249.

Toronto: Italian Government Travel Office, 175 Bloor Street East, Suite 907, Toronto, Ontario M4W 3R8, Canada; email: *enit.canada@on.aibn.com*, tel: (416) 925-4882, fax: (416) 925-4799.

London: Italian State Tourist Office, 1 Princes Street, London WIB 2AY, England; email: *italy@italiantourism.co.uk*, tel: (020) 7408-1254, fax: (020) 7493-6695.

Sydney: Italian Government Travel Office, Level 4, 46 Market Street, Sydney NSW 2000, Australia; email: *italia@italiantourism.com.au*, tel: (61292) 621.666, fax: (61292) 621.677.

Rome: ENTE Nazionale Italiano per il Turismo (Italian Government Travel Office), Via Marghera, 2/6, Rome 00185, Italy; email: *sedecentrale@cert.enit.it*, tel: (06) 49711, fax: (06) 4463379.

MAPS

Detailed maps of Tuscany and Umbria are essential and we recommend purchasing them in advance of your trip, both to aid in the planning of your journey and to avoid spending vacation time searching for the appropriate maps. We like the regional Michelin maps (1 cm = 4 km) Tuscany and Umbria map 563. You might also want to consider the *Michelin Tourist and Motoring Atlas of Italy,* a book of maps with a scale of 1:300,000 (1 cm = 3 km). We sell the Michelin atlas and regional maps in our online store at *www.karenbrown.com.* Another fine choice is the Touring Club Italiano Map Central that can be purchased in Italy. Even the smallest town or, better, *localita* is listed in the extensive index.

PLACES TO STAY

To help you select the type of accommodation you are looking for, the bottom of the description gives one of the following classifications:

B&B: A private home that offers bed & breakfast.

HOTEL: A small, family-run hotel.

SELF-CATERING: Fully furnished accommodation with limited laundry and cooking facilities. No meals are included. These are typically rented by the week, but shorter stays are often available.

RESERVATIONS

Advanced reservations are strongly recomended. It is important to understand that once reservations for accommodation are confirmed, whether verbally by phone or in writing, you are under contract. This means that the proprietor is obligated to provide the accommodation that was promised and that you are obligated to pay for it. If you cannot, you are liable for a portion of the accommodation charges plus your deposit. As a courtesy to your hosts, in the case of cancellation, please advise them as soon as possible. Although some proprietors do not strictly enforce a cancellation policy, many, particularly the smaller properties in our book, simply cannot afford not to do so. Similarly, many airline tickets cannot be changed or refunded without penalty. We recommend insurance to cover these types of additional expenses arising from cancellation due to unforeseen circumstances.

When making your reservations, be sure to identify yourself as a "Karen Brown traveler." The hosts appreciate your visit, value their inclusion in our guide, and frequently tell us they take special care of our readers.

There are several ways to make a reservation:

Email: This is our preferred way of making a reservation. All hotels/bed and breakfasts featured on the Karen Brown Website that also have email addresses have those addresses listed on their web pages (this information is constantly kept updated and correct). You can often link directly to a property from its page on our website. (Always spell out the month as the Italians reverse the American month/day numbering system.)

Fax: If you have access to a fax machine, this is a very quick way to reach a bed and breakfast. If the place to stay has a fax, we have included the number in the description. Following is a reservation request form in Italian with an English translation. (See comment above about spelling out the month.)

Reservation Service: If you want to pay for the convenience of having the reservations made for you, pre-payments made, vouchers issued, and cars rented, any of the bed and breakfasts in this guide can be booked through **Hidden Treasures of Italy**, a booking service run by one of the authors of this guide, Nicole Franchini. Further information can be found at the back this book.

Telephone: You can call the bed and breakfast directly, which is very efficient since you get an immediate response. The level of English spoken is given in each bed and breakfast description. To telephone Italy from the United States, dial 011 (the international code), then 39 (Italy's code), then the city area code (including the "0" unless it is a cellular phone number), and then the telephone number. Italy is six hours ahead of New York.

ROADS

Autostrada: a large, fast (and most direct) two- or three-lane tollway, marked by green signs bearing an "A" followed by the autostrada number. As you enter you receive a ticket from an automatic machine by pushing a red button. Payment is made at your exit point. If you lose your card, you will have to pay the equivalent amount of the distance from the beginning of the autostrada to your exit. Speed limit: 130 kph.

Superstrada: a one- or two-lane freeway between secondary cities marked by blue signs and given a number. Speed limit: 110 kph.

Strada Statale: a small one-lane road marked with S.S. followed by the road number. Speed limit: 90 kph.

Raccordo or *Tangenziale*: a ring road around main cities, connecting to an autostrada and city centers.

ROAD SIGNS: Yellow signs are for tourists and indicate sites of interest, hotels, and restaurants. Black-and-yellow signs indicate private companies and industries.

TOLLS: Tolls on Italian autostrade are quite steep, ranging from $15 to $28 for a three-hour stretch, but offering the fastest and most direct way to travel between cities. Fortunately for the agritourist, tollways are rarely necessary. However, if it suits your needs, a *Viacard*, or magnetic reusable card for tolls, is available in all tollway gas stations for €20–€50, or even more convenient, a MasterCard or Visa card can be used in specified blue lanes (the lines for these automatic machines are notably shorter).

SAFETY

If certain precautions are taken, most unfortunate incidents can be avoided. It is extremely helpful to keep copies of passports, tickets, and contents of your wallet in your room in case you need them. Pickpocketing most commonly occurs in cities on buses, train stations, crowded streets, or from passing motorbikes. WARNING: At tollway gas stations and snack bars, **always** lock your car and beware of gypsies and vendors who try to sell you stolen merchandise. In general, **never** leave valuables or even luggage in the car. Also, **never** set down luggage even for a minute in train stations.

TELEPHONES

The Italian phone company (TELECOM) has been an object of ridicule, a source of frustration, and a subject of heated conversation since its inception. More modern systems are gradually being installed, and most areas have touch-tone phones now. Telephone numbers can have from four to eight digits, so don't be afraid of missing numbers. Cellular phones have saved the day (Italians wouldn't be caught dead without at least one) and are recognized by three-digit area codes beginning with 3. We have added cellphone numbers for the majority of properties in the guide. Cellphones offer the B&B owner great flexibility and give guests the advantage of always finding someone "home."

It is now very easy to rent cellular phones for your stay in Italy either through Auto-Europe car rental or directly at airports.

All calls to Italy need to include the "0" in the area code, whether calling from abroad, within Italy, or even within the same city, *cellphone numbers drop the "0" in all cases.*

Dial 113 for emergencies of all kinds—24-hour service nationwide.

Dial 116 for Automobile Club for urgent breakdown assistance on the road.

Dial 118 for Ambulance service.

Remember that no warning is given when the time you've paid for in a public phone is about to expire (the line just goes dead), so put in plenty of change or a phone card. There are several types of phones (in various stages of modernization) in Italy:

Regular rotary phones in bars, restaurants, and many bed and breakfasts, which you can use *a scatti*, meaning you can pay the proprietor after the call is completed.

Bright-orange pay phones, as above with attached apparatus permitting insertion of a *scheda telefonica,* reusable magnetic cards worth €5–€25, or now more rarely, coins.

To call the United States from Italy, matters have been eased by the ongoing installation of the Country Direct System, whereby you can reach an American operator by dialing either 800-172-4444 for AT&T or 800-90-5825 for MCI. Either a collect call or a credit-card call can then be placed. If you discover this system doesn't work from some smaller towns, dial 170 to place a collect call, or, in some cities, try dialing direct (from a *scatti* phone), using the international code 001 + area code + number.

TIPPING

Hotels: Service charges are normally included in four- and five-star hotels only. It is customary to leave a token tip for staff.

Restaurants: If a service charge is included, it will be indicated on the bill, otherwise 10–15% is standard tipping procedure.

Taxis: 10%.

WHEN TO VISIT

Many places to stay are open only from Easter through November. If you are traveling outside this time, however, it is often worth a phone call to find out if they can accommodate you anyway (at very affordable rates). The best time to travel is without a doubt during the spring and fall months, when nature is in its glory. You can enjoy the flowers blossoming in May, the *vendemmia*, or grape harvest, at the end of September, the fall foliage in late October, or olive-oil production and truffle hunts in November and December. The vast majority of Italians vacation at the same time, during the month of August, Easter weekend, and Christmas, so these time periods are best avoided, if possible.

Staying in Bed & Breakfasts

All of the bed & breakfasts featured in this guide have been visited and selected solely on their merits. Our judgments are made on charm, setting, cleanliness, and, above all, warmth of welcome. The most important thing to remember is that you will be staying in the private homes of families who run their bed & breakfasts without hiring additional personnel aside from family and farmhands. Do not expect the service of a hotel. **Rooms may not necessarily always be cleaned daily**. Nevertheless, do anticipate a comfortable and enjoyable stay, because the proprietors will do everything possible to assure it. Cost will vary according to the level of service offered.

Bed & breakfast accommodation should not be thought of strictly in terms of the British or American definitions of bed and breakfasts, as in Italy they vary greatly according to each proprietor's interpretation of the concept. The bed and breakfasts in this guide have been described in terms of the criteria used in their selection—warmth of hospitality, historic character, charm of the home, scenery, proximity to sites of touristic interest, and quality of cuisine. Obviously, all of these attributes are not always found in each one. Most of them have an average of six rooms situated either within the family's home or in a separate guesthouse. Unless otherwise indicated in the bottom description details, all bedrooms have private bathrooms. Furthermore, we have tried to include only those with en suite bathrooms. Having another bed or two added to a room at an extra charge for families with small children is usually not a problem. According to laws of the European Community, all new or renovated establishments must now offer facilities for the handicapped. It is best to enquire about the individual bed and breakfast's facilities when making reservations to see if they have accommodation that is suitable for you.

Bed and breakfasts often serve only a continental breakfast of coffee, tea, fresh breads, and jams. However, many prepare a buffet breakfast plus other meals and offer (sometimes require) half or full board plans. Half board means that breakfast and dinner are both included in the daily per-person room rate. Full board includes the room and all three meals and is less common, since most guests are out and about during the day, or prefer one lighter meal. Dinner is a hearty three-course meal, often shared at a common table with the host family, and normally does not include wine and other beverages. Menus might be set daily, according to the availability of fresh produce, or a limited choice may be given. Some farms have a full-fledged restaurant serving non-guests as well. Travelers who are not guests at a particular bed and breakfast may take advantage of this opportunity to sample other fare (it is advisable to reserve in advance). When a listing offers dinner by arrangement we indicate this with the icon 🔺. If a property has a restaurant, we use the icon 🍴 .

A highlight of the bed and breakfast experience is without a doubt the food. Most travelers would agree that a bad meal is hard to find in Italy, a country world-famous for its culinary skills. In the countryside you'll be sampling the traditional regional recipes from which Italian cuisine originates. Since, whenever possible, all of the ingredients come directly from the farms where you'll be staying and are for the most part organically grown (watch for the certificate), you'll discover the flavorful difference freshness can make. Even the olive oil has a special certificate of quality (DOP) similar to that of wines (DOC). A peek into the farm kitchen is likely to reveal pasta being rolled and cut the old-fashioned way—by hand. Many country cooks prefer to prepare food using traditional methods, and not rely on machines to speed up the process. Guests are usually welcomed into the kitchen for a look around and actual cooking lessons are becoming very popular.

Staying in Hotels

We visit hundreds of hotels and choose only those we think are special. It might be a splendid villa or a gorgeous palace but there is a common denominator—they all have charm. Each listing is very different and occasionally the owners have their eccentricities, which all adds to the allure of these special hotels. We have tried to be candid and honest in our appraisals and attempted to convey each hotel's special flavor, so that you know what to expect and will not be disappointed. All hotels are places that we have inspected, or stayed in—places that we enjoy. It is difficult to find hotels in Italy furnished in a simple style. Italian hotels frequently reflect a rather formal opulence and tend toward a fussy style of decor. There are some exceptions. In a few instances (which we note in the hotel's description) the hotels are decorated with a more rustic ambiance using country antiques, but this is not the norm. When antiques are used, they are very often the fancy, gilded variety.

Staying in Self Catering Accommodation

Since more and more travelers are learning that it is much more advantageous to stay for longer periods in one place (distances are so short between towns within a specific region), apartment-type accommodations with fully equipped kitchenettes are flourishing. Apartment accommodation is offered either within the farmhouse along with other units for two to six persons, or as a full house rental for six to ten persons. They are rented by the week from Saturday to Saturday throughout the country, the exception being during the low season. No meals are included unless there is a bed and breakfast on the premises which also has a restaurant or makes special arrangements for breakfast or dinner. Rates include use of all facilities, linens, and often utilities. There is usually an extra charge for heating and once-a-week cleaning. Average apartments for four persons run approximately $800 weekly, a rate hotels cannot beat.

Romantic Tuscany

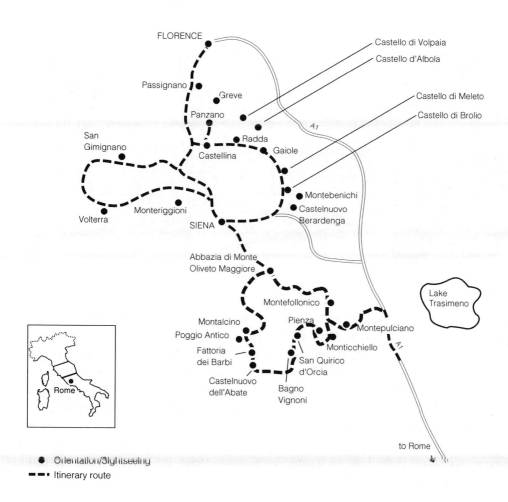

FLORENCE

Castello di Volpaia
Castello d'Albola

Passignano
Greve

Castello di Meleto

Panzano

Castello di Brolio

San
Gimignano

Radda

Castellina
Gaiole

A1

Montebenichi
Castelnuovo
Berardenga

Monteriggioni

Volterra
SIENA

Abbazia di Monte
Oliveto Maggiore

Lake
Trasimeno

Montefollonico

Montalcino
Poggio Antico
Pienza
Montepulciano

Fattoria
dei Barbi
San Quirico
d'Orcia
Monticchiello

Castelnuovo
dell'Abate
Bagno
Vignoni

A1

Rome

to Rome

● Orientation/Sightseeing
--- Itinerary route

21

Romantic Tuscany

Florence, Ponte Vecchio

Nothing can surpass the exquisite beauty of the countryside of Tuscany—it is breathtaking. If you meander into the hill towns any time of the year, all your senses are rewarded with the splendors that this enchanting area of Italy has to offer. Almost every hillock is crowned with a picture-perfect walled town; fields are brilliant with vibrant red poppies; vineyards in all their glory and promise lace the fields; olive trees dress the hillsides in a frock of dusky gray-green; pine forests unexpectedly appear to highlight the landscape. As if these attributes were not enough, tucked into the colorful villages is a treasure-trove of some of the finest small hotels, B&Bs and rental accommodation in Italy. If this is still not sufficient to tempt you away from the normal tourist route, remember that the food and wines are unsurpassed.

Pacing: To explore the hill towns of Tuscany you need at least a week (in addition to the time you allocate to Florence). We recommend a minimum of four nights in the heart of Tuscany's Classico Wine Region, which stretches from Florence south to Siena. This will give the minimum time needed to enjoy the tranquil beauty of the hill towns and to sample the delicious Chianti wines. The second suggested stop is southern Tuscany where we suggest three nights to explore the stunning small towns that dot the hillsides, visit breathtaking monasteries, and taste more of Italy's superb wines: Vino Nobile, grown near Montepulciano, and Brunello, grown near Montacino.

Tuscany is laced with narrow roads that twist through the picturesque countryside. Take a detailed map so that if you get lost, you can find your way home, but part of the joy of Tuscany is to be unstructured. Enjoy the freedom to discover your own perfect village, your own charming restaurant, and your own favorite wine. Although in your wanderings you are sure to find some very special places that we have missed, we share below some of the towns we find irresistible and vineyards that are especially fun to visit.

A convenient place to begin your journey is in **Florence**, Tuscany's jewel. Magnificent art is not confined to the city limits of Florence and you will see impressive cathedrals and museums hosting spellbinding works of art throughout Tuscany. Be generous with your time and do not rush Florence—there is too much to see. You must, of course, pay a visit to Michelangelo's fabulous **David** in the **Galleria dell'Accademia** located just off the **Piazza San Marco**.

During your explorations of Florence, you will cross many times through the **Piazza della Signoria**, located in the heart of the old city. Facing this characterful medieval square is the 13th-century **Palazzo Vecchio**, a stern stone structure topped by a crenellated gallery and dominated by a tall bell tower. It was here that the *signoria* (Florence's powerful aristocratic ruling administrators) met for two months each year while attending to government business. During this period they were forbidden to leave the palace (except for funerals) so that there could not be a hint of suspicion of intrigue or bribery. Of course, you cannot miss one of Florence's landmarks, the **Ponte Vecchio**.

Spanning the Arno in the heart of Florence, this colorful bridge is lined with quaint shops just as it has been since the 14th century.

Palazzo Vecchio, Piazza della Signora, Florence

Don't miss the fantastic museums and cathedrals—the world will probably never again see a city that has produced such artistic genius. Florence's Duomo is one of the largest in the world. The cathedral's incredible dome (over 100 meters high) was designed by Brunelleschi. Climb the 464 steps to the top of the dome for a superb view of Florence. The **Baptistry** has beautiful mosaics and its bronze doors by Ghiberti were said by Michelangelo to be worthy of serving as the gates to paradise. The main door shows scenes from the life of John the Baptist, the north door shows the life of Jesus, and the east door shows stories from the prophets of the Old Testament. The **Uffizi Museum** (housed in a 16th-century palace) is undoubtedly one of the finest museums in the world. You can make advance reservations at the Uffizi Museum but you must prepay for the tickets by postal wire in euros (tel: 055 29 48 83) or call Hidden Treasures (888) 419-6700. Also, do not miss the **Pitti**

Palace with its fabulous art collection, including paintings by Titian and Raphael. NOTE: In addition to regular hours, museums stay open during June, July, August, and September until 11 pm. Be sure to buy a guidebook and city map at one of the many magazine stalls and study what you want to see. We just touch on the many highlights. Florence is best appreciated by wandering the historic ancient streets: poke into small boutiques; stop in churches that catch your eye—they all abound with masterpieces; sit and enjoy a cappuccino in one of the little sidewalk cafés and people watch; stroll through the piazzas and watch the artists at their craft—many of them incredibly clever— as they paint portraits and do sculptures for a small fee. End your day by finding the perfect small restaurant for delicious pasta made by mama in the back kitchen.

Monteriggioni

CHIANTI CLASSICO WINE REGION

This idyllic area lives up to every dream of Tuscany—hills crowned by picture-perfect villages, medieval walled towns, straight rows of towering cypresses, romantic villas, ancient stone farmhouses, vast fields of brilliant poppies, forests of pine trees, vineyards stretching to the horizon. Instead of moving about, packing and unpacking, choose a place to stay anywhere within the area and use it us your hub for exploring this utterly beguiling region of Italy. Below we give suggestions for towns to visit and some of our favorite wineries.

SUGGESTED SIGHTSEEING: TOWNS TO VISIT

Monteriggioni: If you are looking for a town that is truly storybook-perfect, none can surpass the tiny, magical hamlet of Monteriggioni. It is such a gem that it is hard to believe it is real and not a creation by Disney! You can spot it from afar, nestled on the top of a small hill, with 14 towers punctuating the perfectly preserved enclosing walls. No cars are allowed here, so you have to park in the designated area below the walls before walking up to the town, which is composed almost entirely of a main square with small streets radiating from it. On the square you find a Romanesque church, restaurants, boutiques, and shops selling olive oil, cheeses, and wine. It takes only a few minutes to stroll from one end of the town to the other but I assure you, you will be enchanted. As a bonus, Monteriggioni produces its own fine wine, Castello di Monteriggioni.

Passignano in Chianti: Passignano in Chianti is rarely on a tourist route, but we can't help mentioning this tiny hamlet that exudes such a tranquil beauty. For sightseeing, there really isn't much to see except the **Badia a Passignano Abbey**, founded by Benedictine monks in the 11th century. The abbey is set in a pocket of lush landscape and dominates the village, which is no more than a cluster of houses and a restaurant. However, as you drive into the valley, approaching from the west, the abbey with its towering ring of cypresses has such an idyllic setting that it is one of our favorites—a photographer's delight. The abbey can be visited on Sundays at 3 pm; tours leave from the church (please check to verify the abbey is open the Sunday you want to visit). Fine wines, produced by the abbey's vineyards, can be purchased at the Osteria, tel: (055) 80 71 278.

Radda: Located in the very heart of the Chianti wine region, Radda makes a good base of operations. However, not only is the town very conveniently located for sightseeing, it is also extremely quaint and some of its walls are still intact. It was in Radda in 1924 that 33 producers gathered to create a consortium to protect a very special blend of wine that was known as **Chianti Classico**. Only vintners who maintain the standards of the consortium are allowed to proudly display its symbol of the black rooster.

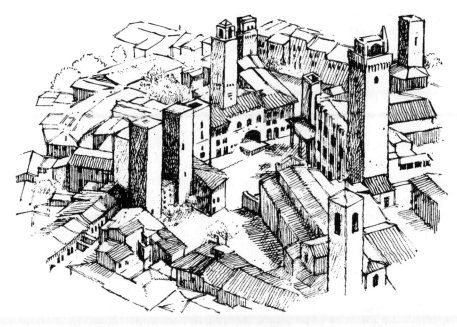

San Gimignano

San Gimignano: During your exploration of Tuscany, one town you must not miss is San Gimignano. What is so dramatic about San Gimignano is that at one time the walls of the town were punctuated by 72 towers. During the Middle Ages it was a status symbol for noble families to build their own personal towers for their protection—the higher the tower, the greater the image of wealth and importance. It is amazing that 14 of the original towers are still standing. They make a striking silhouette, soaring like skyscrapers, and on a clear day you can see them on the horizon from far away. San Gimignano is truly a jewel—plan to spend at least a day here. There are many shops and marvelous restaurants tucked along the maze of streets. On Fridays there are walking tours with English-speaking guides that leave from the Porta San Giovanni at 11 am (best check with the tourist office to be sure the time and day haven't changed). One of our favorite restaurants in San Gimignano is the delightful **Ristorante Dorando,** which has great food served in cozy rooms with coved ceilings that create the ambiance of an old wine cellar. Located on Vicolo del Oro 2, a small side street just off Piazza Duomo, tel: (0577) 94 18 62. Another favorite, **Ristorante Il Pino**, offers mouthwatering homemade pastas—some of the best we have ever eaten. Located on Via Collolese, 8–10, just down the street from L'Antico Pozzo, tel: (0577) 94 04 15.

Siena: This is an entrancing walled hill town that deserves many hours to savor its rich delights—you should allow yourself at least one full day here. The ramparts are perfectly preserved with a series of massive gates guarding a meticulously maintained medieval stronghold. Drive as close as you can to the main square, park your car, and set out to explore on foot. You cannot drive into the center of the city, but there are designated parking areas (marked by "P") near each of the gates. One of the most convenient is the parking at the Porta Romana. Once you leave your car, strike off for the giant **Piazza del Campo**. This central piazza is immense and, instead of being square, is fan-shaped and slopes downward like a bowl. Eleven streets surrounding the square converge into it like spokes of a massive wheel. Like the Spanish Steps in Rome, the Piazza del Campo is a favorite for tourists who linger here just enjoying the medieval ambiance. It is in this gigantic piazza that the colorful **Palio delle Contrade** (dating back to the 11th century) takes place twice a year, on July 2 and August 16. The horse race is only a part of a colorful spectacle of medieval costumes, impressive banners, and parades, and the festivities extend beyond the actual date of the races. Monopolizing one side of the Piazza del Campo is the 13th-century Gothic **Palazzo Pubblico** (Town Hall) whose graceful arches are embellished with Siena's coat of arms. The Palazzo Pubblico is open as a museum where you can stroll through the governor's living quarters.

Although Siena looks like a large city, it is easily negotiable on foot and most of the museums are in one small area. After visiting the Piazza del Campo, most of the other major places of interest are just a few minutes' walk away, clustered about the Piazza del Duomo. There are excellent tourist signs that will guide you along the maze of narrow streets to all the museums.

You absolutely must not miss Siena's 12th-century **Duomo**, facing the Piazza del Duomo. This is one of Italy's most astounding cathedrals. Not only is its exterior breathtaking, but once you enter, you will be overwhelmed by its dramatic black-and-white, zebra-striped marble columns. Don't miss the intricately carved, 13th-century panels depicting the life of Christ on the octagonal pulpit. Also, be sure to see the **Piccolomini Library**. You need to buy a ticket to enter, but it is well worth it. This relatively small room is totally frescoed with gorgeous murals in still-vibrant colors portraying the life of Pope Pius II. The cathedral also has 59 fabulous inlaid-marble mosaic panels on the floor depicting religious scenes. However, some of the most precious of these are covered to protect them and are on display only from the end of August to the first of October.

After visiting the Duomo, the following museums are just steps away. One of our favorites is the **Ospedale di Santa Maria della Scala**, located across from the entrance to the Duomo. At first glance, it is difficult to truly appreciate its wealth of things to see. The museum goes on and on—it is enormous. Just when you think you have finished, a discreet sign will lead you ever downwards to a lower level and a stunning array of artifacts. The building, dating back to the 800s, was originally constructed as a hospital. Be sure not to miss the former infirmary with its lushly colored frescoes by the master Domenico di Bartolo depicting scenes of patients being treated by their doctors. Another nearby museum is the **Baptistry**, a small museum that, as its name implies, houses the baptismal font for the Duomo. In addition to its beautifully frescoed walls and vaulted ceiling, of prime interest is the 15th-century baptismal font, which is adorned by religious scenes cast in bronze by some of Italy's most famous Renaissance masters, including one panel by Donatello. The **Museo dell'Opera Metropolitana** is worth a visit if for no other reason that to see the sublime *Maestá* by Duccio, painted in 1311. The central scene of the Virgin Mary is truly awesome. For art lovers, the **Museo Civico** must not be missed. Here you will see stunning masterpieces by Ambrogio Lorenzetti, Spinello Aretino, and Simone Martini. It is overwhelming to ponder how Italy could have produced so many geniuses. NOTE: There is a ticket valid for three days that allows you entrance into many of Siena's sightseeing attractions—this is a bargain compared to buying individual tickets.

Volterra: Just a short drive from San Gimignano, Volterra is a delightful, non-touristy town enclosed by still-intact, 12th-century walls. Like so many of the cities founded by the Etruscans, Volterra is built upon the flat top of a steep hill. As you drive toward the city, the landscape becomes increasingly barren, since the soil is not conducive to growing grapes or olive trees. Instead, alabaster is king here and objects made of alabaster are sold in all of the shops. Not to be missed is the alabaster museum called **Museo Etrusco Guaracci**, which has a fabulous collection of works of art, including sculptures and beautiful vases, displayed with great taste in a series of interlinking rooms that show the art to perfection. There is an adjacent shop selling many alabaster items. The whole town is a jewel whose charm is best experienced by strolling through the narrow cobbled streets. Its main square, **Piazza dei Priori**, the heart of the town, is surrounded by fine examples of beautifully preserved medieval buildings and with its towers, splendid town hall (the oldest in Tuscany), and Romanesque church, it is considered by some to be one of the finest squares in Tuscany. Stroll to visit one of the main gates, the **Porta all'Arco**, the origins of which date back to the 7th century B.C. During World War II, the loyal citizens of Volterra buried the stones of the gate to keep the Nazis from blowing it up.

Suggested Sightseeing: Wineries

The production of wine plays an enormous role throughout Tuscany, and between Florence and Siena (where **Chianti Classico** is produced) you are constantly reminded of this as you pass through vast rolling hills splendidly adorned with neatly tended vineyards. The Chianti Classico area covers over 172,000 acres, with Siena and Florence being the two "capitals" of the region. Included in the area are the towns of Castellina, Gaiole, Greve, Radda, and some of Barberino Val d'Elsa, Castelnuovo Berardenga, Poggibonsi, San Casciano Val di Pesa, and Tavarnelle Val di Pesa. Even if you are not a wine connoisseur, it would be a pity not to make at least one winery stop both for the fun of observing the production process and for an understanding of the industry that is so central to the soul and character of Tuscany. Many of the wineries also have gift shops and sell marvelous olive oils and cheeses in addition to wine.

As you meander through the countryside you see signs with Chianti Classico's black rooster symbol and you can buy directly from the producer where you see *Vendita Diretta*. In some cases there are also tours of the winery (these are sometimes free, but sometimes there is a charge). A *Cantina* sign means that the winery has a shop where wine is sold and can usually be sampled. One of the delights of touring the back roads of Tuscany is just to stop on whim. When you spot a *Vendita Diretta*, drive in, introduce yourself, and sample some wines. You might well discover one that will become one of your favorites.

Some of our favorite wineries to visit are:

Castello di Brolio: If you visit only one winery, Castello di Brolio should be it since this is not only one of the oldest wineries the world, but also where Chianti wine was "born." Although the production of wine in Tuscany dates back to Etruscan times, the enormously wealthy Ricasoli family, owners of the Castello di Brolio since 1167, are responsible for the special blending of grapes we now consider "Chianti Classico." At one time the enormously powerful Ricasoli family owned most of the land and castles lying between Florence and Siena. The remote family castle, Castello di Brolio, had largely been abandoned when Bettino Ricasoli decided to move into it (so the story goes) after becoming jealous at a winter ball in Florence when his young bride danced a bit too closely to one of her young admirers. Thinking it best to take his wife away from temptation, he rebuilt the huge, remote, crenellated castle, replanted the vineyards, and experimented with the blending of grapes, coming up with the original formula that forms the basis of what is known today as Chianti Classico. The fortified castle tops a high, forested hill. You leave your car in the designated parking area and climb for about 20 minutes up a path or on the road through a parklike forest to the castle gates. Open daily from 9 am to noon and 3 pm to sunset. The castle is located about 10 kilometers south of Gaiole. Tel: (0577) 74 90 66.

Castello di Volpaia: The 12th-century Castello di Volpaia, located on a narrow lane about 7 kilometers north of Radda, is one of our favorite places for wine tasting. Plan to spend a day on this outing, with ample time to meander through the countryside en route, tour the winery, taste the superb wines, and enjoy a wonderful lunch at the winery's excellent restaurant, La Bottega. Although the winery is called *Castello* it really isn't located inside a castle at all, but rather in various medieval stone houses in a picture-perfect village wrapped by vineyards where you find a small church, a cluster of houses, La Bottega Ristorante, and the wine tasting room. You need to preplan this wine tour and also make reservations for lunch since both are very popular and usually booked far in advance. There is a fee for the tour based on the number of people in the group. Tel: (0577) 73 80 66, *www.volpaia.com.*

Castello d'Albola, wine tasting

Castello d'Albola: The Castello d'Albola, a spectacular property just a short drive north of Radda on a gentle hill laced with grapes, is owned by the Zonin family, who have restored the entire medieval complex beautifully. This is an intimate, extremely pretty place to taste wines and take a tour. What we particularly like about the Castello d'Albola is that it is in such a beautiful setting and offers delightfully informal, friendly, free tours. Drive up the hill to the castle, leave your car in the parking area, and walk into an inner castle courtyard, off which you find the wine tasting room and cantina. Before or after wine tasting, your hostess leads you on a short, professional tour showing you how fine wines are produced. The owner has other enormous estates as well as the Castello d'Albola and is one of the largest producers of wine in the world. Tours start at noon, 3 pm, and 5 pm daily. The cantina is open for complimentary wine tasting Monday through Friday from 10:30 am to 6:30 pm. Tel: (0577) 73 80 19, *www.albola.it*.

Castello di Meleto: Another favorite destination for wine tasting is the beautiful Castello di Meleto, which has an idyllic setting in the gentle hills near the town of Gaiole. Just across from the dramatic castle you find a pretty wine tasting room and gift shop where fine wines and olive oils produced on the estate can be purchased. On request, tastings of olive oil and aromatic vinegars can be arranged. What makes this a very special experience is that there is an added bonus: not only can you sample wines, but you can also visit the beautiful interior of the castle. In addition to splendidly frescoed rooms, the castle has one exceptionally intriguing feature—a whimsical private theater complete with its original stage settings. Call ahead, tel: (0577) 73 80 66, to find out the time and cost of the guided tours of the cellars and castle. The Castelo is also a recommended place to stay.

SOUTHERN TUSCANY

The area of Tuscany that lies south/southeast of Siena is famous for its superb wines. A great bonus is that these vineyards are in one of Italy's most picturesque regions, filled with quaint villages and amazing abbeys, thus making your adventures even more enchanting. Whereas Chianti Classico wine is renowned in the area between Florence and Siena, the vineyards farther south also produce some of the mostly highly regarded wines in the world, the most famous of these being **Vino Nobile**, grown near Montepulciano, and **Brunello**, grown near Montacino. There are many wineries open to the public where wine can be tasted and purchased. Many wine tastings are free, although some wineries charge a minimal fee. As you drive through the countryside look for signs reading *Cantina* (wine shop) or *Vendita Diretta* (direct sales).

Romantic Tuscany

LOOP VISITING WINERIES, ABBEYS, AND QUAINT VILLAGES

We suggest a loop that covers some of our favorite wineries, medieval towns, and picturesque abbeys. It would be impossible to squeeze everything in this itinerary into one day unless you rush madly from place to place. Therefore, if your time is limited, don't stop at each place suggested but just choose a few of the sightseeing suggestions below that most appeal to you. But better yet, take several days and follow the itinerary in its entirety, covering a small section each day at a leisurely pace.

This loop begins in **Montepulciano**, a rare jewel of a walled hill town that not only oozes charm in its narrow, cobbled streets but is also center stage for the delicious Vino Nobile di Montepulciano. This wealthy town was home to many aristocrats who built magnificent palaces here. The heart of the city is the **Piazza Grande** where you find the dramatic 13th-century **Palazzo Comunale** accented by a stone tower. Also facing the square is the picturesque **Palazzo Contucci**, fronted by a charming Renaissance well decorated with the Medici coat of arms and highlighted by two stone lions. Leading off the Pizza Grande are small streets that crisscross the town, connected by staircases.

A masterpiece you absolutely must not miss when visiting Montepulciano is the **Temple of San Biagio**, a stunning church located on the west edge of town. You can walk from town, but it is a long way down the hill and then back up again, so you might want to drive, especially in hot weather. Made of creamy travertine, the church's façade is extremely picturesque and its elegant interior is equally lovely—nothing cluttered or dark but rather light and airy, with fine marble pastel-colored walls.

Within Montepulciano there are many boutiques, restaurants, and cantinas selling wine. Our favorite wine shop here is an extremely special one, the very old **Cantina del Redi**, located just down the street from the Piazza Grande with its entrance next to the Palazzo Ricco. Once you enter, an ancient staircase leads ever deeper into the hillside, passing rooms filled with huge wooden casks of wine. When you finally reach the lowest level, you wind your way through more casks until you arrive at the cantina where you can sample and purchase wine. When finished, you discover that you have descended quite a way down the hillside and the main entrance to the winery faces onto a lower terrace.

Another of our favorite wineries, **Dei**, is just a few kilometers outside Montepulciano's city walls. What is especially fun about this winery is that it is family-owned and managed by the lovely daughter, Maria Caterina Dei, who still lives in the beautiful family villa on the property. Maria Caterina is passionate about wine and with great professionalism can explain about the production of the Dei wines, which have won many awards. Before taking over the family's vineyards, the multi-talented Maria Caterina trained in music and the theater, and sometimes she entertains the guests during wine tours. There is a fee for tours, depending upon what is requested. Lunches and wine tasting can be prearranged. Call in advance for tours: Dei, Villa Martiena, Montepulciano, tel: (0578) 71 68 78.

Leaving Montepulciano, take the S146 west toward Pienza. After driving about 3 kilometers, take a small road on the left marked to **Monticchiello**. You soon arrive at a sweet, tiny, charming walled town whose allure is its unpretentious, non-touristy ambiance. Park your car in the designated area outside the main gate. As you enter through the gate, you will see on your left **La Porta**, a charming restaurant with an outside terrace sitting on the town walls—a great place to stop for lunch. As you stroll through Monticchiello (it won't take you long), take a look inside the 13th-century church where you will see a beautiful altarpiece by Pietro Lorenzetti.

From Monticchiello, continue on the back road to **Pienza**. This is one of our favorite walled hill towns in Tuscany, a real gem that mustn't be missed. The town is perched on the top of a hill and is pedestrian-only so you need to park your car outside the walls. It is no wonder that the town is so perfect even though so tiny: it was here in the 15th century that Pope Pius II hired a famous architect, Bernardo Rossellino, to totally redesign the town where he was born, making it into a masterpiece. You will find many restaurants if you are inclined to dine.

Leaving Pienza, take S146 west to **San Quirico d'Orcia**, a very attractive small medieval town with a lovely Romanesque church. If you stop to see the town, you must not miss its lovely garden, called **Horti Leonini**. An entrance about a block from the main square leads into a tranquil Renaissance garden, originally designed as a beautiful resting place for the pilgrims who stopped here on the road to Rome. This cool oasis with clipped box hedges and shade trees makes an interesting stop. If you are hungry, the **Osteria del Leone** makes a good choice for lunch.

From San Quirico d'Orcia, head south on S2 for about 6 kilometers and watch for a small road to the right leading to **Bagno Vignoni**. This is a most unusual, very small town, known for the curative value of its hot sulphur springs. In the center of town, you find what would have been the town square made into a huge sulphur bath built by the Medicis. The pool is surrounded by picturesque medieval buildings that complete the interesting scene.

Leaving Bagno Vignoni, don't continue on the S2, but take S323 directly south for 12 kilometers and then turn right following signs to Montalcino. In a few minutes you come to **Castelnuovo dell'Abate** where, just a few minutes outside town, you will find the superb Romanesque **Abbey Sant'Antimo**, whose origins date back to the 9th century when it was founded as a Benedictine monastery. The abbey—a simple, pastel-pinkish stone church serenely set amongst fields of olive trees—makes a beautiful picture. Try to arrive at 11 am or 2:45 pm when the Benedictine monks, clad in long, pure-white robes, gather at the altar to chant their prayers in Latin. This is a haunting, beautiful experience. The singing lasts only a short time, and the times might vary from the ones we mention above, so to confirm the schedule call, tel: (0577) 83 56 59.

Leaving Castelnuovo dell'Abate, drive north on the road for Montalcino. In a few minutes you will see a sign to the **Fattoria dei Barbi**. Turn right and follow a small road up the hill to the Barbi winery, an excellent winery to visit. It is extremely pretty with many gardens and a charming cantina where you can sample the vineyard's fine wines and purchase wine and other gift items. Its restaurant serves wonderful meals made with only the freshest products, accompanied, of course, by their own wines. Free tours of the winery are given hourly from 10 am to noon and 3 pm to 5 pm, tel: (0577) 84 82 77, *www.fattoriadeibarbi.it.*

After your visit to the Fattoria dei Barbi, continue north for 5 kilometers to **Montalcino**, which is world famous, along with Montepulciano, for its superb wine, Brunello di Montalcino. There are many places in town where wine can be tasted and purchased. In addition to wine, the town is famous for its fine honey, which can be purchased in many of the shops. Montalcino is fun for wandering—it is not large and you can in no time at all cover the area within the walls by foot. On the east edge of town is an imposing 14th-century fortress.

From Montalcino, head south on the road to Grosetto for a little over 3 kilometers to another of our favorite wineries, **Poggio Antico**. Excellent tours are offered and, of course, you can also sample the superb wines. These tours are very popular so you should reserve in advance at tel: (0577) 84 80 44. For dining, the winery's **Ristorante Poggio Antico** serves outstanding Tuscany cuisine. Reservations for the restaurant are also highly recommended—tel: (0577) 84 92 00, email: rist.poggio.antico@libero.it.

After visiting Poggio Antico, retrace your way north to Montalcino and continue on for 9 kilometers to where the road intersects with the S2. Turn left here, going north toward Siena. In 10 kilometers, turn right on S451 and continue for another 10 kilometers to the **Abbazia di Monte Oliveto Maggiore**. Founded in the early 14th century by wealthy merchants from Siena as a Benedictine retreat, this fascinating abbey is well worth a detour. Be prepared to walk since you must park your car and follow a long path through the forest to the abbey's entrance, which is through a gatehouse crowned by a beautiful della Robbia terra-cotta. Once through the gate, you continue through the woodlands to the huge brick complex. After visiting the church, it seems you could wander forever through the various hallways. Before you get too distracted, however, ask directions to the cloister because you don't want to miss this marvel. Here you find 36 frescoes depicting scenes of the life of St. Benedict, some painted by Luca Signorelli, others by Antonio Bazzi.

In the region around the abbey you will come across an entirely different type of landscape, called the *crete*. Here, tucked among the green rolling hills, you unexpectedly come across bleak, canyon-like craters, caused by erosion. These are especially out of character as the surrounding scenery is so soft and gentle.

From Abbazia di Monte Oliveto Maggiore, weave your way through the small back roads to Montepulciano. Follow signs to San Giovanni d'Asso, then Montisi, then Madongino, then **Montefollonico**. Take time to stop in Montefollonico because this is another "sleeper"—a quaint, small, medieval walled town that is fun to explore. For the gourmet, there is a superb restaurant on the edge of town called **La Chiusa.**

From Montefollonico, go south on S327. When you come to the S146, turn left to complete your loop back to Montepulciano.

Florence

The Haunting Beauty of Umbria

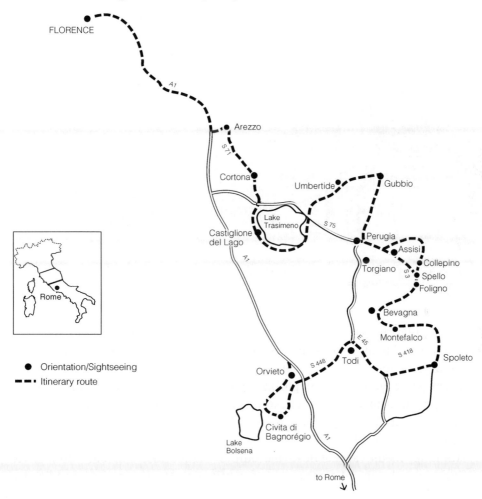

FLORENCE

A1

Arezzo

S71

Cortona

Umbertide

Gubbio

Lake Trasimeno

S 75

Castiglione del Lago

Perugia

Assisi

Collepino

A1

Torgiano

S3

Spello

Foligno

Rome

Bevagna

Montefalco

E 45

Spoleto

S 418

● Orientation/Sightseeing

▪▪▪ Itinerary route

Orvieto

S 448

Todi

Civita di Bagnorégio

A1

Lake Bolsena

to Rome

The Haunting Beauty of Umbria

Assisi

Tuscany is so popular that travelers frequently forget to visit Umbria, snuggled just "next door." Although similar in many ways to Tuscany, Umbria has its own haunting beauty and the advantage of fewer tourists. This is a region seeped in history and imbued with romantic charm. Here you find a beguiling landscape—a blend of rolling hills, craggy forests, rushing rivers, lush valleys, chestnut groves, and hillsides laced with vineyards. Adding further to Umbria's magic is that its hills and valleys radiate a soft mellow light, gleaming gently in the sun. It is not just the landscape that makes Umbria so delightful. It also has stunning medieval castles, incredible cathedrals, ancient monasteries, art treasures, fine wines, beautiful ceramics, and captivating towns perched on hilltops.

Pacing: You can conveniently follow this itinerary either before or after a tour of Tuscany. If you already have visited Tuscany on a previous trip to Italy, this itinerary stands alone. After the finishing the itinerary, you can loop back to Florence by heading north on the A1, or head south on the A1 to Rome. Whichever way you choose, in order to capture its beauty and many sightseeing possibilities, you need at least five nights in the Umbria region: We suggest three nights in the eastern part of Umbria. Choose a place to stay and in use it as a hub from which to journey out each day to explore a different sightseeing target. Next, loop south and choose a place to stay for two nights in the western part of Umbria, somewhere near Orvieto.

EASTERN UMBRIA

NOTE: This itinerary of Eastern Umbria is much too long for one day. Use it only as a framework for how the most interesting towns can be looped together. Once you choose which town you are going to use as the hub for your explorations, tailor the itinerary to visit the places mentioned in the itinerary that most appeal to you.

As you depart from Florence you are bound to run into a lot of traffic, but there are many signs to the expressway. Follow signs that lead to the A1 and take it south toward Rome.

Arezzo: About 65 kilometers after leaving Florence you come to a turnoff to **Arezzo,** located about 10 kilometers east of the highway. Arezzo is still in Tuscany, but since it is so close to Umbria and "on the way," now is the time for a visit. Arezzo has a rich history dating back to the Etruscan era, but is not as quaint as some of its smaller neighbors. It is well known as one of the largest gold centers in Europe and has many shops selling gold jewelry. Arezzo is also famous for its **Antique Fair** that is held in the Piazza Grande on the first Saturday and Sunday of every month. Here you find many unusual items such as antique coins, jewelry, furniture, stained glass remnants, paintings, light fixtures, handmade linens, pottery, trunks, etc. The fair is considered one of the most important ones in Italy and so popular that people come from far and near to browse the rich collection of antiques. Arezzo was the birthplace of Guido Monaco who around the year 1000 A.D. devised musical notes and scales. One of Arrezo's famous inhabitants was the powerful 14th-century poet Pietro Aretino who took great glee in writing scandalous poetry about the rich and famous. Aretino's greatest skill was gentle blackmail, extorting great sums from princes and popes who paid him not to expose their indiscretions in poetry.

Cortona: From Arezzo follow S71 south to Cortona, a gem of a walled town terraced up a steep hillside covered with olive trees and vineyards. Like Arezzo, Cortona is still in Tuscany, but fits more conveniently into the itinerary for Umbria since it is on the route. Stop to enjoy the atmosphere of this medieval town: its narrow, twisting, cobbled streets, jumble of small squares, lovely boutiques, excellent restaurants, and colorful buildings are delightful. The heart of the town is the **Piazza della Repubblica**, the main square, which has many narrow streets feeding into it. If you are up for walking, climb the twisting streets to the old fortress standing guard over the town.

Lake Trasimeno: Leaving Cortona, continue driving south on S71 toward Lake Trasimeno. In about 11 kilometers you come to a four-lane expressway. Do not get on the highway, but instead continue south on S71, which traces the west shore of Lake Trasimeno, Italy's fourth largest lake, which is fed by underground channels linked to the Tiber river basin. Fascinatingly, the early Romans built these underground waterways many centuries ago. Follow the road south for 9 kilometers to **Castiglione del Lago**, the most interesting town on the lake. Built on a high rocky promontory that juts out into the water, the old walled city with its battlements and towers has lots of character. Artifacts and tombs nearby indicate it was originally an Etruscan settlement, but what you see today dates from the Middle Ages. In the 1500s it was the dukedom of the Corgna. In the church of Santa Maria Maddalena you can see a 16th-century panel with paintings of the Madonna and Child by Eusebio da San Giorgio. Also visit the Palazzo del Capitano del Popolo, the Palazzo della Cornna, and the Leone fortress.

Umbertide: Continue the loop around the lake then take the road toward Magione, which is just before the junction with the expressway heading to Perugia. In a few minutes, you see the four-lane expressway, but do not get on it. Instead, continue over the highway and follow the back roads through the countryside to Umbertide. Stop for a short visit to this small, 10th century town that hugs the banks of the Tevere River. In addition to the castle, you might want to visit the Church of Santa Maria della Reggia, which is an intriguing octagonal, three-tiered building topped by a cupola. Another church, the Holy Cross, is famous for its lovely painting by Signorelli, called *Deposition from the Cross*.

Gubbio: Leaving Umbertide, take the road that passes over the highway E45 and continue on to Gubbio. This splendidly preserved, medieval walled town is perched high on the slopes of Monte Ingino. The setting is superb and the view from the plaza that sits like a shelf overlooking the countryside is breathtaking. The narrow, cobbled streets and walkways lacing the hillside are delightful to explore. The town is filled with architectural masterpieces, one of these, the Basilica, dominates the town. There is much to see including the Cathedral, the Consuls Palace, the Piazza Pensile, the Pretorio Palace, and the Santa Maria Nuova church where you can see Ottaviano Nelli's *Madonna del Belvedere*. Outside the city walls, nestled below the town, there are the remains of a Roman theater—another reminder of how important the city was in its prime.

Perugia: From Gubbio head south on S298 in the direction of Perugia. There is a turnoff to Perugia, which is surrounded by many modern commercial buildings. If time is short, bypass Perugia (which is not as pristine as many of Umbria's other jewels) and continue on to the junction of S75 and continue east following signs to Assisi. However, if you want to "see it all," Pergugia has many delights. Perugia is a large medieval city surrounded by ramparts. An important Umbrian city since Etruscan days, the old town has at its heart the **Piazza IV Novembre**, a beautiful square with an appealing fountain, the **Fontana Maggiore**, built in the late 13th century. Although Perugia is rich in history and has a delightful medieval core, it is surrounded by modern commercial development and is not one of our favorites since it does not exude the romantic appeal and the intimacy of some of the other hill towns in Umbria.

Assisi: Coming from either Perugia or Gubbio, take S75 east following signs for Assisi, one of our favorite targets in Umbria. Built up the steep slopes of Mount Subasio, this magical city is a tribute to St. Francis. Although he was born into a family of wealth, after several visions in which Christ appeared to him, St. Francis left his privileged life. He was obviously a person with a deeply poetic soul and his tender teachings of reverence for the beauties of nature and kindness to all animals and birds still appeal to us today. To remember your visit, you might want to buy a statue of St. Francis to bring home. You will find statues in all sizes and price ranges in the many shops. Even if it were not for the lingering memory of the gentle St. Francis, Assisi would be a "must see" for it is one of the most spectacular hill towns in Umbria. Perhaps there are a few too many souvenir shops, but this is a small price to pay for the privilege of experiencing such a very special place. The town walls begin on the valley floor and completely enclose the city as it climbs the steep hillside to the enormous castle at its summit. Assisi with its maze of tiny streets is a marvelous town for walking (you must wear sturdy shoes) and it is great fun as you come across intriguing little lanes opening into small squares. When you stop to rest, there are breathtaking vistas of the lovely Umbrian fields stretching out below. Along with many other historic buildings, Assisi's most famous monument, **St. Francis' Basilica,** was severely damaged by an earthquake in September 1997. However, almost all of the repairs have now been completed and the town looks remarkably "back to normal." The basilica, which also houses a monastery, faces onto a large square bound by columns forming vaulted covered walkways. In addition to the monastery, there are two basilicas—upper and lower. Both are adorned with excellent frescoes that were unfortunately damaged by the earthquake. Also while in Assisi, visit

Santa Chiara (St. Clara's Church). Clara, a close friend of St. Francis, founded the Order of St. Clare. Go into the church to view the lovely frescoes of Santa Clara and her sisters. Part of the enjoyment of Assisi is just to stroll through its narrow, cobbled streets—the whole town is like a living museum. If you have time, hike up to the **Rocca Medioevale**, an enormous 14th-century fortress perched on the hillside overlooking the city. From here you have a magnificent bird's-eye view of Assisi and beyond to the enchanting Umbrian countryside sweeping out to the distant hills.

Collepino: From Assisi you can continue on the S75 in the direction of Foligno. However, if you feel adventuresome and enjoy getting off the beaten path, there is a narrow twisting, very scenic back road that leads through the hills making a loop from Assisi that ends up back on the S75 in Spello, about 5 kilometers before Foligno. The driving is difficult, but you can enjoy the beauty of the rugged forested mountains, an area of Umbria seldom seen by tourists. The road begins at the upper part of Assisi. Follow signs in the direction of Gualdo Tadino, but before you get there, take the road marked to Armenzano where you continue on following signs to Spello. After going through Armenzano, the road passes the adorable secluded hamlet of Collepino, which oozes charm with its winding cobbled streets and stone houses. It is so tiny that you quickly see it all. After Collepino, it is 7 kilometers on to Spello, where the road joins the S75, which you take going south.

Bevagna: Five kilometers south of Spello you come to **Foligno** where we suggest leaving the S75 and taking instead the back roads to enjoy the lovely villages and scenery. From Foligno take the S316 toward Bevagna, which you reach after about 8 kilometers. Bevagna is an enticing, intimate, charming walled village, founded by the Romans. In addition to just enjoying the allure of the town, there is much to see including a stunning 19th-century opera house, the beautiful San Michele church, well-preserved mosaics in the old Roman baths, and a paper press making paper just as it has been for centuries. If it is mealtime, there is a wonderful place for lunch, L'Orto degli Angeli.

Montefalco: From Bevagna, take the road marked to Montefalco (located 7 kilometers from Bevagna). Montefalco is a walled town that crowns a hill with sweeping views of the Umbrian countryside. The town is a maze of small, narrow streets. For sightseeing, the main attraction is **San Francisco**, a church now converted into a museum that displays some of the finest work of Benozzo Gozzoli, including the fresco *Life of St. Francis*. Also, a delicious wine, *Sagrantino*, is produced here.

Spoleto: From Montefalco, loop back to the main road, S75, and continue south following signs to Spoleto. Not only is medieval Spoleto dramatically perched atop a hill, but it also has an almost unbelievable bridge dating from Roman times. This **Ponte delle Torri**, spanning the deep ravine between Spoleto and the adjoining mountain, was built over an aqueduct existing in the 14th century. This incredible engineering wonder is 230 meters long and soars 81 meters high. It is supported by a series of ten Gothic arches and has a fort at the far end as well as a balcony in the center. The 12th-century **Cathedral** in Spoleto is also so lovely that it alone would make a stop in this charming town worth a detour. The exterior of this very old cathedral, with its beautiful rose window and intricate mosaics, is truly charming. Although a great sightseeing destination at any time of the year, Spoleto is very popular in late June and early July when it hosts the world-famous Spoleto Festival, featuring great music, dance, and theater. During the festival season rooms are usually more expensive and almost impossible to secure so should be booked far in advance.

Torgiano: Torgiano, in the center of a rich wine region, has a lovely small wine museum. You would never dream that such a tiny town could boast such a gem, but it is not a coincidence: the Lungarotti family owns the vineyards for many kilometers in every direction. Signor Lungarotti furnished the museum with artifacts pertaining to every aspect of wine production from the earliest days, creating an interesting and beautifully displayed collection worthy of a detour by anyone interested in wines. In the center of town, the Lungarotti family owns, **Le Tre Vaselle**, a charming choice for lunch.

Duomo, Orvieto

WESTERN UMBRIA

From Spoleto, a scenic route connecting the eastern part of Umbria to the western part of Umbria is to take the S418, which twists west from Spoleto for 25 kilometers through beautiful hills to the E45. Turn north on E45 for about 21 kilometers and turn west on S448, following signs to the A1 and Orvieto.

Todi: The picture-perfect village of Todi makes a great midway stop between Spoleto and Orvieto. It is located near the junction of E45 and S448 and is well signposted. This adorable small town crowning a hilltop like icing on a cake is one of our favorites. No, there isn't much to see—it is the town itself that is so picturesque. It is just fun to wander the twisting cobblestone streets, enjoy the medieval ambiance, and stop to enjoy a cappuccino in one of the sidewalk cafés. As you stroll through the small village, watch for the Cathedral, the People's Square, the intimate San Ilario Church, and the Roman/Etruscan Museum.

Leaving Todi you come to the A1, don't get onto the freeway, but instead follow signs to Orvieto. NOTE: When deciding on a town in the area to use as a hub for sightings, don't limit your choice to those in Umbria. You will also find a rich selection of places to stay very nearby in Tuscany.

The Haunting Beauty of Umbria

Orvieto: Originally founded by the Etruscans, Orvieto later became a prosperous Roman city, famous for its production of ceramics. Orvieto is spread across the top of a hill that drops down on every side in steep volcanic cliffs to the Umbrian plain 200 meters below—you wonder how the town could ever have been built! Drive as far as you can up to the town, park your car, and proceed on foot. Have a good map handy because you pass so many churches and squares that it is difficult to orient yourself—Orvieto is a maze of tiny piazzas and narrow twisting streets. Continue on to Orvieto's center where a glorious **Duomo** dominates the immense piazza. You may think you have seen sufficient stunning cathedrals to last a lifetime, but just wait—Orvieto's is truly special, one of the finest examples of Romanesque-Gothic architecture in Italy. It is brilliantly embellished with intricate mosaic designs and accented by lacy slender spires stretching gracefully into the sky. Within the Duomo, you absolutely must not miss the **Chapel of San Brizio;** here you find frescos by Fra Angelico and Luca Signorelli. Also of interest in Orvieto is **St. Patrick's Well**, hewn out of solid volcanic rock. Pope Clement VII took refuge in Orvieto in 1527 and to ensure the town's water supply in case of siege, he ordered the digging of this 62-meter-deep well. It is unique for the 70 windows that illuminate it and the two spiral staircases that wind up and down without meeting. Other sights to see include the Papal Palace, the Town Hall, and the archaeological museum.

Civita di Bagnorégio: Although **Civita di Bagnorégio** is not in Umbria, it's located just southwest of Orvieto, so it conveniently ties in with this itinerary. If you are a photographer and love picturesque walled villages, few can surpass the setting of this small town. Take the N71, which twists west from Orvieto toward **Lake Bolsena**. Stay on N71 for about 20 kilometers and then turn left heading to Bagnorégio. Go into town and follow signs to Civita, which crowns the top of a steep, circular-shaped, rocky outcrop. There is no road into the village—the only access is by walking over a long, narrow suspension bridge that joins the two sides of a deep ravine. Once you arrive, you will find a few shops, some Etruscan artifacts, a church, and a restaurant. However, the main focus is the town itself with its narrow arcaded alleyways and a dramatic 180-degree view of the desolate, rocky canyons that stretch out around the town with a haunting beauty.

Orvieto

Places to Stay in Tuscany

One of the most attractive features of Florence is that its surrounding countryside hugs the city limits, giving the possibility of staying in the tranquil foothills of Chianti. In the nearby village of Antella warm hosts Azelio and Luisa have completely restored their part of an enormous estate divided into three 14th-century villas. The downstairs area includes a large living/dining room, main kitchen, and separate kitchenette for guests' use during the day. The vaulted antique cantina below displays an enviable collection of reserve wines. Up a steep flight of stairs are the four well-appointed guestrooms, all with superb views over countryside all the way to Brunelleschi's cupola. Three regular doubles are individually decorated with country antiques and one has a hydrojet bathtub. The real treat is the large junior suite with its high wood-beamed mansard ceilings, sitting area, and canopy bed. Originally the outdoor loggia, it retains its columns and seven windows looking out to both sides of the property. A country breakfast is served either in the small breakfast room or in the garden. Do not miss a chance to sample one of Luisa's delectable Tuscan meals or, better yet, cooking lessons. *Directions:* Leave the A1 at Firenze Sud. After the toll, turn first right for Siena and after about 1.5 km turn left for Antella. In Antella the Via Montisoni starts from the square with the church on your left.

VILLA IL COLLE
Hosts: Azelio & Luisa Pierattoni
Via Montisoni 45, Antella–Florence, (FI) 50011, Italy
Tel & Fax: (055) 621822
Cellphone: (347) 8778178
4 Rooms, Double: €110–€150
Minimum Nights: 2
Open: all year, Credit cards: MC, VS
Other Languages: good English
www.karenbrown.com/colle.html
B&B

Val di Colle is an authentic stone farmhouse whose origins go back 500 years. The unique character of the home derives from the cleverly restored work of owners Giovanni and Anna who purposely left the architectural features undisturbed while installing carefully concealed modern amenities. Small flights of stairs on either side of the house, lead to charming guestrooms. The open living room space has a loft hall passing through more bedrooms. Simple antique furnishings appropriately accent the exposed stone walls and slate floors and contrast with the modern colorful art paintings adorning the walls(including a Warhol and a Mirò), collected over years of travelling. A breakfast room with wood beamed ceiling greets guests in the morning when the first meal of the day is served on crisp white linen tablecloths. This passion for fine linens is a tradition (past family business) and continues in bedroom sheets and bedspreads. The large property extends over the surrounding hillsides dotted with olive trees. A golf driving range and 9-hole pitch and putt course will open in the spring. At the reception desk staff are on hand to suggest day trips and guided tours of Arezzo. A 2-bedroom apartment for families is also available. *Directions:* Located 4 km south of the city center. Exit from the A1 autostrada at Monte San Savino and continue 10 km to Arezzo. Follow signs to Bagnoro then left to the end of the road—Val di Colle.

VAL DI COLLE   New
Hosts: Giovanni & Anna Palleggi
Località: Bagnoro Arezzo
Arezzo, (AR) 52100, Italy
Tel & Fax: (0575) 365167
10 Rooms, Double: €210–€240
1 Apartment: €420
Open: all year, Credit cards: all major
Other Languages: some English
www.karenbrown.com/valdicolle.html
B&B

Borgo Argenina has all the elements of a "bestseller" bed and breakfast: the perfect location in the heart of Chianti surrounded by vineyards, very comfortable accommodation in an ancient stone farmhouse, glorious countryside views, and, above all, Elena, the Borgo Argenina's gregarious hostess. She left behind a successful fashion business in Milan and bought an entire abandoned village, restoring two of the stone houses for herself and the bed and breakfast. She chose the best artisans in the area and literally worked with them to create the house of her dreams. Everything from painting stenciled borders in rooms through restoring furniture to sewing quilted bedspreads was executed exclusively by Elena herself. The downstairs living rooms and breakfast room are beautifully done in rich cream and soft yellows that complement perfectly the brick-vaulted ceilings and terra-cotta floors. Elena is up at dawn baking cakes for breakfast accompanied by classical music. Every little detail has been attended to in the pink-and-blue bedrooms adorned with white eyelet curtains, patchwork quilts, and dried flower arrangements. Three bedrooms have kitchen facilities and across the way is a very comfortable three-bedroom, independent house. *Directions:* Follow S.S.408 from Siena for Montevarchi and after 15 km turn off to the right at Monti. Just before Monti and S. Marcellina there is a sign on the right for Argenina.

BORGO ARGENINA
Host: Elena Nappa
Localita: Argenina-Monti
Argenina–Gaiole in Chianti, (SI) 53013, Italy
Tel: (0577) 747117, Fax: (0577) 747228
7 Rooms, Double: €150–€200
3 Houses: €200–€400 daily
Minimum Nights: 3, Open: all year
Credit cards: all major, Good English, French
www.karenbrown.com/argenina.html
B&B, SELF CATERING

Bagno Vignoni is a charming little village whose unique piazza is actually an ancient stone pool with thermal water. In medieval times the large bath was divided for men and women who came to soak in the rejuvenating waters, hoping to cure such ailments as arthritis and rheumatism. Today, tourists come to view this remarkable place and take advantage of these same curative properties in the nearby falls or modern pool facilities. With the success of their wine bar (enoteca) here, it was only natural that the young Marinis should open a bed and breakfast for travelers. The stone building dates to the 1300s and was thoughtfully restored after having been abandoned for more than 30 years. The eight double bedrooms and large living room with loft and grand piano are very cozy and purposely old-fashioned in feeling. The beamed guestrooms and nice new bathrooms each have their own theme and corresponding soft pastel color schemes and are romantically appointed with lace curtains and pillows, antique beds and armoires, and painted stencil borders. Breakfast is served across the way in the historic enoteca, which was once part of the Capuchin friars' monastery. With its informal and warm hospitality, it is no wonder that the bar is a favorite place for artists and writers. *Directions:* Bagno Vignoni is 5 km south of San Quirico. Park in the town lot and walk the short distance to the locanda.

LA LOCANDA DEL LOGGIATO
Hosts: Sabrina & Barbara Marini
Piazza del Moretto 30, Bagno Vignoni, (SI) 53023, Italy
Tel: (0577) 888925, Fax: (0577) 888370
Cellphone: (335) 430427
8 Rooms, Double: €130–€150
Minimum Nights: 2
Open: all year, Credit cards: MC, VS
Other Languages: some English, French
www.karenbrown.com/loggiato.html
B&B

After many years of traveling to Italy at any opportunity, Jennie and Alan left England to move to Tuscany and fell in love immediately with Villa Mimosa, a rustic, 18th-century home with a shady front courtyard facing the village street and the church. They have created three sweet bedrooms and one attic mansard suite for four persons, each with a different theme and with lovely mountain views. A cozy sitting room and a library with grand piano are reserved upstairs for guests and decorated with the Pratts' own antiques imported from England. Jennie and Alan delight in sharing their passion for this part of the country known as Lunigiana (very near the Cinque Terre coastal area and one hour from both Parma and Lucca) and give their guests lots of personal attention, while making them feel right at home. Guests are treated to breakfast on the terrace overlooking the pretty garden and swimming pool with the Apennine Mountains as a backdrop and delight in Jennie's creative cuisine straight off the Aga, based on fresh garden vegetables and local recipes. Tea and homemade cakes are served in the shady garden. *Directions:* Leave the A15 autostrada (Parma-La Spezia) at Pontremoli from the north or Aulla from the south and take the autostrada SS62 to Villafranca, then Bagnone. Enter town through the yellow gateway, then over the bridge. Turn left following signs for Corlaga, and the villa is on the right 50 meters before the church.

VILLA MIMOSA
Hosts: Jennie & Alan Pratt
Localita: Corlaga, Bagnone, (MS) 54021, Italy
Tel & Fax: (0187) 427022
Cellphone: (335) 6264657
4 Rooms, Double: €80–€110
Dinner served on request
Open: all year, Credit cards: none
Other Languages: fluent English
www.karenbrown.com/mimosa.html
B&B

Casa Sola is just that—an ancient villa standing alone atop a hill on a gorgeous 400-acre vineyard estate in the heart of Chianti. The gracious Gambaro family produces prestigious Chianti Classico Riserva, Supertuscan-Montarsiccio, and extra-virgin olive oil of the highest quality. There are six large guest apartments on two floors of a rose-covered stone farmhouse down the road from the main villa. All the apartments consist of living room, kitchen, bedrooms, and baths, with private entrances and garden (flowers match the color scheme of each apartment!). The apartments are furnished stylishly with selected country antiques, and details such as botanical prints hung with bows, eyelet curtains, fresh flowers, and a bottle of wine are welcome touches. Number 5, for up to eight people, is the most spacious with four bedrooms, fireplace, and magnificent views over the Barberino Valley and cypress woods. Il Capanno in the converted barn is a delightful "nest" for honeymooners. An inviting swimming pool overlooks the valley surrounding the main villa. Wine-cellar visits with wine tasting are organized once a week and marked hiking trails lead guests through picture-perfect landscapes. *Directions:* From the Autostrada del Sole going towards Florence, exit at Firenze Certosa joining the Firenze-Siena Superstrada. Exit S. Donato in Poggio and go beyond San Donato. After 50 meters, look for the sign for Casa Sola on the right.

FATTORIA CASA SOLA
Hosts: Count Gambaro family
Localita: Cortine
Barberino Val d'Elsa, (FI) 50021, Italy
Tel: (055) 8075028, Fax: (055) 8059194
6 Apartments: €550–€2,100 weekly (Jul & Aug)
€70–€84 daily (2 people), Minimum Nights: 2
Open: all year, Credit cards: all major
Other Languages: good English, French, Spanish
www.karenbrown.com/fattoriacasasola.html
SELF CATERING

Strategically positioned midway between Siena and Florence sits the square stone farmhouse with cupola (actually one of the bedrooms!) dating from 1700 owned by Gianni and Cristina, a couple who have dedicated their lives to the equestrian arts. The Paretaio appeals particularly to visitors with a passion for horseback riding, for the de Marchis offer everything from basic riding lessons to dressage training, and day outings through the gorgeous surrounding countryside. In fact, the Paretaio is recognized as one of the top riding "ranches" in Tuscany, with more than 30 horses. On the ground floor is a rustic living room with country antiques, comfy sofas, and piano enhanced by a vaulted brick ceiling and worn terra-cotta floors, off which are two bedrooms. Upstairs, the main gathering area is the dining room, which features a massive fireplace and a seemingly endless wooden table. This room gives access to more bedrooms, each decorated with touches such as dried flowers, white lace curtains, and, of course, equestrian prints. A vast collection of over 300 pieces with an equestrian theme is displayed about the home. Il Paretaio also organizes courses in Italian and is an excellent base for touring the heart of Tuscany. The swimming pool gives splendid views over olive groves and vineyards. *Directions:* Head south from Barberino on route 2 and after 2 km take the second right-hand turnoff for San Filippo. Continue on 1.5 km of dirt road to the house.

IL PARETAIO
Hosts: Cristina & Giovanni de Marchi
Localita: San Filippo, Barberino Val d'Elsa, (FI) 50021
Tel: (055) 8059218, Fax: (055) 8059231
Cellphone: (338) 7379626
8 Rooms, Double: €65–€98
2 Apartments: €400–€800 weekly
Open: all year, Credit cards: none
Other Languages: good English, French
www.karenbrown.com/ilparetaio.html
B&B, SELF CATERING

When the Caccettas and three other families purchased the 250-acre property over 20 years ago, they were true pioneers in agritourism. After restoring the land and historic 16th-century hunting lodge, today they have a self-sufficient organic farm producing top-quality Chianti, white and rosé wines, grappa, and virgin olive oil. First in Europe to be awarded certification (Uni En Iso) as an "organic agricultural park" for quality and comprehensive agritouristic activity, they also host agro-environmental and cultural activities in their small theater, "del Carbone". Spacious guestrooms are divided between the main house, with two suites and three bedrooms, and an adjacent house. All are decorated with care using lovely family antiques, which blend in perfectly with the overall refined ambiance. The cozy common rooms include a living room with fireplace and stone walls, card room, small bar area, and dining rooms where breakfast and dinner are served. A set four-course dinner of traditional Tuscan recipes using primarily fresh vegetables and herbs is offered. During warmer months a buffet breakfast and dinner are served outside under the pergola overlooking deep woods. A pool, tennis courts, hiking trails, and horseback riding at a nearby stables are all available. *Directions:* Exit the Siena-Florence highway at San Donato, go through Tavarnelle and Barberino. Turn right at La Spinosa sign (Via XXV Aprile) and take the dirt road to the end.

LA SPINOSA
Hosts: Caccetta, Presezzi, Ossola & Videsott families
Via Le Masse 8, Barberino Val d'Elsa, (FI) 50021, Italy
Tel: (055) 8075413, Fax: (055) 8066214
Cellphone: (055) 8075822
9 Rooms, Double: €150–€180
Minimum Nights: 2
Open: Mar to Nov, Credit cards: MC, VS
Other Languages: good English
www.karenbrown.com/laspinosa.html
B&B

The Locanda, a pale-yellow and brick house dating from 1830, sits on the border between Tuscany and Umbria and is an excellent base from which to explore this rich countryside. The villa's dining room features a vaulted ceiling in toast-colored brick, an enormous fireplace, French windows opening out to the flower garden, and antiques including a cupboard adorned with the family's blue-and-white china. The upstairs quarters are reserved primarily for guests, and contain five comfortable rooms all off one hallway and an inviting sitting room and library. The cozy bedrooms have mansard ceilings, armoires, lovely linens, and private bathrooms with showers. Additional guestrooms are located on the ground floor of the converted barn between the house and a small garden, where a swimming pool has been added. These are more spacious, private, and modern in decor. Cordial hostess Palmira assists with local itineraries. Excellent regional fare including divine vegetarian dishes with local produce is prepared by chef Walter Redaelli who is happy to give cooking classes. Siena is only 45 kilometers away, and the quaint medieval and Renaissance villages of Pienza, Montepulciano, and Montalcino are close by. *Directions:* Exit from the Rome-Florence autostrada at Val di Chiana. Head toward Bettolle, then bear right toward Siena. Follow signs for La Bandita.

LOCANDA LA BANDITA
Host: Palmira Fiorini
Via Bandita 72
Bettolle, (SI) 53040, Italy
Tel & Fax: (0577) 624649
Cellphone: (335) 6945920
8 Rooms, Double: €85–€105
Open: Mar to Dec, Credit cards: all major
Other Languages: good English
www.karenbrown.com/locandalabandita.html
B&B

Luisa left her fashion business in Parma and settled in this peaceful spot 3 kilometers from the coast. The stylish, impeccable home clearly reflects the personality of the warm and reserved hostess who tastefully designed both the exterior and interior of this lovely accommodation. Each of the four corner bedrooms upstairs has its own large private terrace and beautiful floral-tiled bathroom and all offer beds made with linen sheets and splendid views over fruit orchards and olive groves to the sea. While the hostess occupies the cupola, guests have a independent entrance to the upstairs rooms, giving utmost privacy to all. Common areas include the living room and open kitchen with large arched window and doors looking out to the surrounding garden. An ample fresh country breakfast with cakes all prepared by Luisa is served here at one long table. A separate cottage next to the main house offers a double room and beamed living room with stone fireplace and kitchen, and a second apartment is available within another cottage next door. Day trips include Elba Island, Volterra and San Gimignano, Lucca, Siena, private beaches, Etruscan itineraries, visits to the wine estates of Bolgheri, and biking in the nearby nature park. Sweet and simple. *Directions:* Exit from Aurelia on route 1 at Bibbona and turn left. Pass through La California and turn left for Bibbona. Podere Le Mezzelune is before town, well marked to the left. Pisa airport is 40 km away.

PODERE LE MEZZELUNE
Hosts: Luisa Chiesa family
Via Mezzelune 126, Bibbona, (LI) 57020, Italy
Tel: (0586) 670266, Fax: (0586) 671814
Cellphone: (329) 3712287
4 Rooms, Double: €166–€176
2 Apartments: €170– €180 daily
Minimum Nights: 3, Open: all year
Credit cards: MC, VS, Other Languages: French
www.karenbrown.com/mezzelune.html
B&B, SELF CATERING

The prestigious Monsignor della Casa property extending over 600 acres is a true country resort with all the trimmings in the beautiful area north of Florence called Mugello. This is the land from which such masters as Giotto, Cimabue, and Fra Angelico came and was the actual home of 15th-century writer and Vatican secretary, della Casa, whose portrait hangs in Washington's National Gallery. The Marzi family meticulously restored a cluster of six stone farmhouses on the vast estate next to their own stately villa. The refined bi-level apartments exude pure Tuscan charm and can accommodate from two to six guests. Two individual villas, each with private swimming pool, can take a group of twelve to sixteen. The finest linens and fabrics were chosen to accent exposed stone walls, brick floors, and wood-beamed ceilings. Spend your days touring or in any of a variety of activities for every age and interest: biking, hiking, or horseback riding in the nearby woods, golf, swimming in one of two pools, tennis, volleyball, and children's playground. An elegantly rustic restaurant and wine bar serves guests in the evening with cordial host Alessio making sure nothing is overlooked. The "wellness center" offers sauna, steam bath, Jacuzzi, and other services. Indulge! *Directions:* From Borgo San Lorenzo follow signs for Faenza. Just after the turnoff for Scarperia turn right for Mucciano, coming first to the resort (3 km total). 27 km from Florence.

MONSIGNOR DELLA CASA
Hosts: Marzi family
Via di Mucciano 16, Borgo San Lorenzo, (FI) 50032
Tel: (055) 840821, Fax: (055) 8408240
21 apartments: €405–€2,625 weekly
2 Villas: €1,590–€4,600 weekly
Minimum Nights: 2, 7 in high season
Open: all year, Credit cards: all major
Other Languages: good English
www.karenbrown.com/monsignor.html
SELF CATERING

Tall cypress trees protect the cluster of ancient stone farmhouses making up the idyllic Iesolana property, situated atop 300 acres of cascading vineyards, olive groves, and sunflowers, with 360 degrees of breathtaking Tuscan views. After years of meticulous restoration of the three ochre-stained houses, eight high-level apartments are offered, most with private terraces. Apartments have from one to four bedrooms and are elegantly appointed with rustic furnishings, country fabrics, and modern kitchens and baths that harmonize beautifully with the cool stone floors and original wood-beamed ceilings. Among the many services available are individual telephones, satellite TV, barbecue facilities, swimming pool, and mountain bikes for leisurely rides. The impeccable landscape is studded with terra-cotta pots overflowing with brightly colored geraniums. The fabulously restored barn now hosts a stylish wine bar for tastings of Iesolana's own wines, oils, and honey. Breakfast and dinners of regional cuisine are also served in the comfortable restaurant with outdoor seating as an option. A state-of-the-art meeting room is available for groups. Centrally located for day trips to Siena, Florence, and Rome, this is the perfect spot for relaxing and exploring. *Directions:* Leave the A1 at Valdarno for Montevarchi, Bucine (8 km). From town follow signs up to Iesolana, passing over a stone bridge (2 km) to the end of the road.

BORGO IESOLANA
Host: Giovanni Toscano
Localita: Iesolana
Bucine, (AR) 52021, Italy
Tel: (055) 992988, Fax: (055) 992879
9 apartments: €490–€2,100 weekly, €100–€380 daily
Minimum Nights: 2, 7 in high season
Open: all year, Credit cards: all major
Other Languages: good English
www.karenbrown.com/iesolana.html
SELF CATERING

The Ripolina farm property is a vast 500-acre farm comprised of several different brick farmhouses. Self-catering apartments (two for up to ten people) and individual guest bedrooms are divided among five farmhouses dotting the soft hills of the property. Two very charmingly authentic apartments are found within the Pieve di Piana, a cluster of houses grouped around an ancient church with bell tower dating to the 9th century. The richly historic Pieve sits on a hill and enjoys panoramic views of vineyards and fields of grain and sunflowers extending as far as the eye can see. Hostess and owner Laura Cresti resides in the house called S. Ferdinando where there are two apartments with two bedrooms with a separate entrance. Five rooms are next door in the Ripoli house, each being individually appointed with appropriate country local antiques. Walls are painted in warm earth colors and the upstairs loggia, a typical open porch with four large arched windows, has been enclosed and transformed into the breakfast room. A full country breakfast buffet includes fresh coffee cakes, fruit, cereals, yogurt, and cheeses. This is strikingly beautiful countryside chock-full of hilltowns to explore. A beautiful swimming pool and bicycles are available for guests. *Directions:* From Siena (25 km) take the S.S.2 to Buonconvento and turn right in town following signs for Bibbiano. After crossing the river, turn right at La Ripolina and drive up to the main house.

LA RIPOLINA
Host: Laura Cresti
Pieve di Piana, Buonconvento, (SI) 53022, Italy
Tel & Fax: (0577) 282280
Cellphone: (335) 5739284
7 Rooms, Double: €75–€90
7 apartments: €35–€60 daily (per person)
Open: all year, Credit cards: MC, VS
Other Languages: good English, French
www.karenbrown.com/laripolina.html
B&B, SELF CATERING

The beautiful Montebelli property, situated in Maremma, with its more wild Tuscan landscapes, covers 300 acres of mountain, hills laden with vineyards and olive groves, and sunflower fields, all close to the sea. The Filotico family divides their time and energy between their guests and production of wines and olive oil. The main guesthouse, orginally a centuries-old mill, holds most of the comfortable guestrooms, while the remaining accommodation is spread out in two one-story wings, each with individual entrance. Rooms are decorated tastefully with typical Tuscan antiques and include the amenities of a regular hotel. The half-board requirement allows guests to sample the marvelous cuisine by candlelight of the region (with a Neopolitan touch, as is owner's origins), within the characteristic dining room featuring the stone wheel from the original press or out on the spacious patio. This is unexplored territory, full of historical treasures and Etruscan remains. Scenic walks or biking on marked trails (a must for the views!), a swimming pool, tennis courts, horse riding, and courses in cooking, yoga and wine are all available. *Directions:* From the north, exit at Gavorrano Scalo from Aurelia S.S.1, following signs for Caldana. Just before Caldana, turn at the Montebelli sign and take the dirt road to the end.

MONTEBELLI
Hosts: Carla Filotico family
Localita: Molinetto, Caldana, (GR) 58020, Italy
Tel: (0566) 887100, Fax: (0566) 81439
21 Rooms, Double: €216–€236*
*Includes breakfast & dinner
Minimum Nights: 2
Closed: Jan to Mar, Credit cards: MC, VS
Other Languages: good English
www.karenbrown.com/montebelli.html
B&B

The Villa Bellaria, situated right in the picturesque village of Campagnatico with its stone streets and houses and magnificent views over the Ombrone Valley and up to Mount Amiata, retains the authentic flavor of a noble country home from centuries past. Credit goes to gracious hostess Luisa who oversees the 900-plus-acre property, once belonging to such powerful families as the Aldobrandeschi and Medici. It was partially destroyed during World War II and completely restored by the Querci della Rovere family. Talented Luisa runs not only the hospitality activity but the entire farm as well, while her husband produces Morellino wine from another property. With its large surrounding balustraded park with cypress-lined trails and swimming pool, one forgets that it is all part of the actual town (with its many conveniences). The spacious bedrooms with family antiques and two of the apartments are situated within the main villa while the other newer but characteristic ones are spread out on three floors in the transformed olive-press building. They have either one or two bedrooms, bathroom, and sitting room with kitchenette and are appointed with the family's country furniture. This is a lovely base for exploring the area. *Directions:* From Siena (55 km) or Grosseto (20 km) exit from highway 223 at Campagnatico and continue for 4 km to the town. The villa is the second right in town—drive up to a green gate.

VILLA BELLARIA
Host: Luisa Querci della Rovere
Campagnatico, (GR) 58042, Italy
Tel: (0564) 996626, Fax: (0564) 996626
Cellphone: (335) 6097438
4 Rooms, Double: €60–€80
10 apartments: €500–€1000 weekly
Minimum Nights: 2, Open: all year
Credit cards: all major, Other Languages: good English
www.karenbrown.com/bellaria.html
B&B, SELF CATERING

The Canonica a Cerreto property is truly a marvel to behold, with an extraordinary combination of features. Perfectly located in lower Chianti and equidistant to most of Tuscany's highlights, it offers not only very comfortable accommodation in a fascinating historic dwelling but also seemingly endless vistas of gorgeous countryside, and welcoming and gracious hosts. Iron gates open up to an entrance lined with gorgeous terra-cotta pots in the form of lions, overflowing with geraniums and oleander plants giving accents of color to the façade of the ancient stone church and attached canonica, the summer residence of the Vescovo of the Duomo of Siena. Within the walls is a complex including the family's residence, three guest apartments in the monks' former rooms, quarters for the farmhands, and a cantina. Signora Lorenzi proudly shows guests her museum-caliber art collection and magnificent home where large period paintings adorn frescoed walls and elegant antique pieces are displayed. The apartments, in an elegant country style, are tastefully appointed with antiques and include a bedroom, bathroom, and living area with kitchenette. The largest apartment has two bedrooms, each with its own bathroom. A lovely, secluded swimming pool has superb countryside views. *Directions:* From Siena follow the S.S.408 towards Gaiole and just after Pianella, take the first left (Canonica a Cerreto is marked on most maps).

CANONICA A CERRETO
Hosts: Egidio Lorenzi family
Canonica a Cerreto, Castelnuovo Berardenga
(SI) 53010, Italy
Tel & Fax: (0577) 363261
3 apartments: €730–€1,250 weekly
Minimum Nights: 3, 7 in high season
Open: Apr to Oct, Credit cards: all major
Other Languages: good English, Abitare la Storia
www.karenbrown.com/canonica.html
SELF CATERING

The turreted medieval village of Capalbio, perched on a hilltop, has the double advantage of being close to one of the prettiest seaside spots—Argentario—plus having the beautiful countryside and villages of Maremma to explore. Monica and husband Filippo run an efficient little bed and breakfast operation, having left a long career in the restaurant business. Breakfast, composed of fresh homemade cakes, breads, and jams, is served in the stone-walled dining room or out on the patio. Ten rooms in a row, each with independent entrance from the garden, are situated next door to the main house; while five new bedrooms have been added in the adjacent converted barn. Rooms are nicely decorated in a classic style, and have such amenities as television, telephone, hairdryer, and air conditioning. This comes in handy on hot summer evenings, although there is always a cool breeze passing through (hence the Etruscan name "Iced Woods") and the swimming pool surrounded by a manicured lawn is wonderfully refreshing. The farm property extends over 30 acres of olive groves and fields of grain and oats. Not to be missed is an unforgettable meal at Tullio's famed restaurant in town and the absolutely delightful sculpture park of Niki de St. Phalle 4 km away. *Directions:* From Rome on the coastal highway 1, exit before Capalbio at Pescia Fiorentina. At Pescia stay left for 3 km. Ghiaccio is 1 km after the fork for Manciano.

GHIACCIO BOSCO
Hosts: Monica Olivi & Filippo Rinaldi
Strada della Sgrilla 4
Capalbio, (GR) 58011, Italy
Tel & Fax: (0564) 896539
Cellphone: (339) 5662578
15 Rooms, Double: €75–€105
Open: all year
Other Languages: some English
www.karenbrown.com/ghiaccio.html
B&B

Castelfiorentino is 40 kilometers from Florence, Siena and Pisa, and although its outskirts are very commercial, it is a strategic touring base and the surrounding countryside is lovely. Continuing a long tradition of making guests feel at home—their hotel in Florence has been in the family for four generations—Massimo and Susanna opened this bed and breakfast five years ago after major restoration of two hilltop farmhouses. The completely refurbished rooms, with many modern amenities, new bathrooms, fresh landscaping, and recently installed swimming pool and tennis court, have a very new feeling. Spacious bedrooms are appointed with authentic and reproduction antiques and have colorful Sicilian ceramic tiles above beds, with matching ones in bathrooms. The former barn was converted into a small restaurant decorated with contemporary art, a kitchen with viewing window, and a common living room/library upstairs. The preparation of delectable Tuscan fare using ancestral recipes is another strong tradition and cooking lessons are happily arranged for those eager to take home family secrets. A buffet breakfast is served. The side terrace, overlooking soft hills, is where guests can both enjoy breakfast and watch the sunset in the evening. *Directions:* From Castelfiorentino turn off at signs for Renai (this can be tricky to locate) and follow signs for Locanda Country Inn Le Boscarecce (5 km).

❋ 🍳 ⚗ ⚖ 💳 ☎ ⛾ P ⑪ 🚭 🏊 ⚘ 🏛 ⛴ ⚕ 🚶 🍇 🍴

LE BOSCARECCE
Hosts: Susanna Ballerini & Massimo Ravalli
Via Renai 19, Castelfiorentino, (FI) 50051, Italy
Tel: (0571) 61280, Fax: (0571) 634008
14 Rooms, Double: €90–€145
Minimum Nights: 2
Restaurant closed on Tuesdays
Open: all year, Credit cards: all major
Other Languages: good English
www.karenbrown.com/boscarecce.html
B&B

This idyllic location in the heart of Chianti, the Fattoria Tregole, five kilometers outside the charming village of Castellina, is reached by a gravel road. The ivy-covered stone farmhouse with hexagonal 18th century oratory (one of only two in Tuscany) is on the small road and opens out to the back to unspoiled hillsides covered with woods and vineyards. While husband Catello tends to the production of Chianti wine (visit the cantina with wood barrels for the reserve wines), gracious hostess Edith pays careful attention to her guests. There are five comfortable bedrooms and also two apartments complete with kitchen corner and living room, perfect for 2 to 4 guests. Particular care has been given to the décor, with peach-coloured hand-stencilled walls and trim, soft coloured quilts, antique pieces, painted wrought-iron beds, and dried flower arrangements all complimenting the terracotta brick floors. The breakfast room is set with white porcelain to match the white chairs and tables where Edith serves fresh cakes and breads each morning. With adequate notice an occasional dinner can also arranged. Outdoors the terrace and swimming enjoy inspiring views across the surrounding countryside. A great base for exploring Tuscany. *Directions:* From Castellina, follow south towards Siena and after 5 km turn left for Tregole and it's 1 km to Fattoria.

FATTIORIA TREGOLE   New
Hosts: Edith Kirchlechner & Catello Conte
Località: Tregole 86, Castellina in Chianti, (SI) 53011
Tel: (0577) 740991, Fax: (0577) 741928
5 Rooms, Double: €105–€120
2 apartments: €180-€200
Minimum Nights: 3
Open: all year, Credit cards: all major
Other Languages: good English
www.karenbrown.com/tregole
B&B, SELF CATERING

If your dream is to discover a small luxury hotel in Tuscany that is truly "off the beaten path" look no further—the romantic Locanda Le Piazze is about as remote as you will find. Tucked in the heart of Tuscany's richest wine-growing region, the hotel crowns a gentle hill. In every direction there is nothing but a breathtaking patchwork of vineyards sweeping like the open sea across undulating hills, dotted with enchanting old farmhouses. After three years in which the buildings were totally renovated and a beautiful pool added, the hotel opened to guests in the summer of 1995. It is no wonder the design and decor are in absolutely faultless taste: the owner, Maureen Bonini, has for over 40 years been a design consultant in Florence. All of the hotel's rooms exude sophisticated country elegance. Huge bouquets of fresh flowers highlight white walls, terracotta floors, and beamed ceilings. Each of the guestrooms has its own personality, but all exude a similar comfortable, homelike ambiance. The fabrics used throughout are all from Maureen's good friend, Ralph Lauren. The stunning swimming pool, tucked in the vineyards, is reached by a path through fragrant beds of lavender. *Directions:* From Castellina in Chianti take the road to Poggibonsi, S.S. 429. As you leave Castellina, turn left at the first road, marked to Gagliole, Castellare, and Castagnoli and follow signs to the hotel—a 15-minute drive on a gravel road (ask for directions).

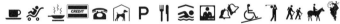

LOCANDA LE PIAZZE
Owner: Maureen Bonini
Localita: Le Piazze
Castellina in Chianti, (SI) 53011, Italy
Tel: (0577) 74 31 90, Fax: (0577) 74 31 91
20 Rooms, Double: €135–€200
Dinner by reservation: €35, light lunches, closed Wed
Open: Apr to Nov, Credit cards: all major
www.karenbrown.com/locandalepiazze.html
B&B

The Tenuta di Ricavo is unique—not a hotel at all in the usual connotation, but rather a tiny, very old, Tuscan hamlet with peasants' cottages that have been transformed into delightful guestrooms. The stables are now the dining room and the barn is now the office. Unlike many of the over-renovated hotels in Tuscany where most of what you see is actually new construction, Ricavo is all real. The guestrooms have been lovingly restored to enhance their original rustic charm and are attractively furnished with country antiques. You enter the large property following a lane through a vast pine forest that leads to the cluster of weathered stone cottages, romantically embellished by climbing roses. Flowers are everywhere and in one of the gardens are two swimming pools. Before it became a hotel, the village was the summer-holiday retreat of a Swiss family who, after World War II, transformed their home into a unique, village-style hotel. However, the Tenuta di Ricavo is not for everyone. It is quiet. It is remote. But it is a haven for the traveler for whom a good book, a walk through the forest, and a delicious dinner are fulfillment. Excellent English is spoken—especially by the gracious owner, Christina Lobrano, whose charming husband, Alessandro, is the talented chef. NOTE: There is a three-night minimum during high season. *Directions:* From Castellina, take the road to San Donato. A long way out of town, the hotel is on your right.

❄ ☕ ⚗ 💳 ☎ 🏋 Y P ⚏ ♨ 🖼 🏃 🚶 🏇 🍇

ROMANTIK HOTEL TENUTA DI RICAVO
Owners: Christina & Alessandro Lobrano
Castellina in Chianti, (SI) 53011, Italy
Tel: (0577) 74 02 21, Fax: (0577) 74 10 14
23 Rooms, Double: €160–€400
Open: Apr to Nov, Credit cards: MC, VS
www.karenbrown.com/tenutadiricavo.html
HOTEL

The Hotel Relais Borgo San Felice, located in the heart of Tuscany, is built within a feudal hamlet consisting of a cluster of stone, ivy-laced buildings linked by quaint cobbled lanes. The various buildings, including a small chapel, have been cleverly converted into reception area, guestrooms, dining rooms, lounges, conference room, and bar. The tiny village is not entirely consecrated to the hotel: local farmers still live in some of the buildings and olive oil and wine are produced. The San Felice wines, produced from grapes grown on the 2,400 surrounding acres, are some of Italy's finest. Although the hotel is secluded deep in the countryside, there is no need for guests to sacrifice any creature comforts. The Borgo San Felice, a member of the prestigious Relais & Châteaux group, is a sophisticated property offering all the amenities and services of a deluxe hotel. Although the façade is rustic, the interior exudes a gracious charm and the guestrooms, which are decorated with soft, pleasing colors, floral fabrics, and many antiques, offer every amenity. When not exploring the wealth of fascinating towns and historic sites round about, guests can relax by a large swimming pool with a view terrace, enjoy a game of tennis, or be pampered at the beauty center. *Directions:* From Florence take S2 south, until the road ends. Follow signs toward Arezzo-Monteaperti to San Felice, which is between the towns of Pianella and Villa a Sesta.

❊ ◪ ✍ 💳 ☎ ⏲ ☂ P ❚❚ ❀ 🐦 🏃 🧍 🐎 🍇

HOTEL RELAIS BORGO SAN FELICE
Manager: Birgit Fleig
Localita San Felice
Castelnuovo Berardenga, (SI) 53019, Italy
Tel: (0577) 39 64, Fax: (0577) 35 90 89
43 Rooms, Double: €290–€570
Closed: Nov to Apr, Credit cards: all major
Relais & Châteaux
www.karenbrown.com/sanfelice.html
HOTEL

The family-run Relais San Pietro is an absolute dream. It offers the finest quality throughout, gorgeous views, excellent location, spectacular swimming pool, and outstanding cuisine, all at remarkably reasonable prices. This gem of a little hotel has the added benefit of superb hospitality: Luigi Protti, your host, radiates a gentle, old-fashioned, welcoming kindness. Upon retirement he and his wife, Antonietta, decided to move back to the peaceful Tuscan countryside and open a hotel. They bought a long-neglected farmhouse only a few kilometers from the town where Signora Protti had been born and a small, intimate hotel. The Protti family recently renovated the 300 year old "Canonica" (priests' house) adding four elegant and spacious suites. The interior of the hotel has a refreshing light, uncluttered appeal. All of the original architectural features such as beamed ceilings and beautiful brick archways have been meticulously preserved. Bedrooms feature beautiful wrought-iron headboards, white bedspreads, excellent lighting, doors painted with regional designs, and superb bathrooms. The romantic dining rooms occupy what were formerly the stables. Signora Protti and her daughter-in-law preside over the kitchen and the food is fabulous. *Directions:* From Cortona, go north on 71 toward Arezzo. At Castiglion Fiorentino, turn right toward Città di Castello. After 6 km, turn left at a sign to Polvano. Go up the hill. Relais San Pietro is on the left.

RELAIS SAN PIETRO
Owner: Protti Family
Polvano
Castiglion Fiorentino, (AR) 52043, Italy
Tel: (0575) 65 01 00, Fax: (0575) 65 02 55
10 Rooms, Double: €170–€300
Closed: Nov 5 to Mar 25, Credit cards: all major
www.karenbrown.com/relaissanpietro.html
HOTEL

The lesser-known area of Tuscany south of Siena makes a delightful discovery and the variety of landscapes within an 8-kilometer drive provides one of the most fascinating excursions in the region. Besides the charming hilltowns of Montepulciano, Pienza, and Montalcino, there are the abbeys of Monte Oliveto and Sant'Antimo, plus the thermal baths of Bagno Vignoni. A perfect base in this richly historical and natural area is the magnificent castle of the Aluffi Pentini family, theirs for the past 400 years or so and practically a village in itself. The family resides in the upper reaches of the castle while guests are accommodated in several separate farmers' houses divided into a combination of apartments with one or two bedrooms, living room, and kitchenette, plus six simply and characteristically appointed bedrooms with country furniture. Rooms facing out have absolutely breathtaking views over the virgin valley. Downstairs is the dining room with wood tables covered with cheery checked cloths, where breakfast and dinner are served using homegrown products. A common space for guests is the old granary, converted into a large cozy reading room with fireplace. This is truly like a place out of a fairytale. *Directions:* The castle is well marked at 5 km from San Quirico d'Orcia. Ripa d'Orcia is marked on most maps.

CASTELLO DI RIPA D'ORCIA
Hosts: Aluffi Pentini family
Localita: Ripa d'Orcia
Castiglione d'Orcia, (SI) 53023, Italy
Tel: (0577) 897376, Fax: (0577) 898038
6 Rooms, Double: €110–€138
8 apartments: €500–€850 weekly
Minimum Nights: 2, 7 in apartments
Open: Mar to Nov, Credit cards: MC, VS
www.karenbrown.com/castellodiripadorcia.html
B&B, SELF CATERING

La Frateria di Padre Eligio, a very special, enchanting hotel, makes an outstanding base for exploring the beauties of Tuscany and Umbria. The guestrooms of this 13th-century convent (founded by St. Francis) are the original guest quarters where the friars lodged passing pilgrims. They are simply, yet tastefully, furnished with antiques. There is nothing to interrupt the enchantment—bathrooms and telephones are the only concessions to the modern era. The silence is sweetened by the song of birds and the air by the fragrance of flowers. A centuries-old forest surrounds the hotel with beckoning paths where you can stroll in perfect stillness. The restoration of this masterpiece of history is superb, but the miracle is how it was accomplished. La Frateria di Padre Eligio, in addition to housing a deluxe hotel, is home to a commune of once-troubled young people who toiled for 12 years to restore the Convento San Francesco to its former beauty. Today these remarkable young men and women awaken at dawn to begin long days of labor. They meticulously groom the gardens, tend the vegetable garden, run the hotel, bake the fresh breads, prepare the meals (exclusively using produce from the farm), and serve in the restaurant. *Directions:* Exit the A1 at Chiusi Chianciano and follow signs to Cetona. Go through town towards Sarteano. Just after leaving Cetona, turn left at sign "Mondo X—La Frateria di P. Eligio." Go about 700 meters to the hotel.

LA FRATERIA DI PADRE ELIGIO
Manager: Maria Grazia Daolio
Convento San Francesco
Cetona, (SI) 53040, Italy
Tel: (0578) 23 82 61, Fax: (0578) 23 92 20
6 Rooms, Double: €220–€280
Open: all year, Credit cards: MC, VS
www.karenbrown.com/padreeligio.html
HOTEL

Il Caggio is a delightful agriturismo farm, distinguishing itself from the many others by the sincere and warm hospitality of its owners, Gabriella and Paolo, and the superb quality of the meals. Conveniently located close to the main autostrada, guests have this corner of Chianti at their fingertips, from Siena, Cortona, Chianti, to Arezzo. Two bedrooms and two apartments are in part of the main stone house and an adjacent house. All are carefully appointed in a creative, country-style with great attention to details and the comfort of guests. All accommodations have private entrances from the exterior. In the rustic main house, the ambience really warms up around Gabriella's dinner table where a non-stop series of aperitifs, pasta specialities, and a dessert buffet are served, accompanied by good local wine. An abundant breakfast with more of Gabriella's homemade, baked cakes awaits guests in the morning. A swimming pool behind the house bordering the woods is available, as well as a six-person hot hydrojet pool. Convinced that their guests will enjoy their stay, their brochure warns: An extended stay here generates a sense of well-being with a tendency to forget about problems, tempting one to postpone going back home! *Directions:* From the A1 autostrada exit at Monte Savino and turn left continuing for 6.7 km to Ciggiano. Turn right and then left at abandoned farmhouse and follow up to the house.

CASALE IL CAGGIO
Hosts: Gabriella & Paolo Magini
Località: Ciggiano
Civitella in Val di Chiana, (AR) 52040, Italy
Tel & Fax: (0575) 440022, Cellphone: (335) 584484
2 Rooms, Double: €90–€130
2 apartments €500–€1,200
Open: all year, Credit cards: all major
Other Languages: good English
www.karenbrown.com/ilcaggio.html
B&B, SELF CATERING

Borgo Elena, located in the hills outside one of our favorite Tuscan towns, Cortona, belongs to Mario Baracchi, whose brother owns the gorgeous inn, Il Falconiere (listed in our Inns guide). In fact, you can reach Borgo Elena by passing through the Falconiere property (stop in for an exquisite meal) on a narrow, steep gravel road that ends at the cluster of stone houses bordered by dense chestnut woods. Here you are totally immersed in nature and complete silence, with hilltop Cortona to one side and the immense Chiana Valley spread out before you. Seven quaint apartments, each with independent entrance, are dispersed among the various stone houses, which were the quarters for the farmhands of the Falconiere estate a century ago. Their original rustic ambiance remains while convenient modern utilities and amenities have been incorporated. The apartments, all charmingly appointed with Tuscan country pieces, accommodate from two to six persons and are all different in layout, most being on two levels. A lovely swimming pool sits higher up and takes in even more of the expansive view. The Borgo Elena is an ideal base for independent travelers who want to settle in one place for easily touring Tuscany's highlights. *Directions:* Instead of going into the center of Cortona, follow signs for Arezzo and drive past Camucia on the outskirts of town to Tavarnelle. Turn right at San Pietro a Cegliolo and drive 2 km up to Borgo Elena.

BORGO ELENA
Host: Mario Baracchi
Localita: San Pietro a Cegliolo
Cortona, (AR) 52042, Italy
Tel & Fax: (0575) 604773, Cellphone: (333) 9319320
7 apartments: €490–€560 weekly
Minimum Nights: 3, Open: all year
Credit cards: none
Other Languages: very little English
www.karenbrown.com/borgoelena.html
SELF CATERING

If you want to find the perfect little hotel to use as a base to explore the wonders of Tuscany and Umbria, look no farther than Il Falconiere—a jewel snuggled in the countryside just a few kilometers outside Cortona. From this convenient location you can venture out each day to such beauties as Siena, Florence, Assisi, San Gimignano, Orvieto, and Pienza, all easily accessible by car. The joy is that you can return each evening to relax by the gorgeous swimming pool, enjoy some of the best food in Italy, then sleep peacefully in the hushed tranquility of the countryside. And what a value! You can stay here for much less than you would pay for a deluxe room in Florence or Rome. Il Falconiere is owned by Silvia and Riccardo Baracchi, a charming, talented young couple who have achieved amazing results from their labor of love and long years of hard work. Riccardo, who inherited the property from his grandmother, was born in the small pretty villa that now houses several of the guestrooms. His wife, Silvia, was born nearby and is the incredibly talented chef whose superb meals have earned their restaurant a Michelin star. The guestrooms are individually decorated with great flair. Many antiques are used throughout, creating a comfortable, quietly sophisticated elegance. Il Falconiere is truly a very special place offering superb quality, charm, and genuine hospitality. *Directions:* Just north of Cortona, signposted off the road to Arezzo.

IL FALCONIERE RELAIS E RISTORANTE
Owners: Silvia & Riccardo Baracchi
Localita: San Martino
Cortona, (AR) 52044, Italy
Tel: (0575) 61 26 79, Fax: (0575) 61 29 27
19 Rooms, Double: €260–€560
Open: all year, Credit cards: all major
Relais & Châteaux
www.karenbrown.com/ilfalconiere.html
HOTEL

The charming medieval Etruscan town of Cortona that gained international fame through Frances Mayes' bestseller, "Under the Tuscan Sun", has subsequently responded to the increased demand for tourist accommodation. The Mancini family decided to completely refurbish their lovely old farm (a village in itself on the site of an Etruscan settlement) to accommodate a variety of needs for the more demanding traveller. The 17th-century private home sits in the middle of its meticulously landscaped gardens boasting 2,500 rose plants and surrounded by ten other stone houses which are now home to the comfortable hotel, Locanda. Featuring a voluminous breakfast room, eight spacious one, two and three-bedroom apartments on two floors of the former olive oil mill and farmer's quarters, there are also two excellent restaurants, a wine bar, a stunning swimming pool with hydro-massage, and a chapel. The décor of all the rooms is in keeping with an air of elegant country ambience. A complete country resort. *Directions:* Exit from autostrada A1 at Valdichiana, proceed towards Perugia. Exit from this highway at second exit for Cortona. Strategically located, Il Melone is well-marked on the main street leading to Arezzo, below Cortona center.

BORGO IL MELONE
Hosts: Carlo Livraga Mancini family
Il Sodo, Case Sparse 38, Cortona, (AR) 52042, Italy
Tel: (0575) 603330, Fax: (0575) 630001
12 Rooms, Double: €125–€270
8 apartments: €1,200–€2,400 weekly
Minimum Nights: 7
Open: Open all year, Credit cards: all major
Other Languages: good English
www.karenbrown.com/ilmelone.html
B&B, SELF CATERING

Cortona, a picturesque walled city in Tuscany, is a favorite with tourists. On the main road that wraps around the east side of the city, the Villa Marsili has the advantages of parking facilities and of being easy to find, and is within walking distance of the center of town. A gated entrance leads into the front courtyard of this handsome yellow villa accented by dark-green shutters and beds of colorful flowers. Inside, the villa has been totally remodeled into a deluxe hotel with every modern amenity. The staff is exceptionally cordial, so even though there is a commercial air, the welcome by the well-trained staff is warm and gracious. The management is happy to help you plan your excursions and they even offer cooking classes. The bedrooms are all tastefully decorated and have all the comforts and appointments of a first-class hotel. Throughout the hotel a quiet, refined ambiance prevails, with soft colors enhanced by antique furniture and ceilings adorned by frescoes. Breakfast is a wonderful buffet of Tuscan specialties. There is no restaurant, but guests can enjoy a complimentary apertif on the garden terrace with a view of the Val di Chiana valley and Lake Trasimeno before walking to a rich selection of restaurants. *Directions:* Located on the east side of Cortona on the road to Arezzo.

VILLA MARSILI
Owner: Valter Petrucci
Viale C. Battisti, 13
Cortona, (AR) 52044, Italy
Tel: (0575) 60 52 52, Fax: (0575) 60 56 18
27 Rooms, Double: €165–€310
Closed: Feb, Credit cards: all major
Abitare la Storia
www.karenbrown.com/villamarsili.html
HOTEL

Casa Palmira, directly north of Florence, was originally a group of rural buildings attached to an 11th-century tower guarding the road to the Mugello area of Tuscany. Stefano and Assunta, the amiable hosts, named their bed and breakfast after the old lady who lived in the house her entire life. She represents perhaps the spirit of the place, reminding everyone of the basic values of simple country living. The seven bedrooms on the top floor are decorated in a fresh, simple, country style, with hardwood floors, dried and fresh flowers, patchwork quilts, botanical prints, and local country antiques. Rooms are accessed by a large open sitting area with skylights and green plants. The hosts' naturally informal style of hospitality has guests feeling so at home that they can't resist assisting as Assunta works wonders in the open kitchen. This is part of a multi-functional space incorporating kitchen, dining room, and cozy living area with wicker chairs and large fireplace. Meals based on fresh vegetables are served either here or out in the garden under the portico. Daily cooking lessons for individuals or weekly cooking courses for small groups are arranged. Transfers from train station or airport are also offered. *Directions:* Halfway between Borgo S. Lorenzo and Florence on route 302 (Via Faentina), 2 km after Olmo coming from Florence (16 km). Casa Palmira is on the right at the sign for Ristorante Feriolo. From the north leave the A1 at Barberino del Mugello.

CASA PALMIRA
Hosts: Assunta & Stefano Mattioli
Via Faentina–Polcanto, Feriolo, (FI) 50030, Italy
Tel & Fax: (055) 8409749, Cellphone: (339) 3331190
7 Rooms, Double: €80–€95
Apartments from €500–€800 weekly
Minimum Nights: 3,
Open: Mar to Dec, Credit cards: none
Other Languages: good English, French
www.karenbrown.com/casapalmira.html
B&B, SELF CATERING

The Bencista is a real find for the traveler looking for a congenial, unpretentious, family-run hotel near Florence that has charm and yet is reasonably priced. The villa, romantically nestled in the foothills with a bird's-eye view of Florence, is owned and managed by the Simoni family who are always about, personally seeing to every need of their guests. Simone Simoni speaks excellent English, and on the day of my arrival he was patiently engrossed in conversation with one of the guests, giving him tips for sightseeing. Downstairs there is a jumble of sitting rooms, bars, and parlors, each decorated with dark Victorian furniture. Upstairs are the bedrooms, which vary in size, location, and furnishings. Some are far superior to others. Many people return year after year to their own favorite room. During the season, reservations should be made well in advance, especially for a room with a view over Florence, as the hotel is beautifully located for sightseeing in both Florence and Tuscany. (If you do not have a car, you can take the bus that runs regularly into Florence from the top of the road.) Two meals (breakfast and a choice of lunch or dinner) are included in the price. One of the outstanding features of the pensione is its splendid terrace where guests can enjoy a sweeping panorama of Florence.

PENSIONE BENCISTA
Owner: Simone Simoni
Fiesole
Florence, (FI) 50014, Italy
Tel & Fax: (055) 59 163
40 Rooms, Double: €176*
*Includes breakfast & dinner
Closed: Dec, Credit cards: MC, VS
www.karenbrown.com/pensionebencista.html
HOTEL

Fiesole, a small town tucked in the green wooded hills above Florence, has long been a favorite of ours. Staying here gives you the best of both worlds—you can enjoy the peacefulness of the countryside while being just a short ride away from Florence. If you are looking for ultimate luxury, nothing can compete with the Villa San Michele, but the Hotel Villa Fiesole offers a delightful alternative for those on a more conservative budget. You can easily spot the Villa Fiesole, set just above the road as it loops up the wooded hillside. Originally a private mansion, the Villa Fiesole was converted into a delightful small hotel in 1995, being equipped with all the finest modern amenities but keeping the overall ambiance of an exquisite home. In this part of the hotel, the rooms vary somewhat in size because of the nature of the building. A new wing has been added and the construction, although obviously recent, was done in excellent taste so that it blends in beautifully with the original villa. Here the rooms are almost identical in size and furnishings. Each is especially spacious and decorated in a most appealing way, using tones of rich blue and whites, giving an overall ambiance of refined good taste. The hotel does not have a formal restaurant but, in addition to breakfast, a light lunch, dinner, and simple buffet supper are available for guests. The Florence bus #7 stops in front of the villa every 20 minutes until 6 pm.

HOTEL VILLA FIESOLE
Director: Simone Taddeifront
Via Beato Angelico
35, Fiesole
Florence, (FI) 50014, Italy
Tel: (055) 59 72 52, Fax: (055) 59 91 33
28 Rooms, Double: €150–€370
Meals for hotel guests only
Open: all year, Credit cards: all major
www.karenbrown.com/hotelvillafiesole.html
HOTEL

It would be difficult to find another hotel with as many attributes as the Villa San Michele—in fact, almost impossible. How could you surpass a wooded hillside setting overlooking Florence, a stunning view, gorgeous antiques, impeccable management, gourmet dining, and, as if this were not enough, a building designed by Michelangelo. The Villa San Michele was originally a monastery dating back to the 15th century and occupied by Franciscan friars until Napoleon turned it into his headquarters. The adaptation of its rooms and public areas to today's standards has been made without affecting the ambiance of serenity and history. Most of the rooms are in the historical building and have been recently renovated and redecorated with taste and somber elegance. Twenty junior suites are located in the Italian garden and two suites in the Limonaia, once the greenhouse for storing lemon plants during the winter. All have stunning views of Florence and the Arno Valley. The lounges, dining rooms, terraces, and gardens are also exquisite. Meals can be enjoyed either in a beautiful dining room or on a lovely veranda that stretches along the entire length of the building. A beautiful swimming pool has been built on a secluded terrace above the hotel. Now a permanent cooking school, the Villa San Michele School of Cookery offers a wide range of gastronomic courses.

VILLA SAN MICHELE
Manager: Maurizio Saccani
Via Doccia, 4
Fiesole
Florence, (FI) 50014, Italy
Tel: (055) 56 78 200, Fax: (055) 56 78 250
45 Rooms, Double: €830–€2700*
*10% tax not included
Open: Mar to Nov, Credit cards: all major
www.karenbrown.com/michele.html
HOTEL

Hotel Albergotto, situated on a corner of the elegant Via de Tornabuoni with its austere Renaissance palazzos and designer boutiques, could not be more central. It existed for the past century as a small hotel once hosting illustrious musical and literary artists like Verdi, Elliot, and Donizetti, but had been virtually forgotten in recent decades. A complete renovation has brought it back to life and it is an excellent choice in the middle price range. From the street entrance you take a red-carpeted flight of stairs to reach the elevator up to the rooms on the top three floors. Beyond the reception desk are two breakfast rooms and a comfortable living room decorated in royal-blue tones with large windows looking out to Tornabuoni. Light-wood floors throughout the hotel give the place a fresh and newer look. Very pleasant, cheerful bedrooms in mustard hues with matching floral bedspreads have amenities such as air conditioning, satellite TV, and mini-bar. The double-paned windows keep out any traffic noise from the main street. Most delightful is the large mansard suite with wood-beamed ceilings and views over the city's rooftops and bell towers. The friendly staff will help you to enjoy your stay. *Directions:* Via de Tornabuoni is three blocks north of the River Arno and two blocks west of Piazza della Repubblica.

HOTEL ALBERGOTTO
Owner: Carlo Martelli
Via de Tornabuoni 13
Florence, 50123, Italy
Tel: (055) 23 96 464, Fax: (055) 23 98 108
22 Rooms, Double: €178–€285
Open: all year, Credit cards: all major
www.karenbrown.com/albergotto.html
HOTEL

The latest arrival in the group of independent city bed & breakfast properties, managed by Lea, is the very charming Antica Dimora Firenze. Located in part of an ancient palazzo owned by the Pandolfini family, just 5 blocks north of the Duomo Cathedral, it has similiar characteristics to the other three bed & breakfasts found in the same area (Johanna, Johlea I and II) owned by the same cordial owner, but offers a touch more. Six rooms are located on the top floor of the ancient, residential building. Each room is individually and tastefully appointed as in a true home, with great attention to detail and guest comfort. A cozy living/reception room with inviting, striped burgundy sofas awaits guests. Breakfast is served in this same reception room or privately in the bedrooms. It is difficult to choose a preference among the six romantic rooms, each completely different in soft pastel color schemes and a unique, additional feature. There are two lovely corner rooms and two quiet ones with small back terraces. All have antique pieces, silk or hand-woven Busatti fabrics and linens, and canopy beds. The color-coordinated bathrooms have marble or brick floors. All are delightful giving the feeling of having your own private apartment in Florence, including the key to the front door! *Directions:* 3 blocks north of San Marco church and square.

ANTICA DIMORA FIRENZE
Host: Lea Gulmanelli
Via San Gallo 72, Florence, 50129, Italy
Tel: (055) 462 7296, Fax: (055) 463 4450
Cellphone: (335) 5344488
6 Rooms, Double: €125–€150
Apartments: €160–€300
Open: all year, Credit cards: none
Other Languages: good English
www.karenbrown.com/dimora.html
B&B

In the new category of accommodation in historic residences, the Antica Torre is at the tiptop of the list. The top floors of this ancient fortified palazzo, in the very center of Florence, has been converted into a luxurious and stunning B&B. An elevator takes guests up to the top-floor sitting/bar area and breakfast room where large windows allow heart-stopping full 360-degree views over Florence's terracotta tiled roofs, major monuments, Arno river, and distant hillside backdrop. Take a closer look by stepping out on the large rooftop terrace complete with turrets to have an eye-level peek at Brunelleschi's grand cupola. On the two floors below you find 12 upscale and extra-spacious bedrooms with many amenities, each featuring more unique views or private terraces. The classically styled rooms have been well appointed in soft hues of gold or celestial blue, many with large open windows, perfect for drinking in the marvelous cityscape, virtually identical to that of the Renaissance period. Attentive and energetic young host, Jacopo, definitely has guests' every comfort in mind, and can arrange anything from special events and dinners on the terrace, to taking over the whole accommodation for family reunions or other gatherings. Magical does not even come close to describing the sensation at sunset from this special perch. *Directions:* The Antica Torre entrance is located half a block north of the Arno river on Via Tornabuoni.

ANTICA TORRE TORNABUONI
Manager: Jacopo d'Albasio
Via Tornabuoni, 1
Florence, 50123, Italy
Tel: (055) 26 58 161, Fax: (055) 21 88 41
12 Rooms, Double: €200–€400
Open: all year, Credit cards: all major
www.karenbrown.com/tornabuoni.html
B&B

The Palazzo dal Borgo–Hotel Aprile, owned by the Cantini Zucconi family for almost four decades, is located in a 15th-century Medici palace behind the Piazza Santa Maria Novella, near the train station and many fine restaurants and shops. The historical building was restored under the strict ordinance of Florence's Commission of Fine Arts. Guests are invited to three complimentary evening lectures a week on Florence's art and history by a professor of the University of Florence. The small and charming hotel is full of delightful surprises: from 16th-century paintings and a bust of the Duke of Tuscany to the frescoed breakfast room and quiet courtyard garden. The old-fashioned reception and sitting areas are invitingly furnished with Florentine Renaissance antiques, comfy, overstuffed red armchairs, and Oriental carpets worn with time. There are 35 bedrooms that vary widely in their size and decor, all with private bathrooms, telephones, mini-bars, carpeted or tile floors, and high vaulted ceilings. A recent extensive renovation has made improvements in facilities while maintaining the original overall charm. Request one of the quieter rooms at the back of the hotel, overlooking the garden. At the desk you find Roberto Gazzini and Sandra Costantini looking after guests' needs. *Directions:* Use a detailed city map to locate the hotel, three blocks north of the Duomo. There is a parking garage.

PALAZZO DAL BORGO—HOTEL APRILE
Host: Riccardo Zucconi
Via della Scala 6
Florence, 50123, Italy
Tel: (055) 216237, Fax: (055) 280947
35 Rooms, Double: €120–€220
Open: all year, Credit cards: all major
Other Languages: good English
www.karenbrown.com/aprile.html
HOTEL

Another nice discovery in the category of small, renovated hotels in Florence is the Botticelli, hidden away on a narrow back street behind the Central Market. Many original features of this 16th-century building, once a private home, have been preserved including evidence of a tiny alley that divided the two now-united buildings. Guests enter into a painted, vaulted reception area appointed with large blue and gold armchairs and side sitting room. Other architectural features so typical of the Renaissance period in Florence are the austere gray stone doorways, beamed ceilings in bedrooms, and the delightful open loggia terrace on the second floor lined with terra-cotta vases of cascading red geraniums. The bedrooms are situated on the three upper floors, with two being up in the mansard and enjoying the best views, and are comfortably and practically decorated with clean wooden furniture and an occasional antique piece blending well with the pea-green fabrics. A full buffet breakfast is offered in the breakfast room with bar just behind the reception area. All the necessary modern amenities such as air conditioning, elevator, modern telephone system, and satellite TV were incorporated during the recent renovation. Fabrizio and his American wife, Janet, run two other hotels in Florence, one being the Villa Carlotta near Piazzale Michelangelo. Very helpful staff. *Directions:* The hotel is one block north of Piazza San Lorenzo and the Medici Chapels.

HOTEL BOTTICELLI
Hosts: Fabrizio & Janet Gheri
Via Taddea 8
Florence, 50123, Italy
Tel: (055) 290905, Fax: (055) 294322
34 Rooms, Double: €110–€225
Minimum Nights: 3 during fairs & New Year
Open: all year, Credit cards: all major
Other Languages: good English
www.karenbrown.com/botticelli.html
HOTEL

Another choice in the now wide selection of city B&Bs is the well-located Dream Domus, a six-bedroom accommodation created from a former apartment in an historic palazzo. The building is conveniently located behind the San Lorenzo marketplace and two blocks from Florence's cathedral. While congenial hostess Perla resides next door, her B&B is on the second floor. The front door opens directly into the main living room where tables are set up side for a hearty buffet breakfast, a prerequisite before setting off to explore Florence with its myriad art museums and attractions. This room looks onto the main street while the six bedrooms off a hall to the back guarantee a peaceful sleep (hence Perla's logo, Parva Domus Magna Quies—small house, big silence. Polished black and white tiled floors lead you to the individually decorated rooms with antique armoires and fancy regal canopy beds. Golden brocade fabrics are mixed with either red, green or blue for the curtains and bedspreads. Comfortable rooms with many hotel style amenities are named after members of Florence's powerful De'Medici family from Lorenzo the great to Cosimo, Giovanni, Caterina, Lucrezia and Maria. An international traveller, Perla thoroughly enjoys taking care of her guests from all over the world and pointing out her favorite spots in Florence. *Directions:* The Via de Ginori is two blocks north of the Duomo cathedral. Garage parking is available.

❄ ☕ 🛉 [CREDIT] ⍭ P 🚭

FLORENCE DREAM DOMUS **New**
Host: Perla Collini
Via de' Ginori, 26
Florence, 50123, Italy
Tel: (055) 295346, Fax: (055) 2675643
Cellphone: (335) 5820093
6 Rooms, Double: €90–€200
Open: all year, Credit cards: all major
Other Languages: good English
www.karenbrown.com/florencedreamdomus
B&B

The Grand Hotel Villa Cora is a mansion, originally built during the 19th century by the Baron Oppenheim as a gift for his beautiful young bride. Among the many romantic tales of the Villa Cora is the one about Oppenheim's wife who, so the story goes, became enamored of one of her many admirers. The jealous baron was so enraged that he threatened to burn the entire mansion, but, luckily for you and me, he was stopped in time from this mad endeavor by his friends, and today this magnificent villa is a stunning hotel. Although only about a five-minute taxi ride from the center of Florence (or a twenty-minute walk), the Grand Hotel Villa Cora is eons away in atmosphere—you feel more like a guest on a country estate rather than in a city hotel. The interior of the hotel is rather ornate and sumptuous. The villa is set in intricate gardens and even has a pool. You can almost hear the sounds of laughter and music drifting through the gardens, and indeed the mansion has always been famous for its dramatic parties: at one time the villa was the residence of Napoleon's wife, Empress Eugenia, whose gay entertaining was the talk of Florence. Now this grand, palace-like home can be yours for days of dreams and romance. Another excellent bonus is free limousine service to/from the heart of Florence.

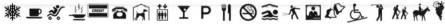

GRAND HOTEL VILLA CORA
Manager: Luigi Zaccardi
Viale Machiavelli, 18/20
Florence, 50125, Italy
Tel: (055) 22 98 451, Fax: (055) 22 90 86
48 Rooms, Double: €300–€900
Open: all year, Credit cards: all major
www.karenbrown.com/hotelvillacora.html
HOTEL

Moderately priced accommodations are rare in Florence, so we were happy to discover the Hotel Il Guelfo Bianco, which combines reasonable rates with a choice location in the heart of Florence. Most importantly, this small hotel has an owner, Alessandro Bargiacchi, whose presence is seen and felt. He speaks only a little English, but his smile and genuine warmth of welcome make guests feel right at home. Everyone who assists him is exceptionally friendly and all converse in several languages, including the gracious manager, Antonella Rocchini. Valentina, Sara and Gaia are also very charming. The inviting lobby sets the tone of the hotel with a bright reception area with exposed brick walls and contrasting abstract paintings and modern light fixtures. There is a lounge bar where guests can relax and enjoy a drink and a reading room with internet access. Breakfast is served in a pretty room with a delightful courtyard that is very popular with guests in pleasant weather. The bedrooms vary in size and shape, as one would expect in an historical 16th-century building. All are decorated with individual antiques and some even have celestial frescos on the ceilings. On a busy street, the more quiet rooms look over a back garden. The Hotel Il Guelfo Bianco is not a deluxe hotel, nor does it pretend to be, but it makes an excellent choice for a friendly, pleasant place to stay in the heart of Florence.

HOTEL IL GUELFO BIANCO
Owner: Alessandro Bargiacchi
Via Cavour, 29
Florence, 50129, Italy
Tel: (055) 28 83 30, Fax: (055) 29 52 03
40 Rooms, Double: €150–€260
Open: all year, Credit cards: all major
www.karenbrown.com/hotelilguelfobianco.html
HOTEL

In our estimation, the Hotel Helvetia and Bristol is one of the finest luxury hotels in the center of Florence. Nothing has been spared to make this showplace a true beauty—the decor is outstanding. The lounges, exquisitely decorated with an elegant, yet extremely comfortable, homelike ambiance, exude quality without flamboyance. Each of the guestrooms is also superbly decorated, and, as in a private home, no two are alike. Abundant use of exquisite padded-fabric wall coverings, with color-coordinated draperies, upholstered chairs, and bedspreads along with lovely antiques make each one special. I fell in love with all of the rooms, but my very favorites were the mini-suites: room 257 in gorgeous shades of muted green and room 363 in lovely golds, creams, and dusty pinks, with a sumptuous marble bathroom with Jacuzzi tub, heated towel racks, plus the added bonus of a tiny terrace. For light refreshments or just relaxing, "Hostaria Bibenrum" is a marvelous retreat—light and airy with a domed, old-fashioned skylight, potted plants, and nostalgic wicker furniture. The Helvetia and Bristol is expensive, but no more so than the other luxury hotels in Florence, and for those who appreciate quality and refinement, it is unsurpassed.

HOTEL HELVETIA AND BRISTOL
Manager: Pietro Panelli
Via dei Pescioni, 2
Florence, 50123, Italy
Tel: (055) 26 651, Fax: (055) 23 99897
67 Rooms, Double: €510–€1650*
*Breakfast not included: €26
Open: all year, Credit cards: all major
www.karenbrown.com/helvetiaandbristol.html
HOTEL

The Hotel Hermitage is a dream of a small, well-manicured hotel housed in a 13th-century palazzo with efficient service and breathtaking views over the city's most famous monuments. The location could not be more central—on a small street between the Uffizzi Gallery and the River Arno. The fifth-floor reception area looking out to the Ponte Vecchio bridge has a cozy living-room feeling with selected antique pieces, Oriental rugs, and corner fireplace. Across the hall is the veranda-like breakfast room dotted with crisp yellow tablecloths and topped with fresh flowers where privileged guests view the tower of Palazzo Signoria. Color-coordinated, air-conditioned rooms, some quite small, others with hydrojet baths, have scattered antiques, framed etchings of the city, and more views. However, the highlight of a stay at the Hermitage is spending time dreaming on the rooftop terrace. The view embraces not only the previously mentioned marvels of Florence, but also the famous dome of the Duomo cathedral and Giotto's tower. Guests are served a continental breakfast under the ivy-covered pergola and among the many flower-laden vases lining its borders. Reserve well in advance. *Directions:* Consult a detailed city map. There is a parking garage in the vicinity. Call for instructions as car traffic in this part of the city is strictly limited.

HOTEL HERMITAGE
Host: Vincenzo Scarcelli
Piazza del Pesce
Florence, 50122, Italy
Tel: (055) 287216, Fax: (055) 212208
23 Rooms, Double: €233–€245
Open: all year, Credit cards: MC, VS
Other Languages: good English
www.karenbrown.com/hermitage.html
HOTEL

The bed and breakfast In Piazza della Signoria is a top-quality B&B hidden away on the corner of Florence's most famous square hosting the imposing city hall, Palazzo della Signoria. Delightful hosts Sonia and Alessandro initially bought the four-story ancient building as an investment but were touched by the magic spell of this very special historic spot just up the street from the house of Dante and decided to restore it and share it with friends. The fascinating restoration project became something of an archaeological adventure, with documents discovered dating back to 1427 along with a pair of woman's shoes from that same period, and 18th-century frescoes uncovered. Up one flight from street level, Sonia, Alessandro, and occasionally their three sons, greet guests in a small reception area. The eight bedrooms, named after Renaissance masters, are spread about the two floors, with the top floor being crowned with three apartments for those able to enjoy this marvelous city for a full week. To-die-for views from this level include the piazza, Giotto's tower, and Brunelleschi's cupola. The new breakfast room with one long table has the same advantage. Impeccably styled rooms with unique personalities display lovely antique furnishings, parquet floors, and rich colors of teal, peach, and rust. None of the innovative designer bathrooms are identical. A real treat. *Directions:* On the northeast corner of the square at the beginning of Via dei Magazzini.

❄ 🍴 ♨ ☕ [CREDIT] ☎ 🛗 ￥ P 🖼 🏌 🚶 🍇

IN PIAZZA DELLA SIGNORIA
Hosts: Sonia & Alessandro Pini
Via dei Magazzini 2, Florence, 50122, Italy
Tel: (055) 2399546, Fax: (055) 2676616
Cellphone: (393) 483210565
8 Rooms, Double: €200–€290
3 Apartments:€320–€380 daily, €1200–€1400 weekly
Open: all year, Credit cards: all major
Other Languages: good English
www.karenbrown.com/piazza.html
B&B, SELF CATERING

The Hotel Lungarno, one of our favorite hotels, is superbly located directly on the River Arno, a few minutes' walk from the Ponte Vecchio. Of more recent construction, the architect has cleverly incorporated into the hotel an ancient stone tower, which houses several romantic suites. The decor is superb, with fine-quality furnishings and gorgeous fabrics accented by an appealing color scheme of blues and creamy whites. The hotel has been totally refurbished with all the latest modern conveniences in smartly styled rooms that have a great appeal. In addition to classic guestrooms are six splendid two-bedroom, two-bath apartments, which are an exceptional value if you are traveling with friends or family. Throughout the hotel a gracious ambiance of understated elegance prevails, enhanced by the admirable management and warm reception. Bountiful bouquets of fresh flowers and an outstanding collection of original 20th century paintings (over 450 works) add the final touch of perfection. If you plan far in advance, you might even be lucky enough to snare a room with a large terrace overlooking the river—these are very special and well worth the extra cost. What a treat to sit on your own terrace in the evening and watch the Arno fade into gold in the setting sun. The alternative is a drink at the Lungarno's sophisticated bar or chic Borgo San Jacopo restaurant, with incomparable river views accompanied by precious Picasso, Cocteau and Rosai paintings. Top-class.

HOTEL LUNGARNO
Manager: Mr. Sandro Alfano
Borgo San Jacopo, 14
Florence, 50125, Italy
Tel: (055) 27 261, Fax: (055) 26 84 37
73 Rooms, Double: €270–€540
Restaurant closed Sun
Open: all year, Credit cards: all major
www.karenbrown.com/lungarno.html
HOTEL

The hills immediately surrounding Florence, dotted with stately villas and country homes dating back to the Renaissance, offered Florentine aristocrats cool respite in summer from the higher temperatures in the city below. The gracious Bulleri family chose this alternative to the city some 30 years ago, and after a successful career in the fashion industry, Claudio and Paola transformed their splendid wooded property into a top-notch inn for discerning guests. Nine very comfortable, immaculate rooms, personally decorated by Paola, have been created in a house across from the family's villa. This includes an elegant main living and dining room with fireplace and large windows looking out over the garden. Classic-style bedrooms have parquet floors, matching fabrics for beds and drapes, and spacious sparkling-white bathrooms. Amenities include satellite TV, mini-bar, safe, air conditioning, and a selection from the wine cellar. A full country breakfast is served out in the gazebo in warmer months. The swimming pool, on a level below the home, has gorgeous hillside views over olive groves. The Bulleris share their personal lifestyle: charming son Lorenzo assists guests with local itineraries, guides and museum or concert ticketing, and Paola conducts cooking lessons, while Claudio accompanies guests to his nearby golf club.

MARIGNOLLE RELAIS & CHARME
Owners: Claudio Bulleri family
Via di San Quirichino a Marignolle, 16
Florence, 50124, Italy
Tel: (055) 22 86 910, Fax: (055) 20 47 396
9 Rooms, Double: €195–€345
Open: all year, Credit cards: all major
www.karenbrown.com/marignolle.html
B&B

Orto de'Medici was named for the Medici family's extensive gardens and orchards that once existed on the site of this hotel. Capable father-and-son team Emilio and Giacomo Bufalini recently took over the reins and took on the challenge of completely refurbishing the family's prim, centuries-old palazzo. Public areas maintain the ambiance of an elegant private home—the frescoed foyer and sitting rooms are graced with portraits, chandeliers, overstuffed armchairs, and Oriental carpets—while services and facilities in bedrooms conform to European Community standards. The spacious upper-floor guestrooms are reached by an elevator and are decorated with classic style. They have matching armoires and beds and all but ten have smart new gray-and-white-marble bathrooms. Several rooms on the top floor have a terrace or balcony with dreamy views over red Florentine rooftops. Perhaps the architectural highlight is the gracious breakfast room (breakfast is a buffet), with high ceilings, original parquet floors, and frescoed panels depicting garden scenes all around. French doors lead from this area to an outdoor terraced flower garden with wrought iron chairs and tables and a lovely view of San Marco church. Wine and cheese tastings are held here in the late afternoon. Dynamic young host Giacomo and his efficient and friendly staff ensure a perfect city sojourn. *Directions:* Four blocks north of the Duomo.

HOTEL ORTO DE'MEDICI
Hosts: Giacomo Bufalini family
Via San Gallo, 30
Florence, 50129, Italy
Tel: (055) 483427, Fax: (055) 461276
31 Rooms, Double: €99–€270
Open: all year, Credit cards: all major
Other Languages: good English
www.karenbrown.com/demedici.html
HOTEL

Palazzo Galletti, housed in an historic Florentine palazzo dating to the 1500s, comes under the newly established accommodation category of Historic Residences, a glorified B&B. Young and enthusiastic partners, Francesca and Samuele acquired the entire upper first floor (historically referred to as the Noble floor and characterized by high ceilings and frescoed walls) with the idea of offering high quality accommodation in a more home-like ambience. Enter from the street through ancient iron gates. Up a flight of stairs is the small reception area, from which a hallway with bedrooms extends and wraps around the center atrium. Softly styled guestrooms, each different from the next, are nicely appointed in beige tones contrasting with colorful abstract paintings. Many have original features such as the magnificent old frescoes in the two corner junior suites (well worth the extra euros!). Amenities abound, from beautiful designer bathrooms in travertine, flat screen tvs, internet connection, air conditioning, and king-sized beds. A fresh buffet breakfast is served down a level in the original kitchen with its vaulted brick ceilings, stone sink and oven all dating to 1550. With all the amenities of a hotel, but the hospitality and ambience of a home, you will feel like a Florentine resident as you return in the evening with your own front door key. *Directions:* Take the Via dell'Oriuolo from behind the Duomo to the end and turn sharp left on Via Sant'Egidio.

*PALAZZO GALLETTI   **New***
Hosts: Samuele Minucci & Francesca Cascino
Cascino Via Sant'Egidio, 12
Florence, 50122, Italy
Tel: (055) 39057501, Fax: (055) 390575212
9 Rooms, Double: €112–€220
Open: all year, Credit cards: all major
Other Languages: fluent English, French
www.karenbrown.com/galleti.html
B&B

The stunning Palazzo Magnani Feroni, an ancient private residence of the Giannotti family, dating back to the 1500s, is on the "left bank" of the River Arno four blocks away from the Ponte Vecchio. The sensation of being in a true palace is captured immediately upon entering the grand foyer with vaulted ceilings, marble busts, statues, and precious period paintings, many from the owners' world travels. This is a unique upscale accommodation in that they have purposefully avoided adding any obvious signs of its being a hotel (a small reception room sits off the main entrance) in order to retain the aura of living in an elegant historical residence. Sumptuous bedrooms with soaring ceilings, mostly enormous suites, have retained their original architectural features and have been appointed with antique and reproduction pieces, gilded framed mirrors, Oriental carpets, brocaded gold fabrics on sofas, and tapestries. Suites on the ground floor look out onto an inner courtyard and one has two walls entirely covered with a fresco depicting a bucolic countryside scene. Breakfast is served in the suites or in the long upstairs dining room with its showcase displaying antique silk fabrics left over from the days when the palazzo was also an antique gallery. Another highlight includes a rooftop terrace with superb views over the city, where in summer the Palace Bar opens every evening.

PALAZZO MAGNANI FERONI
Owners: Dr. & Sra. Alberto Giannotti
Borgo San Frediano, 5
Florence, 50124, Italy
Tel: (055) 23 99 544, Fax: (055) 26 08 908
12 Rooms, Double: €210–€750
Open: all year, Credit cards: all major
www.karenbrown.com/feroni.html
HOTEL

Palazzo Niccolini is one of the few hotels in Florence within a new category called Historic Residences. Dating from the 16th century, this fascinating palazzo has a prime location directly facing the Duomo Cathedral. The Niccolini family, descendents of the original owners, reside in part of the palazzo and have very meticulously restored the building, offering ten elegant, spacious bedrooms and suites for guests. Entered from the street level, the reception area is up one flight of stairs (or elevator) near the grand living room with period paintings, antiques, grand chandeliers. Breakfast is served in the elegant living room, making one feel like a private house guest. Each bedroom is elegantly decorated with antiques and all have sparkling, marble bathrooms; some with frescoed walls or ceilings. However, the "piece de resistance" is the priceless suite upstairs that will leave guests in awe. Open the door, climb up ten steps into the glassed-in living room, and gaze right into the side of Brunelleschi's Cupola. You will never get a better view of the detailed, marble façade and roof tiles. In addition, behind the white sofa (which is located directly in front of the enormous windows) is a two-person hydrojet tub hidden among the plants. The bedroom and bathroom are accessed off to the side. *Directions:* The palazzo is on the corner of the Duomo square and Via dei Servi.

PALAZZO NICCOLINI AL DUOMO
Owners: Filippo & Ginevra Niccolini di Camugliano
Manager: Maura Pedroni
Via dei Servi, 2
Florence, 50122, Italy
Tel: (055) 28 24 12, Fax: (055) 29 09 79
10 Rooms, Double: €250–€500
Closed: Aug 4 to Aug 25, Credit cards: all major
www.karenbrown.com/palazzoniccolini.html
HOTEL

Accommodations in Italy's major art cities has transformed dramatically over the past five years, offering everything from the classic and boutique type hotels, urban bed & breakfasts, and hospitality in historic homes—in all price ranges. The Palazzo Ruspoli is an example of one of Florence's centrally located historic family residences converted into an charming accommodation. Literally around the corner from the Duomo cathedral, one enters the palazzo on a side street, and takes the elevator up one flight to the reception area. Guestrooms are laid out on two wings off this area. An adjacent breakfast room is very inviting with crisp, white linen chairs and French print drapes. The spacious bedrooms with high ceilings have parquet floors, canopy headboards and matching red or blue checked bedspreads, and new bathrooms. Many rooms have views of the famed Brunelleschi cupola. Getting around the city's dense art center is certainly not a problem from this location as you are within easy walking distance to almost everything. The friendly staff is always ready to assist with personal sightseeing arrangements. *Directions:* Half block north of the Duomo cathedral.

PALAZZO RUSPOLI
Owner: Teresa Fichera
Via de' Martelli, 5
Florence, 50129, Italy
Tel: (055) 2670563, Fax: (055) 2670525
20 Rooms, Double: €130–€220
Open: all year, Credit cards: all major
Other Languages: good English, French, German
www.karenbrown.com/ruspoli.html
HOTEL

Country residences of wealthy Florentine families dating back to Renaissance times were all concentrated on the hills above the city. Villa Poggio San Felice is one of these, reached by way of a labyrinth of narrow (unbelievably two-way) winding roads past stone-walled gardens concealing magnificent villas. Livia inherited not only the actual property of her great-grandfather but also a long standing tradition in the hospitality field—he was the founder of two of Florence's most prominent hotels. This bed and breakfast is special as guests are given full run of the main part of the two-story villa with its library, gracious portrait-lined sitting rooms, and high-ceilinged dining room where a full buffet breakfast and dinner are served overlooking the garden through French doors. Hosts Livia and her husband Lorenzo's desire was that their guests experience the true flavor of a noble villa and consequently minimum possible modifications were made. This authentic ambiance prevails throughout the simple bedrooms, which are spread out on the upper floor and contain the family's original furniture. The romantic I Sposi honeymoon bedroom has fireplace, parquet floors, and hunter-green color scheme, while the spacious room Nonni features a large terrace looking out over hills to the famous dome of Florence's cathedral. *Directions:* Ten minutes from the center of Florence. A detailed map is provided.

❄ ☕ ✂ ♨ 💳 ☎ 🏋 P 🚭 🏊 🖼 🔔 🚶 🐎 🍇 🍷

VILLA POGGIO SAN FELICE
Hosts: Livia Puccinelli & Lorenzo Magnelli
Via San Matteo in Arcetri 24, Florence, 50125, Italy
Tel: (055) 220016, Fax: (055) 2335388
Cellphone: (335) 6818844
5 Rooms, Double: €200–€250
Open: Mar to Dec, Credit cards: all major
Other Languages: good English
Abitare la Storia
www.karenbrown.com/borgosanfelice.html
B&B

The Regency, facing out to a park in the most exclusive residential area, is one of Florence's finest luxury hotels and a welcome haven in the overcrowded tourist scene. Gracious hospitality comes naturally to owner Amedeo Ottaviani (also of the Lord Byron in Rome) and his philosophy that every guest should be treated with the best possible personal attention goes hand in hand with the intimate ambiance of the hotel, a former private home. Upon arrival guests are warmly greeted by reception manager, Lara, and invited into one of the cozy English-style sitting rooms richly appointed with fine antiques and paintings, floral-patterned carpeting, and exquisite fabrics in warm red tones. Beyond are two intimate, formal dining rooms, where the house chef is praised for his innovative creations based on Tuscan specialities incorporating the region's top-quality ingredients. The larger glassed-in dining area looks out over the exceptionally lush courtyard garden where romantic candlelit dinners are served in the summer months. Comfortable bedrooms and suites are spread among the top floors and a separate building connected to the main villa. They are uniquely appointed with white furnishings reproduced from original Tuscan antiques, patterned carpeting, and contrasting wall fabrics. Each has its own marble bathroom, with only a handful left to be refurbished. The concierge is on hand to organize museum and concert reservations, and guides.

HOTEL REGENCY
Owner: Amedeo Ottaviani
Piazza Massimo D'Azeglio, 3
Florence, 50121, Italy
Tel: (055) 24 52 47, Fax: (055) 23 46 735
35 Rooms, Double: €275–€880
Open: all year, Credit cards: all major
www.karenbrown.com/hotelregency.html
HOTEL

If you are looking for a hotel in Florence that offers both a fabulous location and reasonably priced, pleasant rooms, the simple Relais Uffizi is for you. The double wood doors of the ancient building are located on the Chiasso del Buco, a quaint narrow back street accessed through an ancient arch from the Chiasso de' Baroncelli, off the Piazza della Signoria. Upstairs in the main reception lounge, the gracious owner, Elisabetta Matucci, or one of her friendly assistants will give you a warm welcome. Because there are so few rooms and the hotel is family-managed, guests are known by name and made to feel like friends. Nothing is contrived or overly sophisticated: instead there is an informal, comfortable ambiance. The heart of the hotel is the lounge where large windows look down upon the famous Piazza della Signoria with its statues and outdoor cafes. From this marvelous perch, you can relax in quiet comfort and enjoy all the drama and activity of Florence unfolding just below you. Although this is a simple hotel with remarkably low rates, no deluxe hotel in Florence can surpass this view of Florence. A maze of hallways leads to the individually decorated guestrooms. They vary in shape and size (number 3 with a canopy bed is especially spacious), but all are attractive in decor and have some antique furnishings. Best of all, they are immaculately clean and offer such amenities as air conditioning, direct-dial phone, mini-bar, hairdryer, and television.

RELAIS UFFIZI
Owner: Elisabetta Matucci
Chiasso de' Baroncelli/Chiasso del Buco, 16
Florence, 50122, Italy
Tel: (055) 26 76 239, Fax: (055) 26 57 909
13 Rooms, Double: €160–€240
Open: all year, Credit cards: all major
www.karenbrown.com/relaisuffizi.html
HOTEL

In the past two years, a new breed of bed and breakfasts has developed in Italy's favorite cities, especially in Florence and Rome. In order to keep costs down and be a competitive alternative to hotels, fewer amenities are offered and breakfast is self-service style in rooms (coffee, tea, breads, jam, cakes) and therefore is more adapted to an independent type of traveler. In fact, it is like having your own home in Florence with keys to the front door. Hostess Lea Gulmanelli had such success with her first B&B that she opened three additional places at a superior level, all in the same neighborhood. At the Johlea three floors of two neighboring 19th-century buildings were restored, producing twelve bedrooms of varying sizes for guests (Johlea I and II). Lea has a real flair for decorating and, as in someone's home, each well-proportioned bedroom retains its own character. All are very cozily appointed in muted soft colors, with an occasional antique, Oriental carpets, paintings by the owner, and original tiled or parquet floors. There is someone on duty all day to assist guests with their needs. Both I and II have a common living room for guests, with Johlea I having a delightful flower-potted terrace with dreamy views over Florence's rooftops to the cupola of the Duomo. Tasteful and very economical. *Directions:* The B&B is located between San Marco Square and Piazza della Libertà, directly north of the Duomo, reached in 12 minutes on foot.

❄ 🍵 🏊 ☎ 👪 🍷 P 🎿 🍇

LE RESIDENZE JOHLEA
Host: Lea Gulmanelli
Via San Gallo 76 & 80
Florence, 50129, Italy
Tel: (055) 4633292, Fax: (055) 4634552
Cellphone: (335) 5344488
12 Rooms, Double: €95–€120
Open: all year, Credit cards: none
Other Languages: good English
www.karenbrown.com/johlea.html
B&B

The refurbished Hotel Silla is located on the left bank of the River Arno opposite Santa Croce, the famous 13th-century square and church where Michelangelo and Galileo are buried. This position offers views from some of the rooms of several of Florence's most notable architectural attractions—the Duomo, the Ponte Vecchio, and the tower of the Palazzo Vecchio. Housed on the second and third floors of a lovely 15th-century palazzo with courtyard entrance, 36 new and spotless double rooms (non-smoking upon request) with private baths are pleasantly decorated with simple dark-wood furniture and matching bedspreads and curtains. Air conditioning and an elevator were recently added necessities. The fancy, cream-colored reception area is appointed in 17th-century Venetian style, with period furniture, a chandelier, and large paintings. Breakfast is served on the splendid and spacious second-floor outdoor terrace or in the dining room overlooking the Arno. The Silla is a friendly, convenient, and quiet hotel, near the Pitti Palace, leather artisan shops, and many restaurants. It offers tourists a good value in pricey Florence. A parking garage is available. *Directions:* Refer to a detailed city map to locate the hotel.

HOTEL SILLA
Owner: Gabriele Belotti
Via dei Renai 5,
Florence, 50125, Italy
Tel: (055) 2342888, Fax: (055) 2341437
36 Rooms, Double: €150–€175
Open: all year, Credit cards: all major
Other Languages: good English, French, German
www.karenbrown.com/hotelsilla.html
HOTEL

The Torre di Bellosguardo is a romantic historic villa nestled on the shelf of a hill with an unsurpassed view of Florence. Below the enormous castle-like home, the tiled rooftops, steeples, towers, and domes of the city seem like a fairyland at your fingertips. It is not surprising that the setting of the Torre di Bellosguardo is so breathtaking: it was chosen by a nobleman, Guido Cavalcanti (a friend of Dante), as the most beautiful site in Florence. The villa is owned today by Amerigo Franchetti who takes great pride in his stunning home and, with a passion for perfection, is restoring the villa to its original glory. The spacious austere guestrooms with views are decorated in authentic period antiques and vary in size as they would in a private home with few frills and bathrooms that are soon to be updated. Other rooms include frescoed ballroom, Orangerie, and upstairs loggia terrace. The most splendid features of the hotel are its incredible setting and meticulously groomed botanical garden, which highlights a swimming pool set on a terrace overlooking Florence, Brunelleschi cupola and all. In summer lunch is served by the swimming pool, otherwise breakfast is the only meal available. For dinner, you must wind down a narrow twisting road to go to a restaurant. If you want to walk into Florence, ask about the "secret" path—a short cut down the hill to the city (15 minute walk). Down a level through an underground tunnel a small pool, sauna and steam room.

TORRE DI BELLOSGUARDO
Owner: Amerigo Franchetti
Via Roti Michelozzi, 2
Florence, 50124, Italy
Tel: (055) 22 98 145, Fax: (055) 22 90 08
16 Rooms, Double: €290–€390*
*Breakfast not included: €20
Poolside lunch in summer
Open: all year, Credit cards: all major
www.karenbrown.com/bellosguardo.html
HOTEL

La Torricella, just on the outskirts of Florence, offers travelers the advantage of staying in a Tuscan home in a quiet residential area, yet with the city easily accessible by public transportation. Marialisa completely restored her great-grandfather's home and converted it into a comfortable and efficient lodging. She decided to offer all the trimmings of a hotel, with amenities such as satellite TVs, mini-bars, and telephones in rooms, plus daily cleaning service. The terraced front of the pale-yellow villa is lined with terra-cotta vases of flowers and intoxicating wisteria vines. Upon entering the home, you pass through a small reception area with brick arches and equestrian prints into the luminous breakfast room where a buffet is served in the morning. Accommodations are scattered about the large, pristine home on various levels and are each similarly appointed in soft-green and mustard hues with sparkling new white bathrooms. Reproduction armoires and desks and wrought-iron beds harmonize well with the brick floors and high, beamed ceilings. Marialisa offers cooking classes, teaching secrets of genuine Tuscan dishes, and is a rich source of information on the area. There is a small pool at the back of the house. *Directions:* From the Certosa exit of the A1, head for the center of the city, turning right at the stoplight in Galluzzo at Piazza Acciaiuoli. Take Via Silvani for several blocks, turning right on Via Vecchia di Pozzolatico just before the fork in the road.

LA TORRICELLA
Hosts: Marialisa Manetti family
Via Vecchia di Pozzolatico 25, Florence, 50125, Italy
Tel: (055) 2321808, Fax: (055) 2047402
Cellphone: (340) 2798856
7 Rooms, Double: €113–€130
1 Apartment: €650–€800 weekly
Minimum Nights: 2, Open: Mar 1 to Nov 20
Credit cards: VS, Other Languages: good English
www.karenbrown.com/torricella.html
B&B, SELF CATERING

The Villa Montartino is actally comprised of two villas: the Villa Montarino and Villa Le Piazzole; both located on the outskirts of Florence with the advantage of being easy to find with convenient parking. Bus and taxi service to Florence are readily available. In the 11th century Montartino was built as a watchtower to ensure safe transit for goods coming into Florence. As you enter the gates and wind up to the enchanting small villa crowning the hilltop, you can quickly see why this site was chosen for protection since the Ema Valley stretches below as far as the eye can see. You feel like a guest in a secluded country estate, yet Florence is only 3 kilometers away. The house has been lovingly restored, with great care taken to retain its original architectural features. Terracotta floors, whitewashed walls, beamed ceilings, handsome wooden furniture, and many beautiful antiques create the ambiance of a noble home. The guestrooms are spacious and the decor luxurious. All rooms have air conditioning, satellite TV, safe, mini-bar, direct-dial phone, and computer line. Added bonuses: a chapel for weddings, pool, Jacuzzi, and steam bath. In the cellar, tastings of their private-label wines and olive oil can be arranged with their English-speaking sommelier. *Directions:* From A1 take the Florence Certosa exit. At the second light turn right on Via Gherardo Silvani for 1.3 km. When the road splits, keep to the right. The hotel is on the left, behind a gated entrance.

VILLA MONTARTINO
Director: Carlotta Ferrari
Via Gherardo Silvani, 151
Florence, 50125, Italy
Tel: (055) 22 35 20, Fax: (055) 22 34 95
7 Rooms, Double: €220–€350
Open: Jan 1 thru Nov 1, Credit cards: all major
www.karenbrown.com/villamontartino.html
B&B

The bed and breakfast boom of the last decade in Italy has brought about a vast variety of accommodation from classic, in-home hospitality to places with many amenities that more resemble small hotels. Il Torrino brings us back to the more traditional example, with four bedrooms offered within the hostess home. The large, old-fashioned family home of Signora Cesarina's grandparents is located in the Montechiari hills between Florence and Pisa east-west and between Volterra and Lucca north-south—a prime touring location. Here you will not find standardized rooms all decorated alike, but rather individual rooms filled with the family's personal belongings, heirloom furniture, and the authentic feeling of a Tuscan home. With her children grown and residing in various parts of the world, the very sweet hostess, Cesarina Campinotti, opened her home to travelers and welcomes guests into the downstairs living room and upstairs breakfast room where an abundant meal is served. A separate garden apartment for two persons has glass doors overlooking the small pool and countryside beyond. The four bedrooms with living room and kitchen can also be rented separately. Here you are in the center of Tuscany and there is a golf course 12 kilometers away. *Directions:* From Forcoli follow signs for Montechiari and Montacchita, continuing past Montacchita up to the group of houses called Montechiari (2 km). Il Torrino has the black iron gate and no sign.

IL TORRINO
Host: Cesarina Campinotti
Montechiari, Forcoli, (PI) 56030, Italy
Tel & Fax: (0587) 629181
Cellphone: (347) 3643411
4 Rooms, Double: €93–€104
1 Apartment: €440–€490 weekly
Minimum Nights: 3, Open: all year, Credit cards: none
Other Languages: very little English, French, Spanish
www.karenbrown.com/iltorrino.html
B&B, SELF CATERING

In the heart of the beautiful Chianti wine region, a cypress-lined lane leads up to the handsome, 13th-century Castello di Meleto, set upon a gentle hill just outside Gaiole. The fairytale-perfect castle with its imposing round watchtowers and arched stone doorway embraced by fragrant roses makes an enchanting stop while exploring the back roads of Tuscany. There is a double treat in store because you can not only sample delicious wines in the attractive tasting room, but also visit the interior of this splendid castle with its walls and ceilings lavishly enhanced by superb frescoes, lovely antique furnishings, and even an adorable baroque theatre dating back to the mid-1700s (call ahead for tour times). The castle also offers nine attractively decorated guestrooms with antique furnishings, five within the castle and four in the chapel house. Breakfast is served each morning in the cozy kitchen with huge open fireplace. The castle gardens stretch out to a line of lacy trees that frame a superb vista of the idyllic Tuscan countryside. There is also a stunning view from the swimming pool, which is bordered on three sides by a flagstone terrace and on the fourth flows seamlessly into the horizon. If you are traveling with friends or family and want a place for a longer stay, the castle offers 11 beautifully furnished stone cottages with well-equipped kitchens and from one to three bedrooms. *Directions:* From Gaiole in Chianti, follow signs to the castle.

CASTELLO DI MELETO
Hosts: Lucia Pasquini & Roberto Garcea
Gaiole in Chianti, (SI) 53013, Italy
Tel & Fax: (0577) 749129
9 Rooms, Double: €125–€148
11 Cottages: €791–€1,700 weekly
Minimum Nights: 2, 7 in cottages
Open: all year, Credit cards: all major
Other Languages: fluent English, German
www.karenbrown.com/castellomeleto.html
B&B, SELF CATERING

The Castello di Spaltenna is a charming hotel nestled within a feudal hamlet in the heart of Tuscany's glorious Chianti wine region. From the castle with its fortified monastery and adjacent church adorned by an 11th-century bell tower, you can look out in every direction to a blissful scene of rolling hills, valleys, and woodlands dotted with castles and medieval villages. Although deluxe in every detail, the hotel reflects its heritage with beamed ceilings, thick walls, stone floors, and watchtowers. The decor too pays tribute to the past, with old oil paintings, tapestries, Persian carpets, handmade wrought-iron beds, and splendid antique furniture. The heart of the hotel is the internal courtyard, which becomes a fairy-tale setting each night for fine dining when tables, softly illuminated by candles, are set with lovely linens and fresh flowers, with a harp playing in the background. On a terrace below the castle guests enjoy a large swimming pool and there is also an indoor pool, which is part of a deluxe spa facility. For those who want ultimate privacy and supreme accommodations: a tower in the adorable village of Vertine has been converted into a suite, complete with a helicopter pad for discreet arrivals, servants' quarters, and even a private pool on the top commanding fantastic views. *Directions:* From Gaiole in Chianti, follow signs to the castle.

❄ ☕ 🛹 CREDIT ☎ 🏋 Y P ‖ ✿ 🏊 🏃 🖼 🔔 👫 🐎 🍇 ❦

CASTELLO DI SPALTENNA
Manager: Guido Conti
Gaiole in Chianti, (SI) 53013, Italy
Tel: (0577) 74 94 83, Fax: (0577) 74 92 69
38 Rooms, Double: €230–€320
Closed: Feb & Mar, Credit cards: all major
www.karenbrown.com/spaltenna.html
HOTEL

The Castello di Tornano, a strategically situated hilltop tower dating back almost 1,000 years, has a 360-degree vista of the surrounding valley and has been of great historical significance in the seemingly endless territorial battles between Siena and Florence. The owners are the Selvolini family and it is Patrizia who welcomes guests to the expansive wine estate. Nine charming suites are situated in the actual castle and its monumental tower. Patrizia has personally taken care of the décor of the house using many of the family's own antiques. The piece d'resistance is the superior suite on the top floor of the tower, offering a unique architectural style and a magnificent view from eight large windows. The tower-top terrace has a 6-person hydrojet pool, a view not easily forgotten. In the stone farmhouse, in front of the tower, 7 one- and two-bedroom apartments are offered guests, each appointed in the typical rustic style of Tuscany. The restaurant serves authentic, traditional meals. The spectacular pool was built inside the ancient moat of the castle. Trails cut across the vineyards and the surrounding woods, enjoyable for walks. It is also possible to ride the owners' horses through the scenic countryside. *Directions:* From the A1 exit at Valdarno, follow the sign to Gaiole. Take the S.S.408 towards Gaiole and pass through the village, following signs for Siena. After 6 km you see the sign for Tornano on the left.

CASTELLO DI TORNANO
Hosts: Patrizia Selvolini & Francesco Gioffreda
Gaiole in Chianti, (SI) 53013, Italy
Tel: (0577) 746067, Fax: (0577) 746094
Cellphone: (335) 7606699
9 Rooms, Double: €140–€460
7 Apartments: €80–€240 daily
Minimum Nights: 2, Open: Mar to Dec
Credit cards: VS, Other Languages: good English
www.karenbrown.com/castelloditornano.html
B&B, SELF CATERING

When dreaming of Tuscany, one usually envisions sweeping fields of vineyards and gentle hills dotted with olive trees. L'Ultimo Mulino has a totally different type of setting, in a heavily wooded nook by a small stream. This small hotel was originally a medieval olive mill and the antique millstone in the lounge stands testament to the hotel's colorful past, as do many architectural features, including 13 dramatic brick arches, which form a vaulted ceiling in the lounge. The primary color scheme throughout is white and blue—seen in the sofas and also in the dining room in the cushions and the table linens and china. The guestrooms all have a rustic ambiance, appropriate to the old mill, with wrought-iron headboards used throughout. The price of the rooms depends upon the size and the amenities. The least expensive rooms are fairly small but those in the upper category are large, and several have their own private terrace. The bathrooms are especially nice, and many have the added luxury of Jacuzzi tubs. All the rooms have air conditioning, direct-dial phones, mini-bars, good lighting by the beds, and satellite televisions. One of the most pleasant features of the hotel is a 20-meter swimming pool built into a terrace above the hotel. *Directions:* From Radda in Chianti, take the road for Gaiole and Siena. About 5 km from Radda, turn left at the sign to L'Ultimo Mulino. The hotel is about midway between Radda and Gaiole.

L'ULTIMO MULINO
Manager: Massimiliano Draghi
Localita: La Ripresa di Vistarenni
Gaiole in Chianti, (SI) 53013, Italy
Tel: (0577) 73 85 20, Fax: (0577) 73 86 59
13 Rooms, Double: €180–€290
Meals for hotel guests (Tues-Sun)
Closed: mid-Nov to mid-Mar, Credit cards: all major
www.karenbrown.com/lultimo.html ,
HOTEL

On the extreme outskirts of Florence, the Fattoressa offers a location for dual exploration of both the city and the Tuscan countryside. One of the many marvelous attractions of Florence is how the countryside comes right up to the doors of the city and just behind the magnificent Certosa monastery you find the 15th-century stone farmhouse of the delightfully congenial Fusi-Borgioli family. They have transformed the farmer's quarters into guest accommodations: four sweetly simple bedrooms plus two triples, each with its own spotless bathroom. Angiolina and Amelio, who have tended to this piece of land for many years, treat their guests like family and, as a result, enjoy receiving some of them year after year. Daughters-in-law Laura and Katia, who speak English, have been a great help in assisting guests with local itineraries. Visitors take meals en famille at long tables in the cozy, rustic dining room with a large stone fireplace (€31 for dinner). Here Angiolina proudly serves authentic Florentine specialties using ingredients from her own fruit orchard and vegetable garden. *Directions:* Entering Florence from the Certosa exit off the Siena superstrada, turn left one street after the Certosa monastery stoplight onto Volterrana. After the bridge, turn right behind the building. The house is just on the left.

LA FATTORESSA
Hosts: Angiolina Fusi & Amelio Borgioli
Via Volterrana 58, Galluzzo, (FI) 50124, Italy
Tel & Fax: (055) 2048418
Cellphone: (339) 8027715
6 Rooms, Double: €70–€90
Open: all year, Credit cards: none
Other Languages: good English, French, German
www.karenbrown.com/lafattoressa.html
B&B

Casa Mezzuola is part of a small group of farmhouses atop a hill 3 kilometers outside Greve where the land was divided into separate smaller properties. Friendly hosts, Riccardo, an antiques and jewelry dealer, Nicoletta, and their two girls live in the main house while hospitality is offered within three apartments for two to four persons in the adjacent stables and fienile where the hay was once stored. The stone walls, beams, and original brick openings to allow air into the barn were all preserved in the tower-like construction housing two of the apartments. A two-story apartment has a tiled kitchen/living area on one floor and bedroom and bathroom upstairs, while the snug studio apartment crowns the top of the tower. They are all nicely furnished with colorful rugs, local country furniture, satellite TV, and fully equipped kitchens. Breakfast is served within the apartments or outside under one of the pergola terraces. Just below the apartments is a swimming pool, which enjoys the expansive vistas, and there are bikes for guests' use. This is a convenient base for travelers in the heart of Chianti. Greve has a full program of festivals, concerts, and events, especially during the summer. *Directions:* Entering Greve from the north (Florence), turn right at the Esso Petrol Station. Follow signs for Mezzuola, Cologne, not Montefioralle. After 3 km of unpaved, bumpy road, you will come across the marked property.

CASA MEZZUOLA
Hosts: Riccardo Franconeri family
Via S. Cresci 30, Greve in Chianti, (FI) 50022, Italy
Tel & Fax: (055) 8544885
Cellphone: (347) 6135020
3 Apartments: €400–€850 weekly, €90–€130 daily
Minimum Nights: 3, 7 Jun to Sep
Open: all year, Credit cards: MC, VS
Other Languages: good English
www.karenbrown.com/mezzuola.html
SELF CATERING

For a simple, sweet, friendly little hotel, the Albergo San Martino offers excellent quality at a reasonable price. Located in the very heart of Lucca, within walking distance of the main architectural and artistic sites, this cheerful inn looked so inviting we had to go in to see if it was as cute inside as out. Named for San Martino Cathedral, which is just steps away, the hotel is painted a soft yellow, which is accented by pretty white shutters. In front, an appealing little garden area with green umbrellas shading tables, chairs, and a sofa is prettily defined by potted trees and plants. You enter into a fresh and tidy lobby with a reception desk to your left and a sitting area and intimate bar to your right. The simply furnished guestrooms offer all the necessary modern conveniences such as: air conditioning, satellite TVs, direct-dial phones, and mini-bars. The professional staff strive to meet the needs of their guests. You can rent bikes near the hotel to tour the town. It is great fun to bike around the wall of the city. *Directions:* Lucca is a maze of tiny streets, so it is best to ask for detailed instructions.

ALBERGO SAN MARTINO
Owners: Andrea Morotti & Pietro Bonino
Via della Dogana, 9
Lucca, (FI) 55100, Italy
Tel: (0583) 46 91 81, Fax: (0583) 99 19 40
9 Rooms, Double: €110–€160*
*Breakfast not included: €10
Open: all year, Credit cards: all major
www.karenbrown.com/albergosanmartino.html
HOTEL

Lucca is decidedly one of the loveliest cities of Italy with its historical churches and circular piazzas interspersed among beautiful shops featuring original storefronts and signage. Besides the well-known summer Puccini Festival (this is his birthplace), there are antiques markets, artisan fairs, and some of the most beautiful formal gardens and villas in Italy surrounding the city. In March the villas and gardens open for a special tour when the area's famed flower, the camellia (tree size), is in bloom. Over the years we have patiently awaited the arrival of a charming place to stay within the city walls and we were eventually rewarded with the Alla Corte degli Angeli. The Bonino family, already very familiar with the hospitality business, took over a private residence in the very heart of Lucca and created ten spacious bedrooms with guests' comfort in mind. The ground-floor reception area includes a lovely dining room with fireplace where an abundant buffet breakfast is served, if not in your own room. Bedrooms on the upper two floors are reached by an elevator, and all follow a specific flower theme, with pastel-colored walls giving an overall fresh feeling. Complementing the well-put-together decor are antique dressers, parquet floors, and amenities such as air conditioning, Jacuzzi tubs, mini-bars, TVs, and Internet access. *Directions:* In the pedestrian-only center of Lucca near the famous Piazza Anfiteatro. Private garage parking can be arranged.

ALLA CORTE DEGLI ANGELI
Host: Pietro Bonino
Via degli Angeli 23
Lucca, (FI) 55100, Italy
Tel: (0583) 469204, Fax: (0583) 991989
10 Rooms, Double: €155
Open: all year, Credit cards: all major
Other Languages: some English
www.karenbrown.com/allacorte.html
B&B

Lucca is an outstanding walled town—truly one of Italy's jewels. If you want to visit Lucca, but prefer staying in the countryside, just a ten-minute drive away sits the sumptuous Locanda L'Elisa, a pretty, deep-lavender villa with white trim peeking out from the trees. The hotel has the appearance of a private home and, happily, this intimate, homelike quality remains even after you step inside where you are warmly greeted. As you look around, it is obvious that this was previously the residence of a wealthy family. Fine antiques, splendid paintings, and luxurious fabrics combine to create a mood of refined elegance. All of the guestrooms are individually decorated, but exude a similar old-world ambiance created with dark woods and opulent materials. The walls are richly covered in damask fabrics that color-coordinate with the draperies and bedspreads. However, the mood changes dramatically in the appealing dining room, found in a glass-enclosed conservatory. During the day, sunlight streams in through the windows and guests can enjoy both excellent cuisine and a view of the trees, green lawn, and colorful, well-tended beds of flowers. In this same garden you find a refreshing swimming pool. The Locanda L'Elisa is a very special luxury hideaway with a gracious warmth of welcome. *Directions:* Take the A11 to Lucca then take N12r (not 12) toward Pisa. Soon after leaving Lucca, watch for a sign on the left for Locanda L'Elisa.

❄ 🖊 CREDIT ☎ 🏠 ⛲ Ⓨ P 🍽 🚭 🏊 🖼 🗡 ⚓ 🏹 🚶 🐎 🍇

LOCANDA L'ELISA
Owner: Alessandro Del Grande
Via Nuova per Pisa, 1952 (S.S. 12B1S)
Massa Pisana, Lucca, (FI) 55050, Italy
Tel: (0583) 37 97 37, Fax: (0583) 37 90 19
10 Rooms, Double: €230–€400*
*Breakfast not included: €16
Closed: Jan, Credit cards: all major
Relais & Châteaux
www.karenbrown.com/locandalelisa.html
HOTEL

It was welcome news to hear that a small deluxe hotel had opened in the historical center of Lucca, one of our favorite medieval walled cities. After years of meticulous restoration, the 12th-century Palazzo Alexander first opened for guests in 2000. Your gracious host and creator of this small inn is Mario Maraviglia, who welcomes guests as friends with hardly a hint of commercialism—there isn't even a hotel sign in front—and his team shares his philosophy. To the left of the marble-floored reception foyer is an ornate, intimate breakfast room and bar, set with small tables and fancy, gold-embellished chairs. Two huge chandeliers enhance the dark, handsome, beamed ceiling. As well as the elevator, a wonderful, very old stone staircase, illuminated by a stained-glass skylight, leads up to the guestrooms, each named after a famous Italian opera. The bedrooms are furnished with antique reproduction furniture in an ornate Venetian style. All the rooms have mini-bars, hairdryers, TVs, direct-dial phones, and elegant marble bathrooms. If you want to splurge, ask for "Tosca" which has a romantic little terrace tucked in the rooftop. At the moment there are only a few rooms, but the building next door has been purchased and soon there will be ten additional suites. *Directions:* The hotel has a parking lot nearby and you can drive through the pedestrian zone to the hotel. Ask for a diagram on how to reach the hotel.

PALAZZO ALEXANDER
Owner: Mario Maraviglia
Via Santa Giustina, 48
Lucca, (FI) 55100, Italy
Tel: (0583) 58 35 71, Fax: (0583) 58 36 10
13 Rooms, Double: €120–€270
Open: all year, Credit cards: all major
www.karenbrown.com/palazzoalexander.html
HOTEL

La Romea is a charming and informal B&B situated in a 14th century palazzo right in the very heart of Lucca's enchanting ancient city center. Walk up to the first floor and enter the spacious apartment with its reception desk, sitting area with black leather sofas, and three breakfast tables all under one beamed ceiling. Warm and friendly hosts, Gaia and Giulio heartily welcome guests. Off the main room are the five guest rooms each decorated and named by color (yellow, red, green, ivory and blue). Individually appointed rooms, each with new bathrooms and amenities such as direct telephone line, television, mini-bar, air conditioning and internet wireless connection, are spacious and well lit with large windows and antique furnishings. Their individual color themes are carried through the wall colour, bedspreads and curtains. Features include stencil painted borders, beams and parquet floors. The celestial blue room is actually a suite, suitable for a family of four. A number of interesting itineraries are suggested and arranged by your knowledgeable hosts, including highlights of the city, wine and villa tours in the outlying countryside. *Directions:* On the corner of the Square Sant'Andrea (12th century church) and Via Ventaglie. A two-minute walk from Lucca's most important sights, the Torre Guingi and Piazza dell'Anfiteatro, plus the lovely Via Fillungo with its many shops and original storefronts.

LA ROMEA New
Hosts: Giulio & Gaia Calissi
Vicolo delle Ventaglie, 2
Lucca, (FI) 55100, Italy
Tel: (0583) 464175, Fax: (0583) 471280
5 Rooms, Double: €100–€160
Open: all year, Credit cards: all major
Other Languages: good English, French
www.karenbrown.com/romea
B&B

The noble Albertario family have four large countryside properties in Umbria and Tuscany that they have opened up to accommodate travelers. Macciangrosso, bordered by ancient cypress trees, is the most beautiful, with its hilltop position overlooking the sweeping valley. The large stone villa, which has been added on to at various times throughout its long history (15th-century origins), belonged to the noble Piccolomini ancestors. You enter through the side gate, walk over a large patio looking onto the delightful rose garden, and climb an external stairway up to the six bedrooms. These are all accessed by a main living room, more like a museum with its rare antique pieces and gilded frame paintings. Bedrooms, each with a small bathroom, are simpler, appointed with wrought-iron beds and coordinated bedspreads and curtains. Other common living areas are the transformed cantina and dining and game rooms. The swimming pool is bordered by a stone wall from the Etruscan period and a tennis court is nearby. Ten apartments of various sizes are found in the rest of the home and in a nearby house next to the chapel. Close to the thermal spas, Macciangrosso is on the edge of Umbria and Tuscany, offering easy access to the highlights of both regions. *Directions:* From Chiusi drive 3 km towards Chianciano. Turn right at the grocery store at the corner with "Via Pignattaia Alta" and go 1.5 km to the house.

MACCIANGROSSO
Hosts: Sonia & Luigi Albertario
Macciano, (SI) 53044, Italy
Tel & Fax: (0578) 21459
6 Rooms, Double: €135
10 Apartments: €440–€950 weekly
Minimum Nights: 2, 4 in apartments
Closed: Nov, Credit cards: MC, VS
Other Languages: good English, French
www.karenbrown.com/macciangrosso.html
B&B, SELF CATERING

It would be difficult for anyone with a passion for the outdoors to resist the challenge offered Federico when he inherited this 1,000-plus-acre estate in the wilderness of Maremma. He and his energetic wife, Elisabetta, plunged in and in two years made this dream come true. The results are notable and very ambitious, with the complete restoration of four stone farmhouses scattered about the vast property comprised of wooded hills, olive groves, and cultivated fields of grain and sunflowers. Guests first arrive at the imposing 1850s main villa, which houses the reception office and private family quarters. Comfortable apartments and rooms (divided among the various farmhouses) are nicely furnished with country pieces old and new and can accommodate from two to ten persons. Guests have the use of four swimming pools, mountain bikes, sauna, exercise and game rooms, Jacuzzi, and massage therapy. They convene at Podernovo where Tuscan meals are served in the exposed-stone dining room with fireplace, or on the patio looking out over the valley and up to Massa Marittima. The Etruscan towns of Massa Marittima, Volterra, Vetulonia, and Populonia are waiting to be explored and you are also close to the seaside. The summer months offer a rich musical program of operas and classical concerts in the main piazza and villas. *Directions:* Drive for 2 km on the gravel road from Massa Marittima where signs indicate Il Cicalino.

TENUTA IL CICALINO
Hosts: Elisabetta & Federico Vecchioni
Localita: Cicalino, Massa Marittima, (GR) 58024, Italy
Tel: (0566) 902031, Fax: (0566) 904896
Cellphone: (347) 6444130
7 Rooms, Double: €75–€85
23 Apartments: €82–€323 daily
Minimum Nights: 2, Open: Mar to Nov
Credit cards: MC, VS, Other Languages: some English
www.karenbrown.com/cicalino.html
B&B, SELF CATERING

The intense, untouched beauty of the Marittima area is gradually drawing attention away from the more popular northern areas of Tuscany, and the Villa Il Tesoro is a prime example of this trend. At first sight, "refreshingly diverse" comes to mind. The Swiss family Guldener, owners of this 300-acre property just 14 km from the seaside, have put their personal mark in the overall concept and detail of this sophisticated country resort. Within the traditional, preserved architecture of a group of stone farmhouses, the décor is contemporary and minimalist in line with the color, space, and nature of the surrounding soft hillsides adorned with olive groves and vineyards. Perfection reigns; from the stunning main sitting room completely open to the mesmerizing landscapes, to the wine bar, the attractive dining room, the circular swimming pool, and the impeccable grounds. With the idea that luxury is space, all similiarly appointed guestrooms are true suites with living areas of varied dimensions, with striped zebra chairs and fluffy cloud-like white beds. "Il Fiore del Tesoro" restaurant chef Heros de Agostinis serves an artful array of mouth-watering dishes inspired by the four seasons and authentic gastronomic culture of the Mediterranean. *Directions:* From the E80 coastal highway, exit at Follonica Est (or Scarlino from the south) and follow to Massa Marittima. Before the town, pass through Valpiana and turn left at signs for the villa.

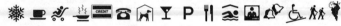

VILLA IL TESORO
Owner: Guldener Family
Localita: Valpiana
Massa Marittima, (GR) 58024, Italy
Tel: (0566) 92 971, Fax: (0566) 92 97 60
19 Rooms, Double: €165–€495
Closed: Jan 9 to Feb 9, Credit cards: all major
Region: Tuscany, Michelin Map: 430
www.karenbrown.com/villailtesoro.html
HOTEL

Florentine sisters Francesca and Beatrice Baccetti eagerly accepted the challenge of converting the family's country home and vineyards into an efficient bed and breakfast. Restoration work began immediately on the two adjacent stone buildings dating back to 1300. All original architectural features were preserved, leaving the five guestrooms and eleven apartments (for two to four people) with terra-cotta brick floors, wood-beamed ceilings, and mansard roofs, and many with generous views over the tranquil Tuscan countryside. The very comfortable and tidy rooms are furnished with good reproductions in country style and feel almost hotel-like with their telephones and modern bathrooms. A beautiful swimming pool with hydro-massage, tennis court, billiards room, and nearby horse stables are at guests' disposal, although finding enough to do is hardly a problem with Florence only 18 kilometers away and practically all of Tuscany at one's fingertips. Breakfast is served at wooden tables in the stone-walled dining room or out on the terrace. Readers give Salvadonica a high rating for service and warm hospitality. *Directions:* From Florence take the superstrada toward Siena for 6 km, exiting at San Casciano Nord. Follow signs for town, turning left at the sign for Mercatale. Salvadonica is on this road and well marked.

SALVADONICA
Hosts: Francesca & Beatrice Baccetti
Via Grevigiana 82
Mercatale Val di Pesa, (FI) 50024, Italy
Tel: (055) 8218039, Fax: (055) 8218043
5 Rooms, Double: €105–€117
11 Apartments: €122–€150 daily B&B
Open: Mar to Nov, Credit cards: all major
Other Languages: good English
www.karenbrown.com/salvadonica.html
B&B, SELF CATERING

The Castelletto di Montebenichi is an enchanting small castle in a tiny, storybook-perfect, medieval village perched on a hilltop in Tuscany, romantically facing a miniature plaza enclosed by a circle of homes built into the old tower walls. This is a sturdy, stone building with a crenellated roof, arched windows, and a row of colorful coats of armor stretching across the top. Inside, it seems as if you are truly stepping back in time—the renovation has been so carefully accomplished that you don't realize any changes have been made (until you see the modern bathrooms). All the fabulous murals have been restored and the floors and beamed ceilings reflect the rich patina of age. The furnishings, too, reflect another era with rich fabrics, beautiful light fixtures, lovely oil paintings, and many fine antiques. Your exceptionally personable hosts, Marco Gasparini and Arnaldo Soriani, want their guests to feel like friends. Everything possible is done to create this ambiance, including an open bar where guests can fix themselves refreshment whenever they want. Breakfast is served in a charming, sunny room with arched windows on three sides. There are also cozy lounges, a stunning library, a swimming pool, a gym with indoor Jacuzzi, and a sauna. This is a non-smoking hotel. No children under 14. *Directions:* Midway between Siena and Arezzo. From the A1, exit at Valdarno and follow signs for Montevarchi, Bucine, Ambra, and then Montebenichi.

CASTELLETTO DI MONTEBENICHI
Owners: Marco Gasparini & Arnaldo Soriani
Montebenichi, (AR) 52020, Italy
Tel: (055) 99 10 110, Fax: (055) 99 10 113
9 Rooms, Double: €250–€300
Open: Apr to Nov, Credit cards: all major
Abitare la Storia
www.karenbrown.com/dimontebenichi.html
HOTEL

Lucca, one of our favorite Italian cities, is well situated near Pisa, with the beautiful Valdera countryside to the south, the Apuane mountain range to the north, the seaside 20 kilometers away, and many splendid villas and famous gardens scattered in the vicinity. The city, however, is directly surrounded by a heavily commercial area until you get to the olive oil and wine country around the charming hilltop town of Montecarlo, 15 kilometers east of town. This medieval stone village with fortress walls has several good restaurants and cafés, its own theater where Puccini was known to put on operas, and many olive-oil-producing farms and wineries close by. A team of three women friends, Antonella, Marta and Miriam, take turns caring for their guests on a rotation basis, alternating with their own family duties. All bedrooms on two upper floors but two have en suite bathrooms and are simply appointed with wrought-iron beds, eyelet curtains and floral bedspreads. A rich and tasty breakfast, made with local and homemade products, is served either out on the front patio where you can observe the daily life of the locals, or in the miniature breakfast room to the right of the reception and mini sitting area (with internet point) where a wine and coffee bar is open all day. You are left a front door key when returning in the evening. *Directions:* From the A11 autostrada, take the Altopascio exit. Head towards Pescia (3 km) and turn left for Montecarlo for another 2 km.

ANTICA CASA DEI RASSICURATI
Hosts: Antonella Romanini,
Marta Giusti & Miriam Keller
Via della Collegiata 2, Montecarlo, (LU) 55015, Italy
Tel: (0583) 228901, Fax: (0583) 22498
8 Rooms, Double: €68–€80
Minimum Nights: 2
Open: all year, Credit cards: MC, VS
Other Languages: good English, French, German
www.karenbrown.com/rassicurati.html
B&B

It is only logical that the Antinori family, one of the most famous wine producers in Italy, has joined the ranks of landowners offering top-quality, agriturismo accommodation. They have done it in grand style, restoring and creating twenty apartments and seven guestrooms within the eight stone houses scattered about the vast property in the center. Chianti is composed of hills, woods, and, of course, infinite vineyards. In keeping with the general countryside ambience, the high-level accommodation is appointed with wood furniture, smart striped or checked fabrics that harmonize well with the brick floors and beamed ceilings. While three of the ancient farmhouses are located up a road across the vineyards, the others are grouped together at the main entrance near the reception room, swimming pool, tennis courts, small gym, and restaurant serving typical Tuscan fare. The Fonte de Medici is heads above the rest with an offering of a wide range of amenities including air conditioning, kitchenette, fireplaces, dishwasher, barbeque, satellite TV, and internet access. Enjoy the classic, Tuscan landscapes coupled with classic Chianti wine and the marvels of this region surrounding you. *Directions:* Exit from A1 at Certosa-Firenze and follow the highway for Siena. Exit at San Casciano and follow for Montefiridolfi, then Badia di Passignano. Follow signs for Fonte de Medici-Antinori to the front gate.

FONTE DE MEDICI
Manager: Gilberto Nori
Località S. Maria a Macerata
Montefiridolfi, (FI) 50020, Italy
Tel: (055) 8244700, Fax: (055) 8244701
Cellphone: (348) 397 96 00
7 Rooms, Double: €162–€189
20 Apartments: €150–€350
Open: all year, Credit cards: all major, Good English
www.karenbrown.com/medici.html
B&B, SELF CATERING

Il Borghetto Country Inn is an absolute dream, an idyllic hideaway in one of the most enchanting areas of Tuscany. It is owned by the Cavallini family who originally bought a farmhouse in the heart of the exquisite Chianti district to use as a family weekend retreat. When the adjacent farmhouse came on the market, they bought it too, restored it to perfection, and opened a tiny hotel. What makes this small inn so special is that it is a family operation. The father, Roberto Cavallini, watches over the operation from Milan, his son, Antonio, is the on-site manager, and the charming daughter, Ilaria, ably helps out. Guests have their own intimate, beautifully decorated lounge, which also serves as the breakfast room (in warm weather breakfast is served outside on the lovely terrace). Rosie Cavallini did all the decorating and every detail is of superb quality with beautiful fabrics, original paintings, abundant displays of fresh flowers, Oriental carpets, and fine antiques. But the best I've saved for last—a sweeping vista of olive groves and vineyards that produce extra virgin olive oil, Chianti Classico and Merlot wine. Tours and wine tasting in the cellar are available, as well as on-site cooking courses which include food and art tours in Florence, Siena and the surrounding countryside. *Directions:* Leave the Florence-Siena expressway at Bargino. Exit, turning right, and then almost immediately, turn up the hill toward Montefiridolfi. 2.6 km after the exit, Il Borghetto is on your right.

IL BORGHETTO COUNTRY INN
Owners: Cavallini family
Via Collina S. Angelo 23
Montefiridolfi, (FI) 50020, Italy
Tel: (055) 82 44 442, Fax: (055) 82 44 247
9 Rooms, Double: €180–€280
Open: Mar to Nov
www.karenbrown.com/ilborghetto.html
B&B

La Loggia, built in 1427, was one of the Medici estates during the centuries of their rule. Owner Giulio Baruffaldi, weary of urban life in Milan, transplanted himself and his wife here and succeeded in reviving the wine estate's splendor while respecting its past, enhancing its architectural beauty while giving utmost attention to the preservation of the historic property. Their informal yet refined hospitality is reflected in the care given to retaining the rustic ambiance of the former farmers' homes, each containing one to three bedrooms, living room, and kitchen, some with fireplace, and adorned with country antiques and original paintings from the Baruffaldis' own art collection. In fact, many important bronze and ceramic sculptures by international artists are displayed throughout the gardens of the villa. Four double rooms have been added, some having a fireplace or hydro-massage bath and steam room. Apart from just basking in the pure romance and tranquillity of this place, you can enjoy a heated seawater swimming pool, horseback riding, and nearby tennis and golf facilities. Other activities include the occasional cooking or wine-tasting lesson, and impromptu dinners in the cellar. The charming hostess Ivana personally takes care of guests' needs. *Directions:* Leave the Florence-Siena autostrada after San Casciano at Bargino. Turn right at the end of the ramp, then left for Montefiridolfi (3.5 km). La Loggia is just before town.

FATTORIA LA LOGGIA
Hosts: Giulio Baruffaldi & Cuca Roaldi
Via Collina, Montefiridolfi, San Casciano Val di Pesa
(FI) 50026, Italy
Tel: (055) 8244288, Fax: (055) 8244283
4 Rooms, Double: €100–€160
11 Apartments: €110–€190 daily
Open: all year, Credit cards: MC, VS
Other Languages: good English, French, Spanish
www.karenbrown.com/laloggia.html
B&B, SELF CATERING

Just opposite the lovely Fattoria La Loggia is a bed and breakfast that was actually one of the farmhouses belonging to the vast vineyard property. Gracious Signora Nadia fell in love with the ancient house and decided to retire here after having the entire place restored, leaving the ground floor for herself and the guests' breakfast room while the upstairs provides apartments of flexible configurations for travelers. The two adjoining apartments to the right (yellow and blue color schemes) can become a three-bedroom apartment with three colourful bathrooms, living room, kitchen, and large fireplace. The two one-bedroom apartments in green hues can be rented separately or adjoined as well. Rooms have a clean, country feeling to them with antique armoires, simple wrought-iron beds blending in nicely with stone walls, wood-beamed mansard ceilings and brick floors so typical in Tuscany. A lovely swimming pool sits close to the house overlooking the soft valley. This is a very easy base from which to visit most of the region's highlights besides being only 20 minutes from Florence and 30 from Siena. *Directions:* Exit at Bargino from the Florence-Siena highway and turn right and then immediately left at the sign for Montefiridolfi. After 3 km look for a stone house with large arched windows on the left side of the road before town.

MACINELLO
Host: Nadia Ciuffetti
Via Collina 9, Montefiridolfi, San Casciano Val di Pesa
(FI) 50020, Italy
Tel & Fax: (055) 8244459
4 Rooms, Double: €210–€225
4 Apartments: €210–€225 daily
Minimum Nights: 3, 7 Jun to Aug
Open: all year, Credit cards: none
www.karenbrown.com/macinello.html
B&B, SELF CATERING

The Villa Sant'Andrea is a prestigious wine estate on a hilltop dominating the Chianti valley. An impressive villa and church are its focal points. So spectacular and strategic is the location that it has been occupied since Roman times. The vast property (over 2,000 acres!) spills down the vineyard-covered terrain to the horizon and includes three typical Tuscan farmhouses, (Zobi, Perticato and Montelodoli) that can be rented weekly or daily, each with its own private swimming pool, Luckily, for those desiring accommodation with breakfast, five quaint country style rooms are also available. Situated within the hamlet and across from the proprietors' gated historic villa, they are hidden by centuries-old cypresses and a lush garden. Wrought iron beds adorned with checked bedspreads and country antiques are authentically Tuscan. Superb views are to be enjoyed from each window. Two common rooms with large open fireplaces are reserved for guests for breakfast or simply lounging. For the more active, mountain bikes are available as well as hiking trails into the scenic countryside, through olive groves, vineyards and oak trees. The marvels of Tuscany are at your doorstep (villages of Chianti, Siena, San Gimignano, Volterra, and everything in between). *Directions:* From the Siena-Florence highway exit at Tavarnelle and follow road for 2 km to Fabbrica and up to the villa entrance.

VILLA SANT' ANDREA   **New**
Hosts: Vicini family
Via di Fabbrica, 63
Montefiridolfi, (FI) 50020, Italy
Tel: (055) 8544254, Fax: (055) 82442030
5 Rooms, Double: €125
3 Houses, €130–€216 daily
Open: all year, Credit cards: all major
Other Languages: English, French
www.karenbrown.com/villasantandrea
B&B, SELF CATERING

La Chiusa, nestled in the hills of Tuscany southeast of Siena, is an old stone farmhouse whose restaurant is so well known that guests come from far and wide to enjoy the meals where everything is fresh, homemade, and delicious. Dania and Umberto Lucherini are the gracious owners and Dania is the talented chef. Almost all the vegetables, olive oil, meats, wines, and cheeses come either from the inn's own farm or from those nearby. The original wood-burning oven still stands in the courtyard in front of the inn, emitting delicious aromas of freshly baking bread. The dining room is large and airy, with an uncluttered simple elegance enhanced by windows overlooking rolling hills. When the weather is balmy, meals are also served on the back terrace, which is ideally positioned to capture a sweeping view. The emphasis here is definitely on the exquisite meals, but there are also bedrooms for guests who want to spend the night. Like the dining room, the guestrooms are perfectly in keeping with the ambiance of the old farmhouse, lovely in their rustic simplicity yet with every modern convenience. In addition to the standard guestrooms, there are some deluxe suites—one even has an olive press in the bathroom! *Directions:* From the highway A1, take the "Val di Chiana" exit. Turn left and follow the signs that lead to Torrita di Siena and then Pienza. About 7 km past Torrita di Siena turn left toward Montefollonico.

LA CHIUSA
Owners: Lucherini family
Managers: Franco Sodi
Via della Madonnina, 88
Montefollonico, (SI) 53040, Italy
Tel: (0577) 66 96 68, Fax: (0577) 66 95 93
15 Rooms, Double: €200–€400
Open: Mar 20 to Nov 25, Credit cards: all major
www.karenbrown.com/chiusa.html
HOTEL

One result of increasing interest in the singular attractions of the Maremma, or southern Tuscany, is the opening or expansion of several noteworthy places to stay. The Villa Acquaviva, once owned by nobility and a small family hotel for some years, was extensively remodeled to include seven guestrooms named for and painted in the colors of local wildflowers. The bedrooms all have private baths and are decorated with country antiques and wrought-iron beds. Breakfast of homemade cakes, breads, and jams can be eaten in the breakfast room near the enoteca. There are ten newer rooms in a stone farmhouse on the property plus eight in another, joined together by a glassed-in reception area. These are our favorites, with beautiful local antiques and colorful matching fabrics adorning beds and windows. Tennis courts and a swimming pool are attractive features of the complex. In the center of the park, in a scenic position by the swimming pool, the restaurant presents typical Maremman dishes made with fresh products from the farm. *Directions:* From Rome, take the Aurelia coastal road, exiting at Vulci. Follow signs for Manciano, then Montemerano. Acquaviva is well marked just outside the village.

VILLA ACQUAVIVA
Hosts: Valentina di Virginio & Serafino d'Ascenzi
Localita: Acquaviva, Montemerano, (GR) 58050, Italy
Tel: (0564) 602890, Fax: (0564) 602895
Cellphone: (335) 7509100
25 Rooms, Double: €102–€168
Minimum Nights: 3
Open: all year, Credit cards: MC, VS
Other Languages: good English, French
www.karenbrown.com/acquaviva.html
HOTEL

Le Fontanelle country house sits in the heart of the Maremma area of Tuscany where, besides being pleasant and well run, it fills a need for the growing interest in this off-the-beaten-track destination. Signor Perna and his two lovely daughters, originally from Rome, searched and found this peaceful haven from the stress of city life, promptly transferring themselves and undertaking major restoration work. Looking over a soft green valley up to the nearby village of Montemerano, the stone farmhouse with its rusty-red shutters offers four comfortable rooms with spotless private bathrooms. The converted barn houses five rooms while the last room is in a separate cottage set in the woods. Sunlight pours into the front veranda-like breakfast room where coffee and cakes are taken together with other guests at one large table. The Pernas assist guests in planning local itineraries including visits to artisan workshops. With due notice, guests can find a wonderfully prepared dinner awaiting them under the ivy-covered pergola in the rose garden. The property is part of a reserve with deer, wild boar, and various types of wildlife, where Porcini mushrooms, wild asparagus, and berries are found in season. *Directions:* From Rome, take the A12 autostrada. Continue north on Aurelia route 1, turning off at Vulci after Montalto. Follow signs for Manciano then Montemerano. Turn left at the bed-and-breakfast sign before town and follow the dirt road for 1 km.

LE FONTANELLE
Hosts: Daniela & Cristina Perna
Localita: Poderi di Montemerano
Montemerano, (GR) 58050, Italy
Tel & Fax: (0564) 602762
Cellphone: (335) 6559699 or (338) 9205641
10 Rooms, Double: €82
Open: all year, Credit cards: MC, VS
Other Languages: some English
www.karenbrown.com/fontanelle.html
B&B

A pleasant alternative to a countryside bed and breakfast is one right in the historical center of the marvelously preserved medieval town of Montepulciano. Most famous for its prized Rosso di Montepulciano wines, its striking charm of the past rivals that of its hilltop neighbors, Pienza and Montalcino. Here Cinzia Caroti offers bed and breakfast on the first floor of a 16th-century palazzo on the main street of town, which is lined with shops and restaurants and is off limits to cars, which adds much to its medieval aura. One flight of wide stairs takes you up to L'Agnolo's reception area. There are three bedrooms off this area and another two off the frescoed dining room with wrought-iron chandelier. The spacious, high-ceilinged rooms have a subdued ambiance, with wrought-iron beds, family antiques, and new white-tiled bathrooms. Better lighting could be used to show off lovely original frescoed ceilings and painted borders. A classic breakfast of cappuccino and fresh croissants is served in the coffee shop below the home, making one feel like a true local resident. Cinzia lives two doors down and is present throughout the day to assist guests and make suggestions from the many sightseeing possibilities in this rich area of Tuscany, bordering Umbria. *Directions:* Park your car nearby (north or east lot) outside the village walls and follow Via di Gracciano running north-south to the middle. There is a small gold name plaque at the door.

L'AGNOLO
Host: Cinzia Caroti
Via di Gracciano nel Corso 63
Montepulciano, (SI) 53045, Italy
Tel: (0578) 717070, Fax: (0578) 757095
Cellphone: (339) 2254813
5 Rooms, Double: €83
Open: all year, Credit cards: MC, VS
Other Languages: very little English
www.karenbrown.com/agnolo.html
B&B

La Dionora is a delightful hotel just outside the walled town of Montepulciano, one of Tuscany's jewels. This appealing small inn, made of tan stone and accented by brown shutters, has a stunning location, crowning a gentle hill with a 360-degree view, with absolutely nothing to mar the beauty and solitude of the setting. As far as the eye can see there are rolling hills covered with forests, fields of sunflowers, olive groves, and, in the distance, the sweet walled village of Pienza. As you approach, it is obvious that this is a well cared for, beautifully managed property. Everything is absolutely meticulous, from the perfectly tended flower beds to the lovingly decorated bedrooms. Three of the guestrooms are located upstairs in the farmhouse with windows that capture the splendid view. The other rooms, each with a private terrace, are in a similar one-story stone building just steps away. All have Tuscan-style antiques enhanced by Ferragamo fabrics. Breakfast is served in the garden in a most attractive stone "winter garden" with arched glass walls on four sides through which the sunlight streams in. Also in the garden is a beautiful swimming pool. Maria Teresa Cesarini, the friendly owner, is ably assisted by Giulio D'Antonio and they are perfect hosts who are very familiar with Tuscany and offer assistance with planning your day. *Directions:* Take N146 from Montepulciano toward Pienza. After 3 km, turn left at the sign for La Dionora.

LA DIONORA
Owner: Mrs. Maria Teresa Cesarini
Via Vicinale di Poggiano
Montepulciano, (SI) 53040, Italy
Tel: (0578) 71 74 96, Fax: (0578) 71 74 98
6 Rooms, Double: €280–€360
Closed: Jan 7 to mid-Feb, Credit cards: all major
www.karenbrown.com/ladionora.html
HOTEL

Montorio is a gem offering everything your heart could possibly desire when dreaming of a perfect holiday in Tuscany: spacious, beautifully decorated guestrooms; a rich selection of restaurants within walking distance; convenient location for exploring Tuscany and Umbria; a glorious setting; spectacular views; cooking facilities in every room; large modern bathrooms; and excellent prices. This characterful, 15th-century golden-stone farmhouse is perfectly located on a hill surrounded by olive groves, vineyards, and cypress trees. The views are awesome, with nothing to disturb the mood of absolute serenity except perhaps for the song of birds and the ringing of church bells. The inn is within walking distance of the marvelous walled city of Montepulciano and through towering cypress trees you can see below the fabulous Renaissance church of San Biagio. In another direction, the adorable walled town of Pienza nestles on a hilltop. Each of the suites has a kitchen or kitchenette and is tastefully decorated with simple Tuscan-style, antique furniture. Centuries-old trees and flowers cascading from terracotta pots embellish the delightful terrace. *Directions:* Just on the north edge of Montepulciano, on the road to Pienza.

MONTORIO
Owner: Stefania Savini
Strada per Pienza, 2
Montepulciano, (SI) 53045, Italy
Tel: (0578) 71 74 42, Fax: (0578) 71 56 35
5 Apartments: €120–€180 daily
Minimum Nights: 3
Open: Feb 1 to Dec 15, Credit cards: MC, VS
Abitare la Storia
www.karenbrown.com/montorio.html
SELF CATERING

Montepulciano, ancient hilltop town and home of the prized "Rosso di Montepulciano" wine, is one of Tuscany's best-preserved marvels. The scenic countryside leads to other enchanting towns, such as Pienza, Montalcino, Sarteano, and San Quirico. Set below the town, behind the Basilica, taking in upwardly sweeping views of Montepucliano, is the lovely San Bruno property. The owners from Milan restored a typical stone farmhouse, drenched in pink cascading geraniums, and found themselves (naturally) with so many houseguests that they created two additional, one-story guesthouses across the informal garden dotted with lavender plants and roses. With guest comfort foremost in mind, large doubles have spacious, travertine bathrooms with hydrojet tub and separate shower. They are impeccably appointed in a refined country décor, using the finest materials and reflecting the innate beauty of these famed landscapes. A borderless, swimming pool awaits guests with a small, side gym and massage room. Home-baked goods are served in the morning until 11:00 in the dining room—located in a separate house incorporating the reception office and a soft-peach/yellow-colored living room with fireplace, inviting white sofas, and enormous glass doors with views. All extras are included in the room rate. *Directions:* From Montepulciano, follow for Basilica San Biagio. Behind church, turn a sharp left on Via Pescaia, then into second gate on left.

RELAIS SAN BRUNO
Host: Alberto Pavoncelli
Via di Pescaia, 5/7, Montepulciano, (SI) 53045, Italy
Tel: (0578) 716 222, Fax: (0578) 715 084
Cellphone: (338) 2557450
7 Rooms, Double: €240–€340
Apartments: €200–€300 daily
Open: Mar to Nov, Credit cards: all major
Other Languages: good English, Spanish
www.karenbrown.com/sanbruno.html
B&B, SELF CATERING

The romantic, ochre-colored, 17th-century Villa Poggiano is truly a gem. The Savini family bought the abandoned mansion, which nestles on a wooded hillside near the charming walled city of Montepulciano, and have tenderly restored it to its original splendor. An intimate, cozy parlor with comfortable chairs grouped around an open fireplace, a sweet breakfast room, and two enormous suites are on the ground floor. A wide staircase leads to four more beautiful rooms. There are also four delightful suites in a separate brick building facing a sweeping panorama of the countryside. The tasteful decor creates a warm, homelike ambiance. Throughout the villa, everything is on a grand scale with handsome fireplaces, sumptuous bathrooms, gorgeous antique furniture, exceptionally spacious rooms, and ornate chandeliers. The villa faces an idyllic Tuscan countryside with olive trees dotting the gentle hillside. Behind the villa is a thick forest with romantic paths meandering through the woodlands. There is also an enormous travertine swimming pool with a granite wall on one side embellished with a large sculpture, while on the other side, lounge chairs are set on a wide terrace outlined by very old cypress trees. The warmth of welcome by Stefania and her charming mother is so genuine you will never want to leave. *Directions:* Take the N146 from Montepulciano toward Pienza and after about 2 km, turn left at the sign for Villa Poggiano.

VILLA POGGIANO
Owner: Stefania Savini
Via di Poggiano, 7
Montepulciano, (SI) 53045, Italy
Tel: (0578) 75 82 92, Fax: (0578) 71 56 35
Cellphone: (338) 402268
9 Rooms, Double: €190–€300
Open: Apr to Nov, Credit cards: MC, VS
Abitare la Storia
www.karenbrown.com/villapoggiano.html
B&B

Monteriggioni is a circular medieval town with turreted fortress walls, mentioned in Dante's Inferno. To the east is an extension of unspoiled land, preserved over the centuries because it was all owned by one proprietor. Within this mix of olive groves and dense woods, in the center of a peaceful forest reserve is the Poggiarello property. The three stone farmhouses dating back to the 1700s are reached by a 2 kilometer dirt road. The Giove family (brother and sister team) bought and restored the property creating apartments for 2-8 people, two doubles, a restaurant and swimming pool plus living quarters for both of their own families. They enjoy entertaining guests and attending to their comfort and ease, offering tasty regional meals, such as fresh pastas and country soups all made with local products and fresh produce. A casual ambience prevails in room dècor which is basic and simple like the stone and beam houses, each with outdoor garden space or a nice wide open view. Another special feature is the Roman hot bath within its own stone house, perfect for a soak after a long day of tuscan touring. Sights in the immediate area include Siena, San Gimignano, Volterra and Chianti. *Directions:* From the Florence-Siena highway, exit at Monteriggioni, turn right at the stop sign and after 1.4 km left for for Abbadia. After 6 km turn left for Scogiano. After 4 km turn left signed Antico Borgo Poggiarello. Go 300m, turn left and follow the dirt road for 2 km.

ANTICO BORGO POGGIARELLO New
Host: Roberto Giove e Paolo Ruggiero
Localita Poggiarello-Srada San Monti
12, Monteriggioni, (SI) , Italy
Tel & Fax: (0577) 301003
2 Rooms, Double: €121–€170
14 Apartments: €100–€246
Open: all year, Credit cards: all major
Other Languages: some English
www.karenbrown.com/anticoborgopoggiarello
B&B, SELF CATERING

Tucked in the gentle Tuscan hills, Monteriggioni is a stunning sight. You will be captivated from afar at your first glimpse: the romantic town crowning the hilltop with its circular stone wall, punctuated by tall towers, still intact. If you have come just to sightsee, you must park your car below the town, but if you are one of the lucky ones who have a reservation at the Hotel Monteriggioni, drive through the portal in the wall to the hotel, which is located at the far end of the little square. It is hard to believe that this lovely small hotel, now so beautiful, used to be a stable. It took three years for the present owners to achieve the miracle you see today. Michela Cagnazzo, the owner, is responsible for the decoration and her taste is faultless. White walls, handsome antique furniture, white slipcovered sofas, and bouquets of fresh flowers create a fresh, appealing country ambiance. The guestrooms are also charming, with the same style of decor as the public rooms. Behind the hotel there is a terrace where breakfast is served, weather permitting. Just beyond is a small swimming pool tucked in the garden with a serene backdrop of the old moat, now filled with olive trees, and the stone walls of the town. The hotel has no restaurant but the Ristorante Il Pozzo next door offers authentic Tuscan cooking, and there are other restaurants nearby. It is a delightful hotel that does credit to a charming village. *Directions:* From the S2 at Monteriggioni, follow signs to the town.

HOTEL MONTERIGGIONI
Owner: Michela Gozzi Cagnazzo
Monteriggioni, (SI) 53035, Italy
Tel: (0577) 30 50 09 or (0577) 30 50 10
Fax: (0577) 30 50 11
12 Rooms, Double: €230
Closed: Jan 7 to end Feb, Credit cards: all major
www.karenbrown.com/monteriggioni.html
HOTEL

After years of working in a hotel in Siena, then owning a wine bar, Marcello and his wife Maria Pia decided to put their hospitality experience into practice and opened the charming Bolsinina bed and breakfast. This is a perfect location for travelers, being so close to Siena (18 km) and having easy access to the main road, which passes through the magical Crete Senesi landscapes with their low, rolling clay hills punctuated by an occasional cypress tree against the horizon, to the hilltowns of Montalcino, Pienza, and Montepulciano. The 18th-century brick house has a courtyard where meals are served in season. To one side are the apartments of varying sizes, and to the other is the large house where the beamed guestrooms are located upstairs, along with a large common living room and loggia terrace with splendid views. Downstairs is an open multi-use space rotating around the center staircase with billiard table, cozy living room with fireplace and two large brick arches, and dining room. Guests reserve in the morning for dinner accompanied by excellent local wines. The house and rooms are filled with local antique country furniture and armoires and there is an immediate "at-home," informal air about the place. An inviting swimming pool is an added bonus. *Directions:* From Siena on the S.R.2, pass Monteroni d'Arbia, Lucignano, and before Buonconvento turn left at Casale-Gaggiolo (km 209). Take the gravel road up to the house.

CASA BOLSININA
Hosts: Marcello & Maria Pia Mazzotta
Localita: Casale, Monteroni d'Arbia, (SI) 53014, Italy
Tel & Fax: (0577) 718477, Cellphone: (338) 2705153
6 Rooms, Double: €85–€150
4 Apartments: €450–€1000 weekly
Minimum Nights: 7 in apartments
Closed: Jan 15 to Mar 15, Credit cards: all major
Other Languages: good English
www.karenbrown.com/bolsinina.html
B&B, SELF CATERING

The island-like promontory of Argentario, facing the islands of Giglio and Giannutri, has always been a favorite seaside haven for Romans. Located on a narrow strip of land connecting Argentario to the mainland is the quaint town of Orbetello. Here you find a charming small hotel, the San Biagio, built within a private residence dating back to 1851. The Magnosi family restored the palazzo, creating the feeling of a nobleman's home, not only in the rich furnishings, but also with the many original architectural features of the palazzo itself. Some of these wonderful features include the arched entrance hall that leads to a small courtyard where breakfast is served, the high-ceilinged rooms with ornate moldings and frescoed borders, and the central staircase leading up to the richly appointed guestrooms that are in the main house, each of which has a luxurious marble travertine bathroom. The family's antique pieces collected throughout Europe adorn the intimate sitting rooms as well as the bedrooms. The adddition of 28 rooms in an adjacent building, with informal restaurant, wine bar, indoor swimming pool and spa is in its final phase ready for opening by beginning of 2006. Although the San Biagio offers no views in a seaside location, it provides top-level accommodation at exceptional comparable rates. *Directions:* From the Aurelia N1, exit at Orbetello and go to the historic center. Facing the church (duomo), Via Dante is the street on its left side.

SAN BIAGIO
Owners: Gianfranco Magnosi family
Via Dante, 34
Orbetello, (GR) 58015, Italy
Tel: (0564) 86 05 43, Fax: (0564) 86 77 87
40 Rooms, Double: €150–€400
Open: all year, Credit cards: all major
www.karenbrown.com/sanbiagio.html
HOTEL

Right next door to the Grazia farm is the very similar property of the Lignana family. Again, a long, straight road takes you off the busy coastal Aurelia highway back to the 700-plus-acre farm and hunting reserve looking out to the distant sea and Mount Argentario. Gracious Signora Marcella and husband, Giuseppe, live in the ivy-covered ancient stone tower and attached villa, while guests reside within seven comfortable self-catering apartments in a converted barn down the road. Spacious apartments have two bedrooms and two bathrooms, living/dining area, and kitchenette. Some apartments have the bedrooms on a second floor, while others have them split between the main floor and an open loft space. They are nicely appointed in a clean and easy style, with fresh white walls, smart plaid cushions on built-in sofas, framed prints, wicker furniture, and wrought-iron beds. An alternative to sea bathing is a dip in the swimming pool, guarded by olive trees. For nature lovers, the area is full of marvelous expeditions on foot or bike, including the National Park of Uccellina, various forts on Mount Argentario, and the islands of Giglio and Giannutri, not to mention the Saturnia thermal spa. *Directions:* From Rome take the Aurelia Highway 1 and turn right at the sign "Piante-Vivaio" (140.5 km after the turnoff for Ansedonia). From the north you must exit at Ansedonia and return to the highway heading towards Grosseto. 140 km from Rome's Fiumicino airport.

IL CASALONE
Hosts: Marcella & Giuseppe Lignana
S.S. Aurelia sud km 140.5
Orbetello Scalo (GR) 58016, Italy
Tel: (0564) 862160, Fax: (0564) 866308
Cellphone: (329) 2167397
7 Apartments: €600–€1,300 weekly
Minimum Nights: 2, 7 in Jul & Aug
Open: all year, Credit cards: none, Good English
www.karenbrown.com/casalone.html
SELF CATERING

The expansive Grazia farm is uniquely located at 3 kilometers from the sea. Gracious and warm hostess Signora Maria Grazia divides her time between Rome and the 300-acre property she inherited from her grandfather. The long cypress-lined driveway takes you away from the busy Aurelia road past grazing horses up to the spacious, rust-hued edifice with its arched loggia. The hosts' home, office, guest apartments, farmhands' quarters, and horse stables are all housed within the complex, which is surrounded by superb country and has peeks of the sea in all directions. From here one can enjoy touring Etruscan territory: Tuscania, Tarquinia, Sovana, Sorano, and the fascinating Roman ruins of Cosa, or stay by the coast on the beaches of Feniglia on the promontory of Argentario. Comfortably modest accommodations, including living area, kitchen, and breakfast basket, pleasantly decorated with homey touches, are offered within five apartments for two to four persons. Maria Grazia can suggest a myriad of local restaurants specializing in seafood or local country fare. Tennis and horseback riding lessons are available. Altogether a delightful combination. *Directions:* Take the coastal Aurelia road from Rome and after the Ansedonia exit turn right into an unmarked driveway immediately after the Pitorsino restaurant.

GRAZIA
Hosts: Maria Grazia Cantore family
Localita: Provincaccia, 110, S.S. Aurelia sud km 140.1
Orbetello Scalo, (GR) 58016, Italy
Tel & Fax: (0564) 881182, Cellphone: (347) 6471779
5 Apartments: €95–€140 daily B&B
Minimum Nights: 3
Open: all year, Credit cards: none
Other Languages: good English, French
www.karenbrown.com/grazia.html
SELF CATERING

Elba is a beautiful small island, easily accessible in one hour by car ferry from Piombino. After exploring Tuscany, or while en route along the coast heading north from Rome, you will find that Elba makes a delightful stopover where you can happily spend several days relaxing and exploring the island's many pretty inlets and picturesque fishing villages. The Hotel Villa Ottone is idyllically nestled in a tranquil park and has its own private beach (there is also a swimming pool). The original part of the hotel is a romantic villa (which belonged to Signor Di Mario's grandfather) facing directly onto the sea. If you want to splurge, ask for a deluxe room in the villa. Some of the guestrooms are located in an attractive building that also houses the reception area and the dining room, while more guestrooms are found in a separate wing nestled amongst the trees. The furnishings throughout are tasteful and everything is immaculately maintained. Be sure to visit the bar, which has a stunning ceiling of intricate plasterwork and lovely frescoes. In high season you need to take the modified American plan (MAP), which includes breakfast and either lunch or dinner and there is a three-night minimum. However, this is no problem as the food is very good and beautifully served. Villa Ottone is a hotel with great personality, overseen with meticulous attention to detail by the gracious Signor Di Mario.

HOTEL VILLA OTTONE
Owners: Di Mario family
Localita: Ottone, Ottone
Isola di Elba, (LI) 57037, Italy
Tel: (0565) 93 30 42, Fax: (0565) 93 32 57
75 Rooms, Double: €160–€310*
*Includes breakfast & lunch or dinner
Open: May to Oct, Credit cards: all major
www.karenbrown.com/villaottone.html
HOTEL

The Villa Le Barone was once the home of the famous Tuscan family, Della Robbia, whose beautiful terracottas are still seen throughout Italy. It was restored after the First World War by Marchesa Maria Bianca Viviani Della Robbia as a wine estate and later converted into a deluxe small hotel by her granddaughter, Duchessa Franca Visconti. Now her cousins, Conte Corso Aloisi and his wife, are the owners. They come frequently to the villa to greet guests and to ensure that the impeccable standards and taste prevail. Staying at the Villa Le Barone is very much like being the guest in a private, elegant home set in the gorgeous Tuscan hills in front of the San Leolino abbey. The lounges are especially inviting, beautifully furnished with charming, family antiques. There are 28 guestrooms, all of which vary in size with modern tiled bathrooms and are individually decorated. Rooms are in the main villa or in renovated cottages and barns. Some have have their own terrace. In addition, there is a lovely swimming pool, romantically set on a terrace looking over the vineyards and rose garden. Wonderful little hideaways are found secluded in the parklike setting where guests can find a quiet nook to read or just to sit and soak in the beauty of the surrounding hills. Dinner is served in the restaurant, which formerly housed the winery. *Directions:* From the center of Panzano, follow signs to the hotel.

VILLA LE BARONE
Owners: Count & Countess Aloisi de Larderel
Via San Leolino, 19
Panzano, (FI) 50020, Italy
Tel: (055) 85 26 21, Fax: (055) 85 22 77
28 Rooms, Double: €190–€300*
*Includes breakfast & dinner
Meals for hotel guests only
Open: Easter to Nov, Credit cards: all major
www.karenbrown.com/villalebarone.html
HOTEL

We look all over for bed and breakfasts that radiate a natural charm like that of Fagiolari, just outside Panzano. Cordial hostess Giulietta has seemingly unintentionally created a haven for travelers just by letting her home be a home. The unique stone farmhouse on three levels is brimming with character and has been restored with total respect for its innate simplicity using stone, terra-cotta brick, and chestnut-wood beams. Entering the front door into the cozy living room with large fireplace, I was impressed by the refreshingly authentic ambiance of this Tuscan home. Two bedrooms are just off this room, the larger having an en suite bathroom of stone and travertine. The main house and former barn, where you find two other good-sized bedrooms, are united by a connecting roof, left open in the middle to allow for an enormous fig tree. Bedrooms hold lovely antiques, book-lined shelves, collections of framed drawings and artwork, embroidered linens, and views of the delightful garden and cypress-lined paths. Overlooking the swimming pool, an adorable one-bedroom house on the property with a bookcase dividing the kitchen and living area is rented out weekly. Giulietta also teaches cooking classes lasting from one to four days. *Directions:* From the piazza in Panzano follow signs to centro and take the left fork for Mercatale. At a half km from the piazza turn left after a pale-green building and follow the gravel road downhill to the end.

FAGIOLARI
Host: Giulietta Giovannoni
Case Sparse 25, Panzano in Chianti, (FI) 50020, Italy
Tel & Fax: (055) 852351, Cellphone: (335) 6124988
4 Rooms, Double: €100–€120
1 Cottage: €840– €910 weekly
Minimum Nights: 3 in cottage
Open: all year, Credit cards: all major
Other Languages: some English
www.karenbrown.com/fagiolari.html
B&B, SELF CATERING

As you wind your way up a steep road through thick woods, you will no doubt wonder as we did how English couple Sonia and Edward ever found the secluded 70-acre property set above the Sieve river valley to the east of Florence. Upon arrival you will be greeted and rewarded with a glass of fresh spring water from the fountain "shower" (la doccia). It is understandable that long ago the farmhouse was originally a farm for the monks of the local abbey—the views are inspirational and the positions of both the house and the swimming pool take full advantage of the expansive panorama encompassing the Rufina wine valley nature reserve. Original features remain intact after a complete restoration of the house that created a variety of high-level accommodation in the form of four bedrooms, three suites with individual kitchenettes, and two attached houses with one bedroom each for weekly stays. The perfectly charming home is filled with lovely antiques (local and imported from England), queen- or king-sized beds, and beautiful linens and tiled bathrooms. Guests can wander about the many common rooms and have a glass of wine in front of a spectacular sunset while Edward works Mediterranean wonders in the kitchen. Prepare to be pampered. *Directions:* 40 minutes from Florence, 5 km from Pelago. Detailed directions are supplied at the time of reservation.

LA DOCCIA
Hosts: Sonia & Edward Mayhew
Localita: Paterno, Ristonchi 19/20, Pelago, (FI) 50060
Tel: (055) 8361387, Fax: (055) 8361388
7 Rooms, Double: €125–€185
2 Apartments: €625–€1,075 weekly
2 Villas: €1,075–€1,175 weekly
Minimum Nights: 3, Open: all year
Credit cards: all major, Fluent English
www.karenbrown.com/doccia.html
B&B, SELF CATERING

The Relais alla Corte del Sole has a superb location—conveniently close to Cortona and Montepulcino, yet snuggled in the tranquil countryside. This gem of a small hotel is owned by the gracious Spiganti family whose famed Tonino Restaurant in Cortona prepares such exceptional cuisine that the late Pope invited the chef to prepare his Christmas dinner. To complement their restaurant, the Spiganti family restored five 16th-century brick farmhouses into an elegantly rustic hotel that is run by their charming daughter, Ilaria, one of the most endearing, gracious hostesses you will ever meet. No two bedrooms are alike and each has been individually decorated with fine brocade fabrics and antiques that enhance the country simplicity of beams and brick floors. The bathrooms have been personalized by a local artist whose whimsical designs reflect the various room names. The restaurant, La Corte del Sole, has a wonderful outside terrace with view. A passion for flowers is evident in the surrounding garden, which leads to a large swimming pool. Bordering Umbria and Tuscany, the Relais alla Corte del Sole is the perfect spot from which to easily explore both regions. *Directions:* Exit the A1 at Val di Chiana and follow signs for Perugia. Take the second Cortona exit towards Montepulciano and drive 7 km to the turnoff for Petrignano-Pozzolo. The hotel is after Petrignano.

RELAIS ALLA CORTE DEL SOLE
Owner: Ilaria Spiganti
Localita: I Giorgi
Petrignano del Lago, (PG) 06061, Italy
Tel: (075) 96 89 008, Fax: (075) 96 89 070
18 Rooms, Double: €160–€312
Open: all year, Credit cards: MC, VS
Abitare la Storia
www.karenbrown.com/allacortedelsole.html
HOTEL

Nestled in the tranquil Tuscan countryside between two enchanting hilltop villages (Pienza and Monticchiello) is another jewel, L'Olmo. You cannot help instantly losing your heart to this very special little hotel. It has the warmth and intimacy of a bed and breakfast, yet the service and amenities rival those of the finest deluxe hotel. This bit of paradise is owned by the Lindo family. A few years ago they left the bustling city of Turin and bought a beautiful 16th-century stone house, which they lovingly restored to perfection, down to the smallest detail, preserving original terracotta floors and wood-beamed ceilings. With superb taste and guests' comfort in mind, five suites were created and appointed with antique chests, locally made wrought-iron beds, and pretty floral fabrics for color. Each has its own travertine marble bathroom and two have a fireplace. There is also a two bedroom, two bath apartment which is great for families. Francesca and her mother Loredana, your exceptionally charming hostesses, tend to guests in a warm and highly professional manner. Downstairs are two cozy sitting rooms leading out to the stone courtyard with tables and flower pots. A full buffet breakfast or gourmet candlelit dinner—upon request—is served in the luminous dining room. Lunch and dinner are also served in the romantic garden pergola. *Directions:* From Pienza drive south, after 6 km turn left to Monticchiello. Follow signs for L'Olmo on your right.

L'OLMO
Owners: Francesca & Loredana Lindo
Monticchiello, Pienza, (SI) 53020, Italy
Tel: (0578) 75 51 33, Fax: (0578) 75 51 24
5 Rooms, Double: €170–€290
1 Apt, Double: €280
Dinner upon request
Open: Apr 1 to Nov 15, Credit cards: all major
Abitare la Storia
www.karenbrown.com/lolmo.html
HOTEL, SELF CATERING

The Relais Il Chiostro is idyllically snuggled inside the stone walls of Pienza, a medieval hilltop village that is one of Tuscany's most perfect jewels. The hotel is built within a stunning 15th-century monastery; a heritage immediately apparent when you step through the massive arched wood doors into an exceptionally beautiful small cloister. The hushed courtyard is framed by a colonnade of marble columns linked by stone arches. The restaurant and the various lounges and sitting rooms occupy the ground floor. Upstairs there are 37 attractive, individually decorated guestrooms with splendid frescoed ceilings featured in some of the suites. The choice rooms overlook the beautiful Tuscan countryside, but views from the other rooms are also delightful—overlooking either the garden cloister or the ancient tiled rooftops of Pienza. One of the most outstanding features of the hotel is its spectacular location. Perched above the valley, the hotel takes full advantage of its position with a terrace garden (where meals are served when the weather is warm) which stretches to the edge of the wall where guests can enjoy an incredible panoramic view of Tuscany at its finest. On a terrace below, a large swimming pool nestles in another garden. *Directions:* Located one block from the main square, Piazza Pio II.

HOTEL RELAIS IL CHIOSTRO DI PIENZA
Manager: Massimo Cicala
Corso Rossellino, 26
Pienza, (SI) 53026, Italy
Tel: (0578) 74 84 00, Fax: (0578) 74 84 40
37 Rooms, Double: €130–€230
Closed: Jan 7 to Mar 15, Credit cards: all major
www.karenbrown.com/ilchiostro.html
HOTEL

Right along the road connecting the hilltowns of Pienza and Montepulciano is the conveniently positioned farm of Felice and Giulia, transplanted from their hometowns in the regions of Marches and Campania respectively. The 18th-century stone farmhouse forms a U with inner courtyard from which you gain access to the breakfast room/bar, stone-walled restaurant with large dividing arch, living room, and upstairs bedrooms divided on both sides. Bedrooms are luminous and spacious, with immaculate bathrooms, pretty bedspreads, and country furniture. The bedrooms on the right side overlook the hilly countryside, swimming pool, and the 100-acre property of woods and fields, which produces its own wine and olive oil. Ancient Pienza can be seen at a distance. The real treat here is Giulia's cooking using the farm's own fresh produce. She has a flair for combining local traditional recipes with her own personal inventions, having homemade pastas as her base. Hard-working Felice relaxes and jokes with guests, often ending the evening playing the guitar. This is an easy-access touring base for the endless itineraries available, including Siena Montalcino and tours of the d'Orcia wine valley, and a great value. *Directions:* Exit from the autostrada at Chiusi and follow signs for Montepulciano, then Pienza. After a total of 25 km, well before Pienza, the iron gates of the Santo Pietro are on the left.

SANTO PIETRO
Hosts: Felice d'Angelo & Giulia Scala
Strada Statale 146, No. 29, Pienza, (SI) 53026, Italy
Tel: (0578) 748410, Fax: (0578) 749877
Cellphone: (347) 0185601
11 Rooms, Double: €85–€93, Apartment: €110–€150
Minimum Nights: 3, 7 in apartment
Open: Mar to Dec, Credit cards: all major
Other Languages: some English
www.karenbrown.com/santopietro.html
B&B, SELF CATERING

The most striking images of southern Tuscany are in the Orcia Valley—enchanting landscapes with soft, rolling hills topped with rows of cypress trees silhouetted against the sky. This alternating with the area called Le Crete Senesi—barren hills made of clay and resembling moon craters—makes for fascinating scenery. Le Traverse, at 4 kilometers from Pienza, is submersed in this peaceful countryside to which your gracious hosts, Pinuccia and Enrico, retired from Milan. Their charming home has been very tastefully restored and all the right touches (such as terry bathrobes and the finest-quality bed linens) added to make guests feel right at home. The stone farmhouse with front courtyard is divided between the couple's own quarters, rooms for their visiting children, and an apartment for guests with independent entrance. The other two bedrooms are situated in the one-level converted barn nearby and are enhanced with the family's country antiques and prints. Huge terra-cotta vases overflowing with geraniums, trailing roses, and azalea plants dot the 50-acre property, which includes a swimming pool. Olive oil is produced as well as jams using homegrown fruit. The intimacy of the place with its three rooms makes you feel like a true houseguest and the area is full of delightful day trips. *Directions:* Follow signs for Monticchiello from Pienza (circular piazza). After 3.3 km turn left on an unpaved road up to a group of cypress trees and the house.

LE TRAVERSE
Host: Pinuccia Barbier Meroni
Localita: Le Traverse, Pienza, (SI) 53026, Italy
Tel: (0578) 748198, Fax: (0578) 748949
Cellphone: (333) 4708789
3 Rooms, Double: €155
Minimum Nights: 2
Closed: Jan 22 to 30, Credit cards: all major
Other Languages: good English, French
www.karenbrown.com/traverse.html
B&B

In a small city near the coast, nor far from the charming town of Lucca and the popular town of Pisa, you will find the Albergo Pietrasanta. Although "albergo" suggests a simple hotel, this small, deluxe property does not fit that definition. Located in the center of Pietrasanta, the building dates back to the 17th century when it was the home of the prestigious and wealthy Barsanti Bonetti family. There is a sophisticated, understated elegance throughout the hotel and a mood of luxury is set as you enter the lobby and register at a lovely antique desk. To the right of the spacious foyer are two splendid lounges which exude the ambiance of a private home, with pastel walls, soft lighting, comfortable chairs grouped around a handsome fireplace, polished terrazzo floors, beautiful paintings, and bouquets of fresh flowers. The far end of the lounge opens through arched doors into one of the hotel's most special features, a romantic garden courtyard, part of which is enclosed in glass to create a "winter garden" where a bountiful breakfast is served each morning. Forming one wall of the courtyard is a separate building, formerly the stables, which has been renovated to house additional deluxe accommodations. As would be expected, guestrooms reflect the same subdued, sophisticated good taste as the public rooms. *Directions:* From the A12, exit at Versilia-Forte dei Marmi and follow signs to Pietrasanta. In town follow signs to the hotel.

ALBERGO PIETRASANTA
Manager: Roberto Esposito
Via Garibaldi, 35
Pietrasanta, 55045, Italy
Tel: (0584) 79 37 27, Fax: (0584) 79 37 28
19 Rooms, Double: €270–€800*
*Breakfast not included
Closed: Nov 20 to Apr 1, Credit cards: all major
www.karenbrown.com/albergopietrasanta.html
HOTEL

For years there was no outstanding place to stay in Pisa, but all that changed dramatically in March 2003 when Maria Luisa Bignardi opened her exquisite, deluxe, small boutique hotel (her family's home since the 1500s) within a few minutes' stroll of Pisa's stunning Piazza dei Miracoli. The Hotel Relais dell'Orologio is truly exceptional in every way—it exudes romance and offers refined comfort, staff to cater to your every whim, a perfect location, gourmet dining, fine wines, lovely decor, and, best of all, the genuine warmth of your elegant, charming hostess. It took eight years of love, imagination, and hard work to restore the long-neglected mansion to its former grandeur and now every detail exudes extraordinary good taste, understated grandeur, and the highest quality. The furnishings are beautiful, with family heirlooms used in the intimate lounges and in the superbly decorated guestrooms, each of which enjoys fine fabrics, excellent linens, quality mattresses, and marble bathrooms. The standard guestrooms are small, so if you prefer more space, we suggest requesting one of the junior suites. In the evening, gourmet meals are served at intimate tables set with fine linens, fresh flowers, and beautiful tableware—all softly illuminated by the glow of candlelight. The Hotel Relais dell'Orologio is truly a gem. *Directions:* Take the North Pisa exit from the A12. When you get into town, follow well-marked signs to the hotel.

HOTEL RELAIS DELL'OROLOGIO
Owner: Maria Luisa Bignardi
Via della Faggiola 12-14
Pisa, (PI) 56126, Italy
Tel: (050) 83 03 61, Fax: (050) 55 18 69
21 Rooms, Double: €212–€620
Open: all year, Credit cards: all major
www.karenbrown.com/relaisorologio.html
HOTEL

As more and more Italians reclaim family property in the countryside or buy and restore their own abandoned castles, people such as the Baccheschi family are moving into more affordable, lesser-known areas. They left behind a successful fashion business to come to the quiet southern part of Tuscany where they bought the ruins of a 13th-century stone castle/convent and have completed putting its pieces back together to form their own private residence and rooms for guests. Two adjacent stunning stone guesthouses are available, plus three suites in the main castle. The smaller house, I Sassi, has one bedroom, a large bathroom, and glassed-in living room taking in the sumptuous view of virgin territory. La Chiesina has a kitchen and spacious living room with parquet flooring, two bedrooms, and two bathrooms. They are appointed sophisticatedly with family antiques and colonial pieces from Indonesia, and are worthy of an article in Architectural Digest. The suites, decorated in the same vein, share a large kitchen and living room. The travertine swimming pool hangs on the edge of the manicured garden, which drops down into untamed landscapes. *Directions:* From the Grosseto-Siena highway 223, exit at Paganico. After 3 km turn right for Sasso d'Ombrone, and right again for Poggi del Sasso. In town watch for street sign Via de Vicarello on the right and follow the road, keeping left at the fork for 3.5 km to the gray iron gate on the right.

CASTELLO DI VICARELLO
Hosts: Aurora & Carlo Baccheschi Berti
Via di Vicarello 1, Poggi del Sasso, (SI) 58043, Italy
Tel & Fax: (0564) 990718
Cellphone: (339) 2546646 or (333) 6914599
4 Rooms, Double: €300–€380
1 House: €700 daily, Minimum Nights: 2
Open: all year, Credit cards: none
Abitare la Storia
www.karenbrown.com/vicarello.html
B&B, SELF CATERING

Thirty-five kilometers northeast of Florence, in a beautiful, hilly area of Tuscany, lies the Rufina Valley, famous for its robust red wine. Crowning a wooded slope is one of the many residences of the noble Galeotti-Ottieri family. The interior of the 15th-century main villa reveals spacious high-ceilinged halls with frescoes depicting family history. The family has also restored several stone farmhouses on the vast property, one of which is the Locanda Praticino whose upper floor contains lovely, simple double rooms with countryside views down one long hall, each named after its color scheme. Downstairs is a large rustic dining and living room with vaulted ceiling, enormous stone fireplace, worn brick floors, and casual country furniture. Full country-fresh Tuscan meals are only €15. A swimming pool and tennis courts, plus the enchanting landscape, make it difficult to tear oneself away for touring. In order to retain the characteristic flavor of farmers' quarters, the properties have an intentionally unrestored, natural air to them. Available for longer stays are three very tastefully decorated apartments. The Petrognano is a tranquil spot where guests may enjoy the gracious hospitality of this historically important Florentine family. *Directions:* From Florence head toward Pontassieve. Continue to Rufina, turning right at Castiglioni-Pomino. Follow the winding road to the property, marked just before Pomino (12 km from Pontassieve).

FATTORIA DI PETROGNANO
Hosts: Cecilia Galeotti-Ottieri family
Localita: Pomino, Pomino, Rufina, (FI) 50060, Italy
Tel: (055) 8318867, Fax: (055) 8318812
8 Rooms, Double: €75–€95
3 Apartments: €350–€800 weekly
Minimum Nights: 2
Open: Apr 15 to Oct, Credit cards: all major
Other Languages: good English, French
www.karenbrown.com/petrognano.html
B&B, SELF CATERING

The Il Pellicano (one of Italy's most idyllic hotels) has been cleverly designed in the traditional villa style and, although not old, looks as though it has snuggled on its prime hillside position overlooking the Mediterranean many years. The façade is stucco, painted a typical Italian russet and set off by a tiled roof. Vines enwrap the building, further enhancing its appealing look. You enter into a spacious, attractive lobby where the sun streams through the windows enhancing the white walls, terracotta floors, and wood-beamed ceilings. The sophisticated and refined ambiance continues with comfy sofas, antique accents, and enormous displays of fresh flowers enlivening every conceivable nook and cranny. The overall impression is one of light and color—and impeccable taste. Beyond the reception area is a spacious terrace where chef Antonio Giuda (one Michelin star) prepares elaborate seafood menus, served outdoors overlooking the dramatic bay and islands. From the terrace, a lawn dotted with cypresses, olive trees, and umbrella pines extends down the hillside to a heated-seawater pool romantically perched at the cliff's edge. From the bluff, both steps and an elevator access a pier at the water's edge. Off the stairs, a large terrace with lounge chairs and mats for sunning has been built into the rocks. The hotel also has a complete spa, tennis courts, boutique, conference room and beauty salon. Exquisite.

IL PELLICANO
Manager: Signora Cinzia Fanciulli
Localita: Sbarcatello
Porto Ercole, (GR) 58018, Italy
Tel: (0564) 85 81 11, Fax: (0564) 83 34 18
51 Rooms, Double: €714–€1488
Open: Apr to Oct, Credit cards: all major
Relais & Châteaux
www.karenbrown.com/ilpellicano.html
HOTEL

Standing proudly on the cliffs overlooking one of Italy's most spectacular coastlines are the remains of a 13th-century Spanish watchtower. The tower has been cleverly incorporated into, and stands as the dramatic symbol for, the Hotel Torre di Cala Piccola, which shares a beautiful small promontory (called Cala Piccola) with luxurious private villas discreetly hidden behind high walls. The hotel looks as though it too might be a private home. The first part of the hotel you see (which houses the informal reception area, lounge, and bar) is a sienna-toned building with red-tiled roof and green shutters, snuggled among silvery olive trees and flowering oleanders. The moderately sized, nicely decorated guestrooms are not in the main building, but instead share romantic stone cottages. Some of the accommodations are designated as one-room apartments with a divider creating a separate sitting area. However, these are a bit cut up and I much preferred the regular doubles. The cottages are strategically placed on the property to capture the view. And what a view! High cliffs drop precipitously down to the sea, forming a series of coves where the rich blue water of the Mediterranean dances in the sunlight. Also capturing this absolutely stunning vista are a lush lawn where, during the summer, dinner is served and, on a lower terrace, a dramatic swimming pool, which seems to almost float high above the sea.

HOTEL TORRE DI CALA PICCOLA
Manager: Stefania Marconi
Cala Piccola, Porto
Santo Stefano, (GR) 58019, Italy
Tel: (0564) 82 51 11, Fax: (0564) 82 52 35
50 Rooms, Double: €230–€430
Open: mid-Mar to Nov, Credit cards: all major
www.karenbrown.com/torredicalapiccola.html
HOTEL

From the moment you enter the grand foyer looking out over the classical Italian garden of this 16th-century country villa, all sense of time and place is lost. The Rucellais' devotion to their estate (in the family since 1759) is apparent, as is their warm hospitality. Guests are given the run of the rambling old home, from the cozy bedrooms, varying in size and decor; antique-filled library; and spacious living room with fireplace, old comfortable sofas, and family portraits to a gracious buffet breakfast room where guests are served at a long table. At the entrance is a duck pond, a large shady area with tables and a 15th-century swimming pool. The family enjoy helping their guests with their itineraries, as well as suggesting cultural events such as art courses, concerts, and tours. Villa Rucellai serves as an excellent base for visiting Florence, Siena, Lucca, and Pisa. The nearby town with its many restaurant choices is conveniently just a 15–20 minute walk away. *Directions:* From Florence take the A11 autostrada, exiting at Prato Est. Follow signs for centro and the railway station. Turn right at the first roundabout onto Viale della Republica. Go straight and under the railway. Circle left onto Viale Borgo Valsugana, keeping the river and railroad to the left. Follow signs all the way for Trattoria La Fontana, then continue 1.5 km on the very narrow Via di Canneto to the entry gate.

❄ ☕ ✄ CREDIT P 🏊 🏌 🚶 🍇 🍷

VILLA RUCELLAI DI CANNETO
Hosts: Rucellai Piqué family
Via di Canneto 16
Prato, (FI) 59100, Italy
Tel & Fax: (0574) 460392
Cellphone: (347) 9073826
11 Rooms, Double: €80–€90
Open: all year, Credit cards: MC, VS
Other Languages: fluent English
www.karenbrown.com/rucellai.html
B&B

Weary of life in the intense financial world of Milan, Guido and Martina packed up and headed for the hills of Chianti and the "good life" that attracts so many there. After a long search they chose the scenic property where La Locanda now stands, primarily for its magnificent position facing out to medieval Volpaia and an endless panorama filled with layers of virgin hills. The results of their meticulous restoration of three simple stone farmhouses are formidable and today fortunate guests can share in their dream. Its remote location among woods and olive groves guarantees total silence and tranquillity and the comfortable, decorator-perfect common rooms and luminous colors harmonize divinely with this idyllic setting. An understated elegance permeates the six bedrooms and the suite. They are tastefully appointed with antiques and smart plaid curtains, and four have the advantage of the views. Breakfast and dinner (except Sundays and Thursdays) are served out on the terrace above the swimming pool whose borderless edge disappears into the landscape. Guido and Martina, natural and gregarious hosts, exude a contagious enthusiasm for their new surroundings. *Directions:* From Radda follow signs for Florence and turn right for Volpaia. Continue on the unpaved road for another 3.8 km after Volpaia village, following signs to La Locanda/Montanino.

LA LOCANDA   Cover painting 2006
Hosts: Guido & Martina Bevilacqua
Localita: Montanino
Radda in Chianti, (SI) 53017, Italy
Tel: (0577) 738833, Fax: (0577) 739263
7 Rooms, Double: €200–€280
Minimum Nights: 2, Open: Apr to Oct
Credit cards: MC, VS, Abitare la Storia
Other Languages: good English, French
www.karenbrown.com/lalocanda.html
B&B

Podere Terreno combines idyllic location and authentic, charming ambiance with delightful hosts Sylvie and Roberto, a Franco-Italian couple, and son, Francesco. The 400-year-old rustic stone farmhouse is surrounded by terra-cotta flower vases, a grapevine-covered pergola, a small lake, and sweeping panoramas of the Chianti countryside. Inside are seven sweet double bedrooms with very small bathrooms, each decorated differently with country antiques and the family's personal possessions, which make the feeling very informal and homelike. Guests convene in the main room of the house around the massive stone fireplace on floral sofas for a glass of house wine before sitting down to a sumptuous candlelit dinner prepared by your hosts. This is a cozy, stone-walled room, filled with country antiques, brass pots, dried-flower bouquets hanging from the exposed beams, and shelves lined with bottles of the proprietors' own Chianti Classico wine. Wine tastings take place within the new cantina. The hosts are experts at suggesting local itineraries and directing guests to the many quaint villages waiting to be explored. *Directions:* From Greve follow signs to Panzano, then go left for Radda and on to Lucarelli. After 3 km turn left at Volpaia and after 5 km turn right at the sign for Podere Terreno.

PODERE TERRENO
Host: Marie Sylvie Haniez
Roberto Melosi & Pier Francesco Rapisarda-Haniez
Via della Volpaia, Radda in Chianti, (SI) 53017, Italy
Tel: (0577) 738312, Fax: (0577) 738400
7 Rooms, Double: €190*
*Includes breakfast & dinner, Minimum Nights: 2
Open: all year, Credit cards: all major
Other Languages: good English
www.karenbrown.com/podereterreno.html
B&B

Both Radda and Greve are excellent bases from which to explore the scenic Chianti wine country with its regal castles and stone villages, in addition to Siena, Florence, and San Gimignano. Radda in particular offers a myriad of possibilities for accommodation, including many private homes with rooms or apartments. The Val delle Corti is the home and vineyard property of gracious hostess Eli Bianchi and her son Roberto where they produce a high-quality Chianti Classico wine. The cozy pale-stone house with white shutters tops a hill overlooking the quaint town. The hosts, who moved here in 1974 from Milan, are extremely active in community affairs and are a superb source for area information. The guest accommodation is a lovely separate little house called il Fienile (hay barn), simply appointed with family antiques and newer pieces, which has a large open kitchen and living space looking out to the vineyards, and two bedrooms and one bathroom on the first floor. Meals can be taken at one of the excellent restaurants right in nearby Radda. *Directions:* Equidistant from Florence and Siena off the N222 Chianti road. Before entering Radda, turn right toward Lecchi-San Sano, then take the first left at Val delle Corti.

PODERE VAL DELLE CORTI
Hosts: Bianchi family
Localita: La Croce
Radda in Chianti, (SI) 53017, Italy
Tel: (0577) 738215, Fax: (0577) 739521
1 Apartment: €100–€150 daily
Minimum Nights: 3
Open: all year, Credit cards: MC, VS
Other Languages: good English
www.karenbrown.com/poderevaldellecorti.html
SELF CATERING

In the very heart of Chianti between Radda, Castellina, and Vagliagli sits the Pornanino farm surrounded by 90 acres of wooded hills and olive groves. Hosts Franco and Lia have carefully restored the main house for themselves plus two stone barns for guests, appointed with the same warm country style as their own home, with antique furniture enhancing beamed ceilings and cotto floors. Il Capannino is completely refurbished and offers a large central room with open kitchen at an upper level, dining room/living room with open fireplace, and two bedrooms with two bathrooms. A large arched glass door opens onto the pergola-covered terrace for outside meals. Il Leccino is similar but has just one bedroom. Guests can also take advantage of the lovely swimming pool overlooking the olive groves. Franco and Lia are part of the increasing breed of "neo-farmers" migrating from major cities in search of a slower-paced lifestyle where the basic values of life are emphasized in everyday living. Franco has become a passionate producer of top-quality olive oil and even conducts small seminars and tastings on the subject. The Lombardis are part of a group of family and friends (called Case Spante) offering similar rentals in the area. *Directions:* The farm is located 9 km south of Radda, 5 km from Castellina, and 4 km north of Vagliagli on route 102 but the turnoff is not marked, so it is best to call ahead. 18 km from Siena and 54 km from Florence.

PORNANINO
Hosts: Lia & Franco Lombardi
Localita: Pornanino 72, Radda in Chianti, (SI) 53017
Tel: (0577) 738658, Fax: (0577) 738794
Cellphone: (347) 7980012
2 Houses: €725–€1,150 weekly
Minimum Nights: 4
Open: all year, Credit cards: MC, VS
Other Languages: good English, French
www.karenbrown.com/pornanino.html
SELF CATERING

The Relais Fattoria Vignale is a superb small hotel idyllically located in the heart of the Chianti wine region. It enjoys the enviable honor of having the best of both worlds—it feels as if you are secluded in the countryside, yet you are right in Radda, one of Tuscany's most picturesque towns. It was the manor house of a large Chianti estate, which still produces fine wines. The hotel sits on the main street, but magically, the back of the hotel opens onto a gorgeous, pristine view of rolling hills laced with vineyards and dotted with olive trees. Some of the guestrooms are in the main manor while others, which also have lovely views, are just across the street. The guestrooms and cozy lounges are tastefully decorated with antiques. Care has been taken in the restoration to preserve many of the enticing architectural features of the manor such as heavy beams, arched hallways, decorative fireplaces, and painted ceilings. Behind the hotel, meticulously kept gardens lead down the hillside to a romantic wisteria- and jasmine-covered terrace where guests enjoy breakfast, or dinner under the stars, with an incredible view. Another bonus of this fine hotel is the heated swimming pool, overlooking the vineyards. The original wine cellars have been transformed into a tavern/winebar. Only 300 meters from the hotel is the Ristorante Vignale, which is owned by the hotel.

RELAIS FATTORIA VIGNALE
Manager: Silvia Kummer
Via Pianigiani, 15
Radda in Chianti, (SI) 53017, Italy
Tel: (0577) 73 83 00, Fax: (0577) 73 85 92
34 Rooms, Double: €165–€385*
Service: 5%
Tavern closed Wed
Open: Apr 1 to Nov 15, Credit cards: all major
www.karenbrown.com/fattoriavignale.html
HOTEL

Nicoletta Innocenti is the delightful owner and hostess of Fattoria La Palazzina, one of our favorite bed and breakfasts. The stately 18th-century villa has 11 lovely guestrooms appointed with antiques, each having its own cool pastel color scheme. The large dining room with checked black-and-white tiled floors looks out to the garden and expansive lawns. A swimming pool hugs the side of the hill overlooking sweeping panoramas. Two of the three apartments within a 17th-century stone farmhouse, Colombaio, have two double bedrooms each, living area with kitchenette, fireplace, and bathroom. The third is a studio apartment for two persons. They are rustically furnished with local antiques and offer gorgeous valley views. The lovely Villa Fonte Emerosa, appointed with period antiques, has three bedrooms, three bathrooms, large living rooms with fireplace, garden, and swimming pool and faces out to the mountains. The 18th-century farmhouse, Casa di Terra, is set among the vineyards and includes three bedrooms, two bathrooms, kitchen, living room, and dining room. This southeast corner of Tuscany offers a rich variety of sites to explore, including the Amiata Mountains and the hilltowns of Montepulciano, Pienza, and Montalcino. *Directions:* From Florence on the A1 autostrada, exit at Chiusi and drive towards Sarteano on route 478, turning left for Radicofani. After 14 km turn left for Celle Sul Rigo then right at the sign for Fattoria La Palazzina.

FATTORIA LA PALAZZINA
Hosts: Innocenti family
Localita: Le Vigne, Radicofani, (SI) 53040, Italy
Tel: (0578) 55771, Fax: (0577) 899647
11 Rooms, Double: €96–€108
3 Apartments: €350–€750 weekly,
2 Houses: €414–€2,582 weekly
Minimum Nights: 2, Open: Apr to Oct
Credit cards: all major, Other Languages: good English
www.karenbrown.com/palazzina.html
B&B, SELF CATERING

With passion and determination, Daniela and her architect husband, Piero, brought back to life the family's ancient property with total respect for its 9th-century origins. This very special place has a rich historical past and a Romanesque church (no longer consecrated) within the home where concerts are held. The complex of stone houses is surrounded by vineyards, woods, and olive groves (from which the family's prestigious olive oil comes), and a garden including a collection of English roses. Hospitality is offered within seven apartments attached to the main house accommodating from two to five persons, simply decorated with the family's country antiques, which live harmoniously with their perfectly preserved centuries-old environment. The authentic dwellings feature living room with fireplace, balconies taking in either the sweeping countryside views down to the sea or out to the woods, wrought-iron beds, and original paintings by Daniela's father, a renowned fresco painter. Besides a swimming pool and massage treatments, painting classes are organized in May and October. Along with Siena and Montalcino, there are plenty of off-the-beaten-track sights to see organized by son Emiliano, and bikes can be rented. *Directions:* From Grosseto take Aurelia route 1 north and exit at Braccagni. Continue towards Montemassi and before town turn right for Caminino and Roccatederighi. After 1 km turn right at the gate for Caminino.

PIEVE DI CAMININO
Hosts: Daniela Locatelli & Piero Marrucchi
Via Provinciale di Peruzzo
Roccatederighi, (GR) 58028, Italy
Tel: (0564) 569736, Fax: (0564) 568756
Cellphone: (393) 3356605
7 Apartments: €600–€1,150 weekly, €120–€150 daily
Minimum Nights: 3 in high season
Open: all year, Credit cards: all major, Good English
www.karenbrown.com/caminino.html
SELF CATERING

The spectacular 2,500-acre hilltop farm property of Montestigliano is a rich combination of woods, cultivated fields, olive groves, and open meadows all surrounding the hamlet dating from 1730. British-born hostess Susan makes sure guests are comfortable in one of the ten independent apartments within the various houses scattered about the property. All retain their original Tuscan character in furnishings and have a combination of two or three bedrooms, kitchen, living room (some with fireplace), and essential modern amenities like washing machines and telephones. The granary has been restored and converted into a farm shop, recreation room, and dining room where meals are served upon request from Monday to Friday. Groups of up to 12 persons have the opportunity to reside in the main villa. Two swimming pools are at guests' disposal, plus many paths and trails. Montestigliano is a marvelous base for getting to know in depth a part of Tuscany whose traditions and lifestyles have remained intact, while still having Siena, San Gimignano, Pienza, Montalcino, and the Chianti area at one's fingertips. Plenty of places to dine are available in Rosia and Sovicille. Susan has also recently arranged weddings in this idyllic setting for groups staying at Montestigliano. *Directions:* From Siena (12 km) take S.S.223 (towards Grosseto). After 12 km, just after a gas station, turn right and after 2 km turn left for Brenna and drive up the unpaved road to the end.

MONTESTIGLIANO
Host: Susan Pennington
Rosia, 53010, Italy
Tel: (0577) 342189, Fax: (0577) 342100
Cellphone: (347) 7778761
10 Apartments: €454–€1,622 weekly
1 Villa: €1,382–€2,957 weekly
Minimum Nights: 5, Open: all year, Credit cards: none
Other Languages: fluent English
www.karenbrown.com/montestigliano.html
SELF CATERING

The Villa Il Poggiale, an intimate, elegant boutique hotel, opened in the spring of 2003. This traditional Tuscan country villa dating to the Renaissance period has had such illustrious proprietors as noble families Corsini, Martini, and Ricasoli-Rucellai, and has been in the Vitta family for the past 50 years. Brothers Johanan and Nathanel have brought the family residence back to its former glory, transforming it from a private country home to an exclusive inn, with no expense spared on beauty, comfort and modern conveniences. On the ground floor you find the splendidly decorated grand main salon plus another smaller one off which three of the generous bedrooms and suites with antique furnishings and lovely new bathrooms are found. Soft-peach, olive-green, and pale-yellow color schemes are displayed in fine fabrics used for bedspreads, draperies, and upholstery. Other frescoed bedrooms upstairs are nicely spaced apart by three additional sitting rooms, the most desirable being those away from the main road. A full buffet breakfast featuring homemade cakes and local specialties is served overlooking the garden, which leads down to the swimming pool with its extraordinary views of the picture-perfect Tuscan landscape. This is a luxurious villa where you will feel like guest in a private home. *Directions:* Drive through San Casciano following signs for Empoli. After 2 km, Villa Il Poggiale is on the left-hand side of the Via Empolese.

VILLA IL POGGIALE
Owners: Johanan & Nathanel Vitta
Via Empolese, 69, Val di Pesa
San Casciano, (FI) 50026, Italy
Tel: (055) 82 83 11, Fax: (055) 82 94 296
24 Rooms, Double: €135–€240
Closed: February, Credit cards: all major
www.karenbrown.com/poggiale.html
HOTEL

The luxurious Villa Mangiacane with its combination historic home, wordly décor, and high-tech amenities is, in a word, magnificent. Owner Glynn Cohen returned from years in South Africa and purchased the 15th century estate which encompasses 600 acres of surrounding land dedicated to the production of Chianti Classico wines and extra virgin olive oil. The stately villa once the residence of the Machiavelli family, is assumed to be the architectural work of Michelangelo. The eight sumptuous bedrooms and suites can be rented separately or as a full house rental and are elegantly appointed with priceless antiques and artwork, finest fabrics and linens, and designer bathrooms. Besides grand but comfortable salons, dining room, library, wine cellars, terraces, swimming pool, and gym, spectacular Renaissance views are awarded at every window. In fact the home was designed on the same axis as the Duomo cathedral in Florence with the long driveway, villa entrance and exit to the back frescoed loggia, all perfectly aligned to frame the famous cupola through a pathway cut in the hilltop woods. Truly amazing. A full staff caters to your every whim and the remaining 18 spacious rooms available for spring of 2006 are in the adjacent house complex. *Directions:* Exit A1 at Firenze Certosa, go straight towards Tavarnuzze. Pass Tavernuzze, drive over a the small bridge named "Scopet" on your right. At the first stop turn right and drive 50 m to the hotel.

VILLA MANGIACANE   New
Manager: Silvia Piazzini
Via Faltignano 4
San Casciano, Florence, (FI) 50026, Italy
Tel: (055) 82 90 123, Fax: (055) 82 90 358
26 Rooms, Double: €250–€2500
Open: all year, Credit cards: all major
www.karenbrown.com/villamangiacane.html
HOTEL

In the southeastern corner of Tuscany is a delightful, yet undiscovered pocket of absolutely stunning countryside. It was only natural that Andrea, with his expert culinary skills, and his lovely wife, Cristina, a born hostess, should open a bed and breakfast close to their vast 1,000-acre countryside property producing olive oil, wine, cereals and vegetables. La Crocetta sits at the crossroads leading up to the charming town of San Casciano, offering eight guestrooms above the restaurant. You enter the small restaurant by way of a front porch, where meals are also served outdoors, into the cozy reception area set around a large sit-in fireplace. Here within the two dining rooms with soft-pink-colored walls Andrea presents his delectable creations featuring homemade pastas with vegetable fillings and other regional dishes using the best local ingredients available. His success has been noted in several restaurant guides. Small guestrooms with varying color schemes, each with a new bathroom, are pleasantly appointed with canopy beds and fresh country fabrics used for bedspreads and curtains. A pool has been added in the front garden. Thermal hot springs with spa treatments and horse-riding facilities are located nearby. Orvieto, Perugia, Siena, and the hilltowns of Montepulciano and Montalcino are all at easy touring distance. *Directions:* From the A1 autostrada, exit at Fabro from the south or Chiusi from the north, traveling towards Sarteano-Cetona, then San Casciano.

LA CROCETTA
Hosts: Cristina & Andrea Leotti
Localita: La Crocetta
San Casciano dei Bagni, (SI) 53040, Italy
Tel: (0578) 58360, Fax: (0578) 58353
Cellphone: (339) 6366336
8 Rooms, Double: €120–€135
Minimum Nights: 2, Open: Mar 30 to Nov 12
Credit cards: MC, VS, Other Languages: good English
www.karenbrown.com/lacrocetta.html
B&B

Perched atop a hill and enjoying a 360-degree view of perfectly unspoiled landscape, including a stunning medieval castle, sits the Le Radici farmhouse. Partners and ex-urbanites Marcello and Alfredo carefully chose this peaceful spot in order to offer accommodation to those who truly appreciate nature and the sense of well-being it inspires. The two farmhouses have been restored, maintaining most of the original rustic flavor, and divided into seven double rooms, three suites, and two apartments. The apartments include one or two bedrooms, living room with fireplace, kitchenette, and bathroom. The tastefully appointed rooms in muted colors are adorned by wrought-iron beds and antique furnishings, complemented by wood-beam and brick ceilings. Special attention has been given to landscaping around the immediate property, which includes vineyards and olive groves. The real treat is the absolutely gorgeous "borderless" swimming pool with cascading water, which fits harmoniously into its surroundings. A romantic candelit dinner showing off Alfredo's passion for cooking is served in the dining room or out on the terrace, using fresh ingredients from the property. The hosts suggest many interesting itineraries in this area, which borders Umbria. One can relax in the thermal waters of San Casciano or venture out to the towns of Orvieto, Todi, or Pienza, among others. *Directions:* From San Casciano follow signs for Le Radici (4 km).

☕ 💳 ☎ 🏠 P ⅋ ♨ 🏕 👫 🐎

LE RADICI
Hosts: Alfredo Ferrari & Marcello Mancini
San Casciano dei Bagni, (SI) 53040, Italy
Tel: (0578) 56033, Fax: (0578) 56038
Cellphone: (338) 5856890
10 Rooms, Double: €150–€204
2 Apartments: €1,078–€1,281 weekly
Minimum Nights: 2, Open: Apr 1 to Nov 6
Credit cards: MC, VS, Other Languages: good English
www.karenbrown.com/leradici.html
B&B, SELF CATERING

Without a doubt, San Gimignano is one of the most picturesque places in Tuscany: a postcard-perfect hilltop village punctuated by 14 tall towers. During the day, the town bustles with activity, but after the busloads of tourists depart, the romantic ambiance of yesteryear fills the cobbled streets. For the lucky few who spend the night, there is a jewel of small inn, the Hotel L'Antico Pozzo. What a pleasure to see a renovation with such excellent taste and meticulous attention to maintaining the authentic character of the original building. The name of the hotel derives from an antique stone well (pozzo), which is softly illuminated just off the lobby. The fact that only the most affluent families could afford the luxury of a private well indicates that this 15th-century townhouse was once a wealthy residence. A timeworn stone staircase leads up to the air-conditioned bedrooms, tucked at various levels along a maze of hallways. Each one of the quietly elegant rooms has its own personality with thick stone walls, terracotta floors, and beautifully framed antique prints, plus satellite television. One of my favorites, number 20, has the palest of pastel-peach-colored walls, windows opening onto the terrace, and a fabulous domed ceiling painted with ancient Roman designs. Number 14 is also outstanding—a very large room with a canopy bed. Another advantage of L'Antico Pozzo is that this is a long time family-run hotel.

HOTEL L'ANTICO POZZO
Manager: Emanuele Marro
Via San Matteo, 87
San Gimignano, (SI) 53037, Italy
Tel: (0577) 94 20 14, Fax: (0577) 94 21 17
18 Rooms, Double: €125–€160
Open: all year, Credit cards: all major
www.karenbrown.com/anticopozzo.html
HOTEL

Il Casale is a highly efficient and very popular bed and breakfast, thanks to warm and dedicated host, Alessandro, who has combined his extensive hospitality experience with a desire to see his great-grandfather's lovely country property restored properly. Six double rooms and two small apartments including bedroom, kitchen/eating area, and bathroom are all housed within the extended stone farmhouse. Another section is reserved for Alessandro and the family who looks after the wine estate. Access to the guest entrance is through a well-kept garden around the back with a small chapel and lovely views over the soft hills. Main areas include a sitting room and beamed breakfast room with fireplace. The spotless home is appointed with scattered antiques and the very comfortable guestrooms, each with a different color scheme, have new bathrooms and either countryside views or garden or interior patio entrance. Infinite attention to details in both the esthetics and service offered is given to guests. The entrepreneurial Alessandro has also restored the stone barn and cantina over in the olive grove, Rocca degli Olivi, creating an apartment, five lovely bedrooms with either mansard or vaulted ceilings and gorgeous views, and a breakfast room. An inviting swimming pool is hidden among the olive trees. Plenty of tourist information is on hand. *Directions:* From San Gimignano follow signs for Certaldo for 3 km. Il Casale is on the left and well marked.

IL CASALE DEL COTONE
Host: Alessandro Martelli
Localita: Cellole 59, San Gimignano, (SI) 53037, Italy
Tel & Fax: (0577) 943236
Cellphone: (348) 3029091
11 Rooms, Double: €95–€108
3 Apartments: €95–€140 daily
Minimum Nights: 3 in apartments
Open: all year, Credit cards: all major
www.karenbrown.com/casaledelcotone.html
B&B, SELF CATERING

Due to the ever-increasing popularity of the stunning medieval village of San Gimignano, accommodations in the surrounding countryside have flourished. The Casanova is a typical square stone farmhouse with wood shutters and red-tile roof, which you'll grow accustomed to seeing throughout Tuscany. The bed and breakfast's exceptional feature is that it enjoys a privileged view of the towers of San Gimignano, an ancient town referred to as the "Manhattan" of the year 1000. Roberto and his wife Monica, who aim to offer quality accommodation at competitive rates, have the bed and breakfast, adding amenities in rooms such as air conditioning, satellite TV, and telephone, and have also installed a swimming pool. Breakfast is served on the outside patio where guests are immersed in breathtaking scenery, before heading out to visit intriguing San Gimignano and the many surrounding villages. This is an authentic wine-producing farm with eight double rooms with private baths and one apartment for two persons. Country furniture characteristic of the region decorates the rooms, whose original architectural features have been preserved. *Directions:* From San Gimignano take the road toward Volterra. After 2 km, turn left at the sign for Casanova, not Hotel Pescille.

CASANOVA DI PESCILLE
Hosts: Monica & Roberto Fanciullini
Localita: Pescille, San Gimignano, (SI) 53037, Italy
Tel & Fax: (0577) 941902
8 Rooms, Double: €90–€100
1 Apartment: €100–€110 daily
Minimum Nights: 2
Open: Mar to Dec, Credit cards: MC, VS
Other Languages: very little English
www.karenbrown.com/casanovadipescille.html
B&B, SELF CATERING

Accidentally coming upon the Casolare, tucked away in the unpopulated hills 8 kilometers past medieval San Gimignano, was a delightful surprise. Just before reaching the bed and breakfast, you'll see a half-abandoned stone convent dating back to 1100. The attractive renovated farmhouse, hosted by Andrea, a former art and antiques dealer, and his Spanish wife, Berta, retains all the features characteristic of the original structure. The five double rooms are extremely comfortable and tastefully appointed. Rooms are divided between the two floors of the house, with one being an independent structure poolside. The suites for two to four persons with terrace and living room have been decorated with refined antiques as well. Original watercolor paintings by a local artist adorn an entire wall in the inviting double living room. An extra bonus is the breathtaking swimming pool, with sweeping countryside panorama, surrounded by a manicured lawn, fruit trees, and terra-cotta pots overflowing with pink geraniums. It provides refreshment after a hot day of sightseeing, while you anticipate another appetizing candlelit meal at dusk under the pergola. Berta is an excellent cook and prepares very special Tuscan menus accompanied by an impressive wine list. This is a truly tranquil haven. *Directions:* From San Gimignano follow signs for Montaione. Staying left at the fork, turn left for Libbiano and take the dirt road to the end.

CASOLARE DI LIBBIANO
Hosts: Berta & Andrea Bucciarelli
Localita: Libbiano 3
San Gimignano, (SI) 53037, Italy
Tel & Fax: (0577) 946002
Cellphone: (349) 8706933
8 Rooms, Double: €110–€160
Open: Apr to Nov, Credit cards: all major
Other Languages: good English
www.karenbrown.com/casolaredilibbiano.html
B&B

San Gimignano is one of the most fascinating of the medieval Tuscany hilltowns. As you approach, this looks like a city of skyscrapers: come even closer and the skyscrapers emerge as 14 soaring towers—dramatic reminders of what San Gimignano must have looked like in all her glory when this wealthy town sported 72 giant towers. Most tourists come just for the day to visit this small town, but for those lucky enough to be able to spend the night, San Gimignano has a simple but very charming hotel, La Cisterna. The hotel is located on the town's main square and fits right into the ancient character of the surrounding buildings with its somber stone walls softened by ivy, arched shuttered doors, and red-tile roof. Inside La Cisterna, the medieval feeling continues with lots of stone, vaulted ceilings, leather chairs, and dark woods. The bedrooms are not fancy, but pleasant, and some have balconies with lovely views of the valley. Renovations added air conditioning in the restaurant and satellite TV (for European channels and CNN). La Cisterna is probably more famous as a restaurant than as a hotel and people come from far and wide because not only is the food delicious, but the dining rooms are delightful. Especially charming is the dining room with the brick wall, sloping ceiling supported by giant beams, and picture windows framing the gorgeous hills of Tuscany.

LA CISTERNA
Owners: Salvestrini family
Piazza della Cisterna, 24
San Gimignano, (SI) 53037, Italy
Tel: (0577) 94 03 28, Fax: (0577) 94 20 80
50 Rooms, Double: €90–€122
Restaurant closed Tue & lunch on Wed
Open: Mar 10 to Jan 10, Credit cards: all major
www.karenbrown.com/cisterna.html
HOTEL

Leaving San Gimignano on the road north towards Pancole-Certaldo, you come across La Fonte, the property of the Bergamasco family. Their daughter Maria now runs it after selling her nearby bed and breakfast, Il Vicario, previously in this guide. This typical Tuscan farmhouse with cupola is surrounded by a nature reserve, vineyards, olive groves, and woods, yet is very close to many major sights and cities. Within the large main house are four fully-equipped apartments with coveted views for longer stays. Three have two bedrooms each with en suite bathrooms and one has one bedroom. Depending on guests' requests, Maria uses the seven bedrooms separately for bed-and-breakfast guests or as four apartments. Maria has enhanced the natural beauty of the home's original features—brick vaulted ceilings and floors—with appropriate country furnishings and smart, colorful fabrics. The cypress-backed swimming pool is nearby, and several patios within the English garden with its extensive lawns offer quiet places for relaxing after touring the many sights of the area. At your fingertips are Volterra, Lucca, the Chianti area, Siena, and many other Tuscan delights. Breakfast can be served outdoors or a pre-ordered tray is brought directly to rooms. *Directions:* 8 km from San Gimignano, 4 km from Certaldo. From Certaldo, take the road south (there are three) towards San Gimignano-Pancole, and at Il Monte turn in at the sign for La Fonte.

LA FONTE
Host: Maria Bergamasco
Via Canonica 4, San Gimignano, (SI) 53037, Italy
Tel: (0577) 944845, Fax: (0577) 945635
7 Rooms, Double: €110
4 Apartments: €90–€170 daily
Minimum Nights: 3
Open: all year, Credit cards: all major
Other Languages: fluent English
www.karenbrown.com/lafonte.html
B&B, SELF CATERING

The increasing popularity of this perfectly intact medieval town and the resulting availability of accommodations have made San Gimignano a hub from which tourists fan out to visit nearby, lesser-known treasures such as Volterra, Colle Val d'Elsa, and Monteriggioni. A pleasant, informal stay can be had at the Podere Villuzza, run by friendly young Sandra and Gianni Dei who opened the doors of their 150-year-old stone farmhouse to guests after extensive modification. Chairs are set up in front where visitors can enjoy the view of vineyard-covered hills leading up to the impressive multi-towered town. Common areas include the rustic living room with ceramic-tiled tables and fireplace where guests convene after a day of touring. While gregarious Sandra pampers guests, Gianni occupies himself with the production of top-quality olive oil. Six double rooms on ground and first floors accessed by several different entrances are furnished in true country style with a mix of wrought-iron beds and antique armoires, complemented by mansard beamed ceilings and stone walls. Rooms have views out over the countryside and town or over back hills. Also available for weekly stays are three small apartments within the house that include a living area and kitchen. A swimming pool just to the left of the farmhouse is a great bonus for guests. *Directions:* Go through town and follow signs for Certaldo. After 2 km turn right and follow signs for Villuzza.

PODERE VILLUZZA
Hosts: Sandra & Gianni Dei
Strada 25, San Gimignano, (SI) 53037, Italy
Tel: (0577) 940585, Fax: (0577) 942247
Cellphone: (335) 7118172
6 Rooms, Double: €95–€102
3 Apartments: €752 (2 people, weekly)
Open: all year, Credit cards: MC, VS
Other Languages: good English
www.karenbrown.com/poderevilluzza.html
B&B, SELF CATERING

The countryside around San Gimignano is becoming like the Alto Adige mountain area where practically every house offers some kind of accommodation, and the competition has created bed and breakfasts with high standards of quality and service. Among these, Il Rosolaccio (the local name for the poppies that cover the hill in springtime) is an 18th-century typical Tuscan farmhouse perched high above the road between Certaldo and San Gimignano. As expected, the view over the vineyards and hillsides is absolutely breathtaking. After a 30-year career running a hotel in Rome, Ingrid Music, with her son Steven, bought and very carefully restored the house which, by tradition, was added on to each time someone in the family got married. All the right ingredients are included for a perfectly delightful stay, with tastefully decorated bedrooms and apartments perfectly in tune with the simple beauty of the preserved farmhouse, warm and discreet hospitality, and marvelous views to be enjoyed either poolside or at sunset with a glass of wine. Common areas include the vaulted dining room and cozy upstairs living room with huge open fireplace and family antiques. *Directions:* From San Gimignano follow signs for Certaldo and after 7 km, turn right at the sign up to Il Rosolaccio. From Certaldo drive in the direction of San Gimignano for 5 km and turn left at Rosolaccio.

IL ROSOLACCIO
Hosts: Ingrid & Steven Music
San Gimignano, (SI) 53037, Italy
Tel: (0577) 944465, Fax: (0577) 944467
Cellphone: (335) 6360715
6 Rooms, Double: €96–€110
6 Apartments: €660–€1,090 weekly
Minimum Nights: 2, Open: Mar to Oct
Credit cards: all major, Fluent English, German
www.karenbrown.com/rosolaccio.html
B&B, SELF CATERING

La Locanda del Castello is a dreamy place to stay recently opened by Silvana Ravanelli, who took on the ambitious project of restoring part of the village's 13th-century castle (the municipal hall is housed in the other half) and transforming it into charming accommodations and a restaurant. The success she had with her previous, much smaller bed and breakfast in this guide created the desire to offer additional, more upscale rooms. She has a real talent for decorating and each individual room has been thoughtfully appointed with the family's antiques, gorgeous fabrics, and beautiful travertine bathrooms. Most have king-sized beds, double sinks, and generous showers. The golden hue chosen for the rooms' walls harmonize perfectly with the surrounding wheat-covered hillsides dotted with cypresses. The brick-vaulted restaurant, originally the olive press, is accessed through a delightful garden with dining tables right at the historic walls of the castle. The chef adds his own creativity to ancient Tuscan recipes using local percorino cheeses, white truffles, and other fresh local products. San Giovanni is right in the middle of some of Tuscany's most picture-perfect scenery. *Directions:* 35 km south of Siena, exit from autostrada A1 at Bettolle-Sinalunga and follow signs for San Giovanni d'Asso. Stairs from the town's main parking lot lead up to the inn.

❄ ☕ CREDIT ☎ ♈ P ⑪ 🖼

LA LOCANDA DEL CASTELLO
Piazza Vittorio Emanuele II, 4,
San Giovanni d'Asso, (SI) 53020, Italy
Tel: (0577) 802939, Fax: (0577) 802942
9 Rooms, Double: €110–€150
Per person half board: €160–€220
Minimum Nights: 3 for half board
Open: all year, Credit cards: all major
Other Languages: good English
www.karenbrown.com/locandadelcastello.html
B&B

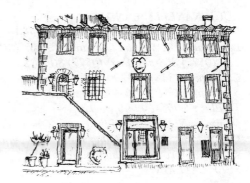

For those seeking a base for exploring the hilltowns of Tuscany while sojourning in very characteristic accommodation with a rich historical past, the Lucignanello is a sublime choice. Imagine residing in one of the cluster of stone houses that make up the quaint village immersed in the type of picture-perfect, timeless Tuscan landscape seen in Renaissance paintings. The illustrious Piccolomini family still owns the 15th-century property where lovers of Italy can live out a dream. Five two-bedroom houses have been masterfully restored, preserving the original architectural features while ensuring modern facilities. The irregularly shaped interiors are filled with lovely antiques, Oriental carpets, beautifully tiled bathrooms, and kitchens with travertine counters, and all but one have large fireplaces. High above the village is a pool set among olive trees with inspiring views. Although breakfast ingredients are supplied, guests are self-sufficient (they find the hamlet's grocery shop and osteria most convenient) but a permanent staff is at their disposal for any suggestions or assistance. A separate five-bedroom farmhouse with private swimming pool is rented out by the week. Country charm exudes from every corner and the ambiance is so authentic you will feel almost Tuscan before you leave! *Directions:* From San Quirico go towards Siena, taking the first right to San Giovanni d'Asso. Two km before town, turn right for the 2-km drive to Lucignano d'Asso.

LUCIGNANELLO BANDINI
Host: Angelica Piccolomini Naldi Bandini
Lucignano d'Asso, San Giovanni d'Asso, (SI) 53045
Tel: (0577) 803068, Fax: (0577) 803082
Cellphone: (338) 5032004
5 Apartments: €1,100–€1,700 weekly
1 Villa: €1,065–€4,000 weekly
Minimum Nights: 2 in high season, Open: all year
Credit cards: MC, VS, Other Languages: good English
www.karenbrown.com/lucignanello.html
SELF CATERING

We instantly fell in love with Il Borro and decided that this gorgeous property would be perfect for those who want to nestle into Tuscany for a week or more in a "home away from home." Il Borro is owned by Ferruccio Ferragamo whose son, Salvatore, personally manages it. This isn't your normal hotel at all—it is a huge estate with vineyards, walnut groves, olive trees, woodlands, and pastures. For such a vast property (1700 acres), it is amazing that there are only twenty-two suites, accommodating from three to six persons. Each has a bedroom (or bedrooms), kitchen, and living room. A wide variety of accommodations is offered: fourteen of the suites are in three houses nestled in the countryside, eight are in individual cottages in the hamlet of Borro, and the last, a romantic, secluded little mill, stands by the river. My favorites are the eight cottages in Borro, an adorable village with a cluster of enchanting stone buildings facing onto narrow, cobbled, pedestrian-only streets. This hamlet, reached by a beguiling stone bridge, is a real town with its own tiny plaza, artisan shops, boutiques, church, cobbler, goldsmith, restaurant, delicatessen and wine bar. Here, the eight guest cottages are tucked among the villagers' homes. No matter where you stay, the decor and accommodations are outstanding, and in the off season prices drop dramatically. *Directions:* When you reach the town of San Giustino Valdarno, follow signs to Il Borro.

IL BORRO
Owner: Ferruccio Ferragamo
San Giustino Valdarno, (FI) 52020, Italy
Tel: (055) 97 70 53, Fax: (055) 97 70 55
22 Rooms, Double: €180–€240
Open: all year, Credit cards: all major
Abitare la Storia
www.karenbrown.com/ilborro.html
HOTEL, SELF CATERING

In the countryside on the main road north of Arezzo (16 km) is the Villa Cassia di Baccano, a newly refurbished accommodation within a stately home and 16th century mill next door. The vaulted brick mill is where a buffet breakfast is served and where the reception area is located. Opposite the villa is a lovely borderless swimming pool overlooking a wide open countryside panorama, while the back opens up to face an umbrella pine tree garden. One and two-bedroom apartments within the main building are spread between two floors and are softly appointed with cool white and beige tones in a minimalist style. Wood floors and sleek travertine bathrooms harmonize well with the soothingly simple décor and canopy beds are made up with the finest linens available. All apartments have fully equipped kitchens and the ground floor accommodation includes a patio out in the garden. Rooms looking north have the same open view as that from the pool. Your hostess, Michela, is on hand to suggest itineraries in Arezzo, exploration of the immediate area or over to Chianti just across the tollway. *Directions:* From A1 autostrada, exit at Valdarno and follow for Terranuova and then S. Giustino Valdarno. The Villa Cassia is on this road just before town.

VILLA CASSIA DI BACCANO   New
Host: Sandro Bartolucci
Via Setteponti Levante, 132
San Giustino Valdarno, (AR) 52040, Italy
Tel: (055) 9772310, Fax: (055) 9772898
13 Apartments: €160–€260 daily
Open: all year, Credit cards: all major
Other Languages: good Engish
www.karenbrown.com/baccano.html
SELF CATERING

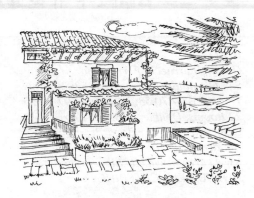

Staying at the Villa Arceno is truly like staying with friends in a sumptuous Italian villa. Although a luxurious property with stunning decor and impeccable service, the hotel exudes the warmth and charm of a small inn. The manager, Gualtiero Mancini, makes everyone feel at home. The mood of grandeur is set as you approach by a seemingly endless private road that winds through lovingly tended vineyards to a classic, three-story, ochre-colored villa. At one time the summer home of royalty, this 17th-century Palladian villa has been masterfully restored, both outside and within. The public rooms are more like lounges in a private home with a sophisticated, yet comfortable, elegance. The individually decorated guestrooms in the main villa are gorgeous—even the standard rooms are enormous and splendidly decorated. All the rooms are so outstanding it is difficult to choose, but I think my favorites are suites 104 and 204, both with sweeping vistas of vine-covered fields. Reveling in the utter peace and quiet, go sightseeing in nearby Siena, explore the wonders of Tuscany, or enjoy the hotel's bicycles, swimming pool, tennis court, and (best of all) the park. Here you can stroll for hours along romantic lanes shaded by rows of centuries-old cypress trees or meander on paths through the forest, passing almost-hidden statues and small temples, to an idyllic, secluded lake. *Directions:* Ask hotel for directions.

RELAIS VILLA ARCENO
Manager: Gualtiero Mancini
San Gusmè, (SI) 53010, Italy
Tel: (0577) 35.92.92, Fax: (0577) 35 92 76
16 Rooms, Double: €330–€500
Open: mid-Mar to mid-Nov
Credit cards: all major
www.karenbrown.com/hotelvillaarceno.html
HOTEL

If you are looking for a place to stay in the heart of Tuscany that is moderately priced, yet does not sacrifice one ounce of charm or quality of accommodation, the family-run Hotel Belvedere di San Leonino is unsurpassable. Ceramic pots of geraniums, trellised grapevines, and climbing roses soften and add color to the weathered stone buildings, which were originally a cluster of 15th-century farmers' cottages. Off the central patio area you find a small reception area, a living room blandly decorated with contemporary furniture, and an attractive dining room with tiled floors, rustic beamed ceiling, and appropriately simple wooden tables and chairs. When the weather is warm, meals are served outside in the garden. Because the rooms are tucked into various parts of the old farmhouses, they vary in size and shape. They also differ in decor, but all have an antique ambiance with wrought-iron headboards, beautiful old armoires, and pretty, white curtains. What adds the icing to the cake is the setting of the Belvedere, nestled in the very heart of the Chianti wine region, surrounded by stunning scenery—in every direction you look there are idyllic, sweeping vistas of rolling hills dotted with vineyards, olive groves, and pine forests. Hotel Belvedere is conveniently located only a short drive from the freeway.

HOTEL BELVEDERE DI SAN LEONINO
Manager: Signora C. Orlandi
San Leonino, (SI) 53011, Italy
Tel: (0577) 74 08 87, Fax: (0577) 74 09 24
28 Rooms, Double: €100–€130
Meals for guests only (closed Tues)
Open: mid-Mar to mid-Nov
Credit cards: all major
www.karenbrown.com/hotelbelvedere.html
HOTEL

Easily accessed off one of the ancient roads leading from Rome to Florence (Via Cassia), Il Rigo farmhouse sits in its own 600-acre estate. It is ideally located as a base from which to explore the scenic landscapes south of Siena with their sparsely vegetated rolling hills. The large, rectangular stone and brick house dates back 500 years. Its inner courtyard sits on a hill overlooking fascinating vistas stretching to the distant horizons. Within are nine country-style bedrooms on both ground and upper floors, divided by several cozy sitting rooms. Country furnishings such as armoires and wrought-iron beds are very much in harmony with the simple, authentic farmhouse. Breakfast or a light lunch or dinner are served in a spacious dining room on the first floor. Ingredients from the farm include organic grains and beans and, of course, extra virgin olive oil and wine. Hostess Lorenza is an excellent cook and has conducted lessons both here and in the States. The Cipolla's live most of the year in the family palazzo (which has been owned by the family since 1684), Casa dell'Abate Naldi, in the charming village of San Quirico, where four lovely bedrooms with antiques are also available for guests. *Directions:* From San Quirico take the SS 2 south for 2 km and turn left at sign for Il Rigo. Continue on dirt road for 3 km up to cypress-lined driveway to the main house.

IL RIGO **New**
Hosts: Vittorio & Lorenza Cipolla
Località: Casabianca
San Quirico d'Orcia, (SI) 53100, Italy
Tel: (0577) 897291, Fax: (0577) 898236
9 Rooms, Double: €96–€104
Open: all year, Credit cards: all major
Other Languages: good English
www.karenbrown.com/rigo.html
B&B

The Residence San Sano is a very special small hotel in San Sano—a picturesque hamlet in the center of the Chianti wine-growing region. We were charmed by the hotel, which is incorporated into a cluster of 16th-century stone houses. A cozy dining room serves guests excellent meals featuring typically Tuscan-style cooking. Each of the bedrooms is delightfully furnished in antiques and each has a name incorporating some unique feature of the hotel, the name evolving from the time during reconstruction when each room was remembered by its special feature. One is called the Bird Room: here birds had claimed the room for many years and had nested in holes that went completely through the wall. With great imagination, the holes were left open to the outside, but on the inside were covered with glass. Another room is named for a beautiful, long-hidden Romanesque window that was discovered and incorporated into the decor and another for an antique urn uncovered during renovation. The hotel has upgraded the property with a beautiful swimming pool and several spacious new rooms overlooking the vineyards.

HOTEL RESIDENCE SAN SANO
Owner: Maurizio Amabili
San Sano, (SI) 53010, Italy
Tel: (0577) 74 61 30, Fax: (0577) 74 61 56
14 Rooms, Double: €130–€160
Minimum Nights: 3
Meals for hotel guests only (closed Sun)
Open: mid-Mar to Feb, Credit cards: all major
www.karenbrown.com/residencesansano.html
HOTEL

Poggio ai Santi has a magnificent view over a green valley down to the sea 4 kilometers away. Francesca has put her heart and soul into the place over the past 20 years with the emphasis being on the comfort and ease of her guests. In order to fulfill the needs of both families and couples she has divided the property into two separate accommodations, conveniently separated by a road. On the left is the Muccheria, two converted farms houses, bi-level family apartments with kitchen facilities, its own swimming pool and play area. On the right is the Poggio ai Santi with the family's stately main house, plus a one-story guest house with five junior-suite-sized rooms, all with independent entrances from the garden. A second guest house with additional suites is being completed further down the hill. An immediate sense of calm and well-being is invoked by the views, the peaceful ambience and immaculate rooms appointed in soft earth tones (bedspreads and matching curtains are changed according to season), plus spacious bathrooms with natural stone tiles and rain showers. The pool area is landscaped primarily with aromatic herbs and lavender. A country breakfast is served out on the veranda overlooking this lovely garden. *Directions:* Exit from the Aurelia freeway SS1 at San Vicenzo Sud and keep driving north to San Vicenzo on the older SS1 Aurelia for 1 km. Follow Take a right turn for San Carlo and continue for 3 km. Poggio ai Santi is just before San Carlo.

❄ ☕ 🎿 🍜 CREDIT ☎ P 🍴 🚭 🏊 🖼 ♿ ⚓ 🐎 🍇 🌷

*POGGIO AI SANTI   **New***
Host: Francesca Vierucci
Via San Bartolo, 100, San Vincenzo, (LI) 57027, Italy
Tel: (0565) 798032, Fax: (0565) 798090
4 Rooms, Double: €100–€300
1 Apartment €450–€1,400 weekly
Minimum Nights: 3 high season in b&b, 7 in apartment
Open: all year, Credit cards: all major
Other Languages: good English
www.karenbrown.com/santi.html
B&B, SELF CATERING

Within the charming, medieval town of Sarteano, just south of the famed Tuscan hilltowns of Montepulciano, Pienza, and Montalcino, is the historic 16th-century home of gracious hostess, Signora Liboria. Although uninhabited for forty years and in dire need of restoration, she fell in love with the home and purchased it eight years ago, complete with frescoed-ceilings, private chapel, and formal garden. A meticulous restoration followed; the prime objective to preserve the home's original flavor and offer three guestrooms for her bed & breakfast activity. Signora thoroughly enjoys walking visitors through the historic, museum-like rooms, each with a mythical theme portrayed in the frescoed-ceilings (Venus, Cupid, Bacchus). Pastel-colored rooms are appointed with a selection of antiques, small object collections, family heirloom paintings, and lace curtains (one made from a wedding veil!) to create a feminine, romantic ambience. The theme continues in the three bedrooms with immaculate bathrooms, tiled rooftop, and hillside views. Royal blue and yellow are the predominant colors in the Contessa room, red in the canopied-bed of the Cardinal room, and roses decorate every object in the third, smallest bedroom. An abundant, country breakfast is served guests, while daily itineraries are arranged for this scenic area. *Directions:* Exit A1 at Chiusi-Chianciano, follow signs for Sarteano, and continue directly into the historic center.

PALAZZO FANELLI
Host: Liboria Albanese
Via dei Lecci 25
Sarteano, (SI) 53047, Italy
Tel: (0578) 268130: (0578) 268130
3 Rooms, Double: €120–€140
Open: all year, Credit cards: none
www.karenbrown.com/fanelli.html
B&B

As more travelers realize how close together destinations of interest throughout Italy are, weekly house rentals to use as a home base for excursions have become more popular. One such ideal base is La Sovana, bordering Tuscany and Umbria and equidistant to Siena, Perugia, Assisi, Arezzo, and many other smaller hilltowns such as Montepulciano, Pienza, and Montalcino—the area where Italy's finest wines are produced. Two stone farmhouses were carefully restored to provide comfortable suites for two to six people. Tastefully decorated with local antique beds and armoires, matching floral bedspreads and curtains, each has a fully equipped kitchenette and eating and living area. Guests can dine by candlelight in the dining room in the main house, whose enormous arched window takes in the expansive view of vineyards, wheat fields, and impeccable landscaping. Giovannella and Giuseppe Olivi, dedicated and amiable hosts, and their two grown children, Riccardo and Francesca, dine with their guests each evening. Potted flowers abound around the pool and Jacuzzi where on Saturday nights a sumptuous barbecue is organized to enable guests to meet one another. Two tennis courts, a small fishing lake, and bikes are available. There are more bi-level suites in a large converted barn in the woods a short walk away from the main farmhouse. *Directions:* Just 2 km from the Chiusi exit of the A1 autostrada. La Sovana is just before Sarteano on the right.

LA SOVANA
Hosts: Giuseppe Olivi family
Localita: Sovana, Sarteano, (SI) 53047, Italy
Tel: (0578) 274086 or (075) 600197
Fax: (075) 5158098, Cellphone: (335) 7258560
15 Rooms, Double: €134–€192
Minimum Nights: 3, 7 in high season
Open: Jan 1 & Apr 1 to Nov 3, Credit cards: none
Other Languages: good English
www.karenbrown.com/lasovana.html
B&B, SELF CATERING

Tenuta La Bandita is set amid 150 acres of woods, olive groves, orchards, and meadows within a beautifully undisturbed area south of Livorno near the sea. Dino and Daniela, with their former business and hotel experience, bought the estate not too long ago and are in the process of gradually bringing it back to its past splendor. The 17th-century main villa is where most of the guest bedrooms are situated. Their idea was to transform the villa into a bed and breakfast while leaving as much as possible of the original structure and atmosphere of the private residence intact. This was made easier by the fact that the home came with ten furnished bedrooms with bathrooms, situated down one long corridor upstairs. The rooms are appointed with original period furniture, chandeliers, and matching golden brocade drapes and bedspreads. Guests can lounge on the front terrace with wide countryside views or in the gracious arched living and dining room downstairs with gray-stone fireplace and framed portraits. Fifteen additional rooms are divided within two adjacent houses, Gliuliui and La Foresteria, between the villa and swimming pool. *Directions:* Exit from S.S.1 at Donoratico and head for Sassetta/Castagneto for 11 km on a winding mountain road. Take the turnoff left for Laderello/Monteverdi (not Sassetta) for 1 km to the La Bandita property. Pass through the gate and go past the first group of private homes to the villa at the end of the road.

TENUTA LA BANDITA
Hosts: Daniela & Dino Filippi
Via Campagna Nord 30
Sassetta, (LI) 57020, Italy
Tel: (0565) 794224, Fax: (0565) 794350
25 Rooms, Double: €90–€195
Minimum Nights: 2
Open: Mar 19 to Nov 6, Credit cards: all major
Other Languages: some English, French, German
www.karenbrown.com/tenutalabandita.html
B&B

Saturnia's thermal waters have been gushing from an underground volcano for over 2,000 years, yet only recently have it and the enchanting surrounding Maremma area become internationally famous, leading to new accommodations springing up. One such is the charming Villa Clodia, once home to nobility, now run by former restaurateur Giancarlo Ghezzi. The villa is a curiosity, seemingly built out of the limestone rock, one side overlooking the street and the other an expansive valley of grapevines and olive trees. Because of its unusual proportions, each room is unique in size and decor. A small winding stairway takes guests up or down to rooms, some of which have been literally carved out of the rock. All bedrooms feature scattered antiques, new bathrooms, and valley views, and a fortunate few boast a terrace. Amenities include air conditioning, TVs, and mini-bars. Breakfast is offered in a sweet, luminous room next to the sitting room. A lush rose garden and fruit orchard surround the inviting star-shaped pool. Advance reservations are a must and weekly stays preferred. *Directions:* From Rome take the Aurelia highway north, turning off to the right at Vulci following signs for Manciano, Montemerano, and Saturnia. Villa Clodia is in the middle of town.

VILLA CLODIA
Host: Giancarlo Ghezzi
Via Italia 43
Saturnia, (GR) 58050, Italy
Tel: (0564) 601212, Fax: (0564) 601305
12 Rooms, Double: €90–€105
Minimum Nights: 4
Closed: Dec 1 to 20, Credit cards: VS
Other Languages: good English
www.karenbrown.com/clodia.html
B&B

The Maremma, a beautiful area in the coastal foothills of southern Tuscany, quite undiscovered by tourists, offers a wealth of sightseeing possibilities: walled villages, Etruscan ruins, archaeological sites, and lovely landscapes. Until recently there were few places to stay that offered much charm, but happily this problem was solved when the Pellegrini family converted a 200-year-old stone farmhouse into a small hotel. Here you will find true Tuscan hospitality. The dining room is the heart of the inn and has tables set in a beamed-ceilinged room filled with sunlight from large French doors opening onto a terrace where meals are served on warm days. The bedrooms in the original house are quite small, but 13 new, very spacious guestrooms and four suites have been built in an annex. There is also a spa offering a number therapies for well being and a swimming pool. Another real bonus is the food: it is wonderful—everything is homemade under the direction of Signora Pellegrini, including marvelous pastas prepared by local housewives, and the hotel even produces its own wines which are served with the meals. Specialties of the inn are Signora Pellegrini's cooking classes and trekking (horseback riding). In the corral below the hotel, horses are groomed each day for guests' use: in fact, special room rates are offered which include riding in the Maremma countryside. *Directions:* From Scansano, take S.S. 322 toward Manciano. The hotel is on the left.

ANTICO CASALE DI SCANSANO
Owners: Massimo Pellegrini & family
Scansano, (GR) 58054, Italy
Tel: (0564) 50 72 19, Fax: (0564) 50 78 05
32 Rooms, Double: €120–€200
Open: Mar to mid-Jan, Credit cards: all major
www.karenbrown.com/anticocasale.html
HOTEL

Another one of Italy's best-kept secrets is the Monte Amiata area in the southern part of Tuscany, offering some of the most spectacular naturalistic landscapes in all of Italy. The mountain's peak reaches a height of 1800 meters and is surrounded by one enchanting village after another, untouched by tourism. Enrico Casini and his wife Stefania took over a vast countryside property here, transforming the four scattered ancient farmhouses into fourteen very comfortable apartments for guests. Appointed in true Tuscan country style, they have either one or two bedrooms, living room, and kitchenette. The main house is the heart of the place where Enrico, a well-known chef and sommelier with international experience, thoroughly expresses himself. His extraordinary dishes combine the freshest produce and top-quality cheeses and salamis of the area with traditional recipes and his own creative touch. The estate also produces top-rated extra-virgin olive oil using ancient methods. Meals are served in one of two attractive dining rooms or out on the porch overlooking an open lawn leading to the swimming pool. *Directions:* 15 km from Montalcino. From the Cassia route 2, exit from the north at S. Quirico or from the south at Radicofani and drive towards Seggiano-Castel del Piano. Turn right 4 km before town at Poggio Ferro-Le Casacce.

LE CASACCE
Hosts: Enrico & Stefania Casini
Localita: Casacce
Seggiano, (GR) 58038, Italy
Tel: (0564) 950895, Fax: (0564) 950970
Cellphone: (347) 5292957
14 Apartments: €620–€1,285 weekly (Jul & Aug)
Open: all year, Credit cards: all major
Other Languages: good English
www.karenbrown.com/casacce.html
SELF CATERING

The Grand Hotel Continental Siena, an elegant small hotel that opened in early 2002, is one of the most exciting properties to come on the scene in Siena in many years. Although there are lovely places to stay on the periphery, there has never been an outstanding hotel in the heart of Siena, within steps of all of its fabulous sights. To say that this need for an exceptional property has now been fulfilled is an understatement: the Grand Hotel Continental Siena is an absolute dream and would be a sensation anywhere in the world. Located just off the Piazza del Campo, the building dates back to 1600 when it was designed as a magnificent palace for the noble Chigi family. After years of labor by countless artisans, the palace has been returned to its original splendor. The grandeur and opulence of the rooms are breathtaking. Fine fabrics, exquisite furnishings, and priceless antiques create a setting of unsurpassed grandeur. At the heart of the palace a central courtyard, protected by a glass roof, allows the sunlight to fill the hotel with sunshine. Off the courtyard the various parlors and ballrooms are gorgeous. A sweeping, wide staircase leads upstairs to the sumptuous bedrooms and suites, some of which feature magnificent, museum-quality, frescoed ceilings. At the nearby "sister" property, the Park Hotel, guests can take advantage of its various amenities, including golf, tennis, and swimming.

GRAND HOTEL CONTINENTAL SIENA
General Manager: Pietro Panelli
Banchi di Sopra, 85,
Siena, 53100, Italy
Tel: (0577) 56 011, Fax: (0577) 56 01 555
*51 Rooms, Double: €310–€540**
**Breakfast not included: €28*
Open: all year, Credit cards: all major
www.karenbrown.com/hotelcontinental.html
HOTEL

So very close to Siena, yet having the advantage of countryside tranquillity, is the elegant Villa dei Lecci of the Albuzza sisters from Milan. The enterprising and energetic pair left their city careers to resettle in Tuscany, totally renovating an abandoned 17th-century country home to create an upscale bed and breakfast and an intimate and romantic retreat for couples. The yellow bedroom downstairs is a suite with large bathroom adjacent to the frescoed dining room where a generous breakfast is served. A candlelit dinner can also be had upon request here or out in the garden gazebo. Upstairs, where the noble proprietors once lived, the quarters are more elaborate, with painted, wood-paneled ceilings and a large living room and library filled with fine antiques. The Victorian-style Peach Room has floral wallpaper, lace curtains, and silver-framed family photos, while the Alcove Suite is done in golden tones and rich fabrics. Adding to guests' indulgence are a hot tub, exercise room, and sitting area on a frescoed veranda. A weeklong cooking program is organized in off-season months. An excellent touring base. *Directions:* Exit the A1 at Val di Chiana and take 326 to Siena. Continue straight on to the Siena Est exit, arriving at Due Ponti. Take a sharp right at Bar Due Ponti onto Strada Pieve al Bozone for 2.6 km, turning left at the crucifix onto an unpaved road, Strada di Larniano. Continue 1.8 km to the end of the road and up to the gate of the stone villa.

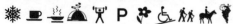

VILLA DEI LECCI
Hosts: Miki & Marika Albuzza
Strada di Larniano 21/1, Siena, 53100, Italy
Tel & Fax: (0577) 221126
Cellphone: (339) 8008711
4 Rooms, Double: €180–€230
Minimum Nights: 3
Open: mid-Mar to Dec, Credit cards: none
Other Languages: good English
www.karenbrown.com/lecci.html
B&B

Siena is a fascinating walled, hilltop city filled with a wealth of fabulous museums, intriguing squares, and breathtaking churches. If you want to stay within walking distance of the all the major sights and your budget precludes a splurge at the deluxe Grand Hotel Continental, the Palazzo Ravizza pensione makes an excellent choice. The brick exterior of the hotel looks quite plain but inside, the beauty of this once-grand 17th-century palace is immediately revealed. Belonging to the same family for 200 years, the mansion exudes the warmth of a home, with an intimate parlor, card room, music lounge, cozy bar, handsome ceiling frescos, old family portraits, and fresh flowers on polished antique tables. The Palazzo Ravizza is a simple hotel and some of the fabrics show a well-worn look, but overall it is well kept and appealing and for the price, it is an excellent choice. The individually decorated bedrooms vary in size, but all are furnished with antiques. The choice rooms are those that overlook the back garden—I especially liked rooms 14 and 11. The most outstanding feature of the Ravizza is its splendid large garden. This is the heart of the hotel where guests enjoy a cold drink at one of the tables on the terrace, relax on one of the benches strategically placed for capturing a sweeping view of the Tuscany hillside, or dine on the terrace in balmy weather. *Directions:* Near the Porta San Marco gate. Ask hotel for exact directions.

PALAZZO RAVIZZA
Owner: Francesco Grottanelli
Pian dei Mantellini, 34
Siena, 53100, Italy
Tel: (0577) 28 04 62, Fax: (0577) 22 15 97
40 Rooms, Double: €160–€250
Open: all year, Credit cards: all major
www.karenbrown.com/ravizza.html
HOTEL

The Park Hotel Siena, a splendidly renovated 16th-century villa, is perched on a hillside on the outskirts of Siena, close to the wonders of this fabulous city, yet with space for tennis, a swimming pool, and even a golf course. Guests can easily slip into the heart of Siena for sightseeing. As soon as you step through the doors into the elegantly appointed reception hall decorated with fine antiques, you will be surrounded by an ambiance of quiet grandeur. Although a deluxe property, the Park Hotel Siena exudes the feeling of a private home, with intimate groupings of finely upholstered sofas and chairs, carved stone fireplaces, handsome oil paintings, and magnificent chandeliers. My favorite room is the lovely dining room, with its tall windows opening onto the terrace. Pastel-colored walls, high, vaulted ceilings, soft lighting, handsome chandeliers, beautiful tiled floors, high-backed dining chairs, and tables set with fine linens and crystals create a mood of gentle romance. As you would expect, the individually decorated, spacious guestrooms are beautifully appointed and furnished with antiques. *Directions:* From the Siena-Florence highway, take the Siena Nord exit. As you follow the road into Siena, there is a sign to the hotel on your right.

PARK HOTEL SIENA
General Manager: Pietro Panelli
Via di Marciano, 18
Siena, 53100, Italy
Tel: (0577) 29 0290, Fax: (0577) 49 020
69 Rooms, Double: €256–€405
Closed: Nov 15 to Mar 15
Credit cards: all major
www.karenbrown.com/parkhotelsiena.html
HOTEL

The Locanda dell'Amorosa, a charming small hotel with great warmth and excellent management, makes a super base for exploring Tuscany and Umbria. From the Locanda dell'Amorosa it is an easy drive to such sightseeing delights as Siena, Pienza, Orvieto, Todi, and Assisi. The Locanda dell'Amorosa is actually a tiny town located a few kilometers south of Sinalunga. You approach along a cypress-lined road that cuts through fields of grapes. Park your car and enter through the gates into the walled 14th-century medieval village where you are greeted by an enormous courtyard with its own little church—exquisite inside with its soft pastels and its lovely fresco of the Madonna. A rustic wine bar next to the church features a selection of the estate's wines and can provide guests a light meal when the restaurant is closed. On the right side of the courtyard are the stables, which have been converted to a stunning restaurant whose massive beams and natural stone-and-brick walls are tastefully enhanced by arched windows, thick wrought-iron fixtures, and wooden tables. The guestrooms, located in a separate building, are tastefully appointed with a few antiques and matching bedspreads and draperies. The rest of this tiny village spreads out behind the main square and the buildings are used for the production of wine. *Directions:* Exit the A1 at Sinalunga. Just before town turn left toward Torrita. After 2 km, the hotel is on your right.

❄ ☕ ✤ ♨ 💳 ☎ ⅄ P ⑂ 🏊 🖼 🔔 🐎 🍇

LOCANDA DELL'AMOROSA
Managers: Carlo Citterio & Alessandra Chervatin
Sinalunga, (ME) 53048, Italy
Tel: (0577) 67 72 11, Fax: (0577) 63 20 01
25 Rooms, Double: €234–€660
Restaurant closed Mon & lunch on Tue
Closed: Jan 7 to Mar 7, Credit cards: all major
Abitare la Storia
www.karenbrown.com/dellamorosa.html
HOTEL

In yet another lesser-known pocket of Tuscany halfway between Siena and the sea is the absolutely stunning 1,000-acre property of the Visconti family. Dating back to the 1400s, in its heyday it was a village in itself, complete with the noble family's main villa, farmers' houses, church, nuns' quarters, oil press, and blacksmith and carpenter's shops. These stone buildings are all attached to the villa in a U-shape formation with a beautiful formal garden within. Terra-cotta pots with lemon trees and red geraniums give spots of color among the greenery. Vitaliano and Vittoria, whose home has been in the same family since its origins, welcome guests in the restored part of the villa where eight bedrooms with private bathrooms have been created including three large triples. All with beamed ceilings and brick floors, they are simply appointed with beds and armoires, looking out either to the garden or woods at the back. Common areas are the living room with enormous fireplace, the dining room where delectable Tuscan country meals are served (€20), and an upstairs loggia with a panoramic view over the countryside, which seems to take in all of Tuscany. Four apartments are available for weekly stays. For those who enjoy spectacular scenery in a very special, historical setting, this is the place. *Directions:* From the Florence-Siena highway exit at Colle Val d'Elsa Sud. Follow signs for Grosseto-Radicondoli-Castelnuova Val di Cecina, then Fattoria Solaio.

FATTORIA SOLAIO
Hosts: Vittoria & Vitaliano Visconti
Solaio–Radicondoli, (SI) 53030, Italy
Tel: (0577) 791029, Fax: (0577) 791015
9 Rooms, Double: €90–€115
3 Apartments: €630– €750 weekly
Minimum Nights: 3
Open: Mar to Nov, Credit cards: all major
Other Languages: good English
www.karenbrown.com/fattoriasolaio.html
B&B, SELF CATERING

If the idea of staying in an extraordinary medieval fortress that crowns a spectacular hilltown far off the beaten path appeals, you will fall in love with the Hotel della Fortezza—it is an absolute jewel. This tiny hotel is in a splendid part of Tuscany called Maremma, little known to the casual tourist, but well worth exploration. There are many walled villages in the hills that lie between Orvieto and the coast, all beckoning you to drive within their walls, but one of the most beautiful of all is Sorano. The town is nestled into a pocket of the hill, a jumble of ancient stone and stucco buildings that form a striking architectural design, and crowning the top of the town is the imposing Orsini Fortress. You enter through an impressive gate, cross a stone bridge over what was once a moat, then pass through a tower gate and into the fortress where you find the hotel. This is not a deluxe hotel nor does it pretend to be, but the interior is extremely appealing, with the guestrooms decorated with great taste, appropriate to the charm of the building. Almost all of the bedrooms have a breathtaking view of the town and beyond to the densely wooded hills. Number 16 is an especially attractive corner room, larger than most, with handsome antique headboards and windows on two sides. However, even the smaller rooms have sensational views. This area is well known for its many walking trails. *Directions:* In Sorano, look for signs to the Fortezza Orsini.

HOTEL DELLA FORTEZZA
Manager: Luciano Caruso
Piazza Cairoli, 5
Sorano, (GR) 58010, Italy
Tel: (0564) 63 20 10, Fax: (0564) 63 32 09
15 Rooms, Double: €120–€200
Closed: closed Jan & Feb, Credit cards: all major
Abitare la Storia
www.karenbrown.com/fortezza.html
HOTEL

La Taverna Etrusca is in an intriguing, picturesque, little-known part of Tuscany called Maremma, where you find ancient towns with very old stone houses, wrapped by dense green woodlands, tucked into the landscape. Throughout this region, hiking, biking, and horseback riding are popular ways to discover the countryside. Etruscan ruins are found everywhere, making this an especially interesting area to explore. This property's emphasis is not as a hotel, but rather as a restaurant. It's housed in a rustic stone building situated in the center of a tiny village that seems to be suspended in time. The restaurant, which specializes in traditional Tuscan and Maremman dishes, faces onto a tiny piazza where a stone church, topped by a whimsical bell tower, sits at one end. Within, the restaurant abounds with medieval allure. High ceilings are enhanced by wood beams and huge stone archways divide the room into romantic dining areas. When the weather is mild, meals are also served outside on the terrace. Many dining guests never realize that there are also a few hotel rooms upstairs. These are small and simply decorated, but are very nice for the price. *Directions:* Located in the center of the village, facing the piazza.

LA TAVERNA ETRUSCA
Manager: Luciano Caruso
Piazza del Pretorio 15
Sovana, (GR) 58010, Italy
Tel: (0564) 61 61 83, Fax: (0564) 61 41 93
8 Rooms, Double: €99
Restaurant closed Wednesdays
Closed: Jan & Feb, Credit cards: all major
Abitare la Storia
www.karenbrown.com/tavernaetrusca.html
HOTEL

It was love at first sight as I drove up the long graveled road through forest and vineyard and suddenly caught my first glimpse of the Borgo Pretale, a tiny cluster of weathered stone buildings nestled next to their medieval watchtower. My first impression was more than justified—this small inn is truly paradise. There are absolute serenity and beauty here with nothing to mar the perfection. Civilization seems far away as the eye stretches over a glorious vista of rolling hills forested with oaks, juniper, and laurel, interspersed with square patches of vineyards. But although this small village is seemingly remote, it is only a short drive south of Siena, thus a perfect hideaway from which to enjoy the magic of Tuscany. The rooms in the tower are showplaces of fine country antiques and splendid designer fabrics, blended together with the artful eye of a skilled decorator. Every piece is selected to create a sophisticated yet rustic elegance. The rooms in the surrounding cottages are furnished in a more "country" style, though maintaining standards of elegance and comfort. The lounge beckons guests to linger after dinner by the roaring fire. A path leads to a groomed tennis court and farther on to a swimming pool on a hillside terrace. *Directions:* The closest town on most maps is Rosia, which is about 5 kilometers southeast of Borgo Pretale. To reach the hotel, go through Rosia and follow signs to Borgo Pretale.

BORGO PRETALE
Manager: Daniele Rizzardini
Sovicille
Pretale, (SI) 53018, Italy
Tel: (0577) 34 54 01, Fax: (0577) 34 56 25
35 Rooms, Double: €205–€240
Open: Apr to Nov, Credit cards: all major
www.karenbrown.com/borgopretale.html
HOTEL

Halfway between Florence and Siena in the heart of the Chianti region is the Sovigliano farm, restored by a gracious couple from Verona, Claudio Bicego and his wife, Patrizia, and daughter, Claudia. Guests have an independent entrance to the four bedrooms with kitchenette, each very much in keeping with the pure simplicity of this typical farmhouse. Exposed-beam ceilings and worn terra-cotta floors, antique beds and armoires, and bucolic views make time stand still here. Besides three apartments (two with air conditioning) in a separate farmhouse, there is also a spacious two-bedroom apartment within the house with kitchen and dining area and fireplace. At guests' disposal are a living room, kitchen with country fireplace, TV, large surrounding garden with swimming pool and hydrojet, exercise trail, and outdoor eating area overlooking the characteristic hills of Chianti. Signor Bicego is actively involved in the production of top Tuscan wines in conjunction with several other wine estates, and also coordinates with other area residents to organize lessons in language, history, and culinary arts with local professors. *Directions:* From Siena, exit the superstrada at San Donato in Poggio; from Florence at Tavarnelle Val di Pesa. Drive through the village of Tavarnelle following the directions to Certaldo-Marcialla. At the end of Tavarnelle, at the fourth traffic circle, veer to the left (blue sign says Magliano), following signs for Sovigliano.

SOVIGLIANO
Hosts: Patrizia & Claudio Bicego
Via Magliano 9
Tavarnelle Val di Pesa, (FI) 50028, Italy
Tel: (055) 8076217, Fax: (055) 8050770
4 Rooms, Double: €130–€160
4 Apartments: €870–€1,400 weekly B&B
Minimum Nights: 3, Closed: Jan 15 to 3
Credit cards: MC, VS, Other Languages: good English
www.karenbrown.com/sovigliano.html
B&B, SELF CATERING

Country tourism has flourished in the last decade, especially in the highly popular region of Tuscany. However, most travelers still flock to the Chianti area, leaving many other parts of Tuscany wide open to discovery. Such is the gorgeous virgin territory of the Valdera Valley between stunning Volterra with its Etruscan origins and Pisa where everything has remained remarkably unspoiled. Affable host Sandro and his family bought a 100-acre farm property here and are restoring the ancient farmhouses piece by piece with guests' comfort foremost in mind. So far, eight neat apartments with one or two bedrooms and five guest bedrooms have been completed within three adjacent stone houses and are tastefully appointed with local antiques. Within one of the houses is the pleasant dining room with large arched windows where breakfast and dinners upon request are served, all prepared by Sandro's mother, who also conducts cooking lessons. Olive oil, wine, fruits, and vegetables all come directly from the farm. There is a beautiful borderless swimming pool and Sandro supplies guests with mountain bikes and a long list of interesting local itineraries. Easy day trips include Florence, Siena, San Gimignano, Lucca, Pisa and Volterra, famous for its alabaster artisans. *Directions:* Il Selvino is located off the main road 439 from Volterra (20 km) between Terricciola and La Sterza at Pieve a Pitti (marked on most maps).

IL SELVINO
Hosts: Alessandro Sgherri family
Localita: La Sterza, Via Pieve a Pitti 1
Terricciola, (PI) 56030, Italy
Tel & Fax: (0587) 670132, Cellphone: (338) 6209229
5 Rooms, Double: €90–€115
8 Apartments: €150–€200 daily
Minimum Nights: 2, Open: all year
Credit cards: MC, VS, Other Languages: some English
www.karenbrown.com/ilselvino.html
B&B, SELF CATERING

The Aiola opened its doors to guests nine years ago when the Campellis restored the farmers' houses on the wine estate's vast property in Chianti. The family's villa with its ancient origins sits across the street from the guest quarters, almost completely hidden by enormous oak and cypress trees, where the bedrooms, one of which sleeps four persons, all have separate outside entrances. Original architectural features have been preserved and rooms are decorated with wrought-iron beds and antique or reproduction armoires. The vineyards come right up to the house and a wide, open view of the hills is offered to the other side. The barn next door includes common areas such as the breakfast room, where Federica's fresh-baked coffee cakes are served, and a living room. Part of the founding members of the Wine Tourism Association, visits to the cellar and the villa, and wine tasting begin right here at the Aiola. Federica and Enrico aim to make each guest feel special, dedicating much time to suggesting itineraries with maps and making reservations at restaurants, museums, and local concerts. At 12 kilometers from Siena and an easy distance from the highlights of the region, the Aiola serves as an excellent touring base. Total silence reigns here, with only the buzz of cicadas breaking it. *Directions:* From Siena follow route 222, then 102 just past Vagliagli—the Aiola property (well marked) is on this same road.

CASALI DELLA AIOLA
Hosts: Federica & Enrico Campelli
Vagliagli, (SI) 53010, Italy
Tel: (0577) 322797, Fax: (0577) 322509
8 Rooms, Double: €95–€120
Open: all year, Credit cards: all major
Other Languages: good English
www.karenbrown.com/laaiola.html
B&B

With great finesse and determination, Lucia and Paolo, an editor and art collector, managed to purchase Villa Campestri, a magnificent Renaissance villa—no easy feat, considering the 400-acre property had been in one family for 700 years. The cream-colored villa with handsome lawns and surrounding cypress woods commands a spectacular view over the immense valley and Mugello mountain range in an area north of Florence known for its concentration of Medici villas. The guestrooms in the villa have been restored to their original splendor, with high Florentine woodworked ceilings, carefully selected antiques, and delightful blue-and-white-tiled bathrooms. The honeymoon suite features a grand, gold-crowned, red canopy bed. Equally characteristic rooms are located in the side wing and small independent house. A sitting room adorned with rich paintings leads to the elegant, stencil-painted dining rooms where original combinations of fresh local produce are served with great attention to detail, accompanied by an excellent selection of wines. They have created Italy's first "Oleoteca" devoted to the culture of olive oil, offering courses in its history, science, and cuisine. Villa Campestri offers refined, romantic accommodations with professionalism and hospitality given by daughter, Viola. *Directions:* Exit A1 at Barberino di Mugello and follow signs for Borgo San Lorenzo, then to Vicchio, then Campestri.

VILLA CAMPESTRI
Owners: Lucia & Paolo Pasquali
Localita: Campestri 19/22
Vicchio di Mugello, (FI) 50039, Italy
Tel: (055) 84 90 107, Fax: (055) 84 90 108
21 Rooms, Double: €144–€310
Open: Mar to Nov, Credit cards: all major
www.karenbrown.com/villacampestri.html
HOTEL

For years Andrea and Silvia have literally opened their entire home to guests, welcoming and re-welcoming "friends of La Volpaia," their bed and breakfast. International guests gather together in the evenings out on the patio or in the converted barn for one of Silvia's delightful meals based on fresh vegetables and meats enhanced with their own extra-virgin olive oil. Conversation is never lacking with meals accompanied by La Volpaia's own Chianti (all beverages are included in the half-board rate). Andrea, a native Roman architect and sculptor, bought the wine estate with its 16th-century farmhouse 19 years ago and his pieces in olive wood are displayed in and about the property. The five cozy bedrooms are appointed with antiques, as is the large living room with fireplace. Beyond the patio where meals are served is the spectacular swimming pool with its heavenly views of what can only be described as a truly classic Tuscan landscape. Horses, personally trained by the hosts, are available for excursions into the surrounding countryside (experienced riders only). Guests are made to feel immediately right at home in this informal setting and so it is no wonder that many become "regulars" to this idyllic spot so close to the highlights of Tuscany. *Directions:* From the town of Vico d'Elsa follow Via della Villa (on the right) for 2 km, turning left at the wooden signpost for La Volpaia.

LA VOLPAIA
Hosts: Silvia & Andrea Taliaco
Strada di Vico 5-9, Vico d'Elsa, (FI) 50050, Italy
Tel: (055) 8073063, Fax: (055) 8073170
5 Rooms, Double: €220*
*Includes breakfast & dinner
Minimum Nights: 3
Open: all year, Credit cards: none
Other Languages: good English
www.karenbrown.com/lavolpaia.html
B&B

Volterra, a walled medieval hilltown, is not as well known as its ever-popular neighbor, San Gimignano, but it too exudes great authentic medieval character. Although not quite as colorful, it benefits from fewer tourists and offers a wealth of museums and many boutiques selling items made of alabaster, for which the town is renowned. Conveniently located within the walled city, very near the gate called Porta Florentina, the Hotel La Locanda is intimate and very attractive. The exterior is a pretty pinkish-beige color with arched doorway, flower boxes at the windows, green shutters, and a wrought-iron light sconce. You enter into a small foyer with gorgeous parquet floors and fresh flowers accenting the antique reception desk. Just beyond are a small lounge and then the cheerful room for breakfast, the only meal served (the restaurant for the hotel, under the same ownership, is the Etruria, just a short walk up the street). Throughout the hotel you find original art, with the work of local artists on display in all of the rooms. An elevator leads up to three floors of guestrooms, all as fresh and pretty as can be. Each level has its own color scheme—green, red, or blue—established by the carpeting and the richly hued, handsome coordinating fabrics used for draperies and bedspreads. The marble bathrooms are excellent and the suites even have Jacuzzi tubs. *Directions:* Inside the city walls, on the street leading to, and close to, Porta Florentina.

HOTEL LA LOCANDA
Owner: Assenza Andrea
Via Guarnacci, 24
Volterra, (PI) 56048, Italy
Tel: (0588) 81 547, Fax: (0588) 81 541
19 Rooms, Double: €85–€250
Open: all year, Credit cards: all major
www.karenbrown.com/locanda.html
HOTEL

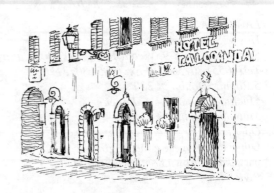

Places to Stay in Umbria

Having made the decision to return to her native Italy after years in Venezuela, Liria elected to do it in style. She bought a 200-acre estate in the virgin hills north of Orvieto and set about restoring the four abandoned stone houses which once made up a farmer's village. Her natural flare for integrating soft muted color tones, gorgeous french fabrics and selected antiques has resulted in a refined and romantic country ambience throughout. The five spacious bedrooms with canopy beds in the main house are tastefully appointed and harmonize well with handmade terracotta brick floors and original stone walls so typical of an Umbrian home. Two 2-bedroom apartments are found in an adjacent house complete with kitchenette and living room for longer stays. Alternatively you could rent an entire two-story house with three bedrooms. Sweeping valley views over soft green hills are enjoyed from any position whether it be out in the lavender garden surrounding the curved swimming pool or on the main terrace where most meals are served. The farm produces organic olive oil, wine, grain, honey and fruits. *Directions:* Directions: From the A1 autostrada exit at Fabro and turn right for Allerona. Pass through the town center of Fabro and continue for 5 km and fork left for Allerona Scalo. After 3.2 km turn right and stay to the right for the next two forks until you come to Monticchio.

I CASALI DI MONTICCHIO   New
Hosts: Liria Costantino family
Vocabolo Monticchio 34, Allerona, (TR) 05011, Italy
Tel: (0763) 628365, Fax: (0763) 629569
10 Rooms, Double: €150–€200
2 Apartments, €1,200–€2,500 weekly
Minimum Nights: 2
Open: all year, Credit cards: MC, VS
Other Languages: good English, Spanish
www.karenbrown.com/monticchio.html
B&B, SELF CATERING

As the road twists and turns ever further into the wooded hills above Assisi, one can't help wondering what treasure awaits at the trail's end, or if anyone could possibly have found this romantic hideaway before you. What a surprise then to finally turn off the graveled road and discover the parking lot filled with luxury cars. In this glorious hillside setting with its sweeping panorama of wooded hills, worldly cares quickly melt away. Although the hotel is built into a cluster of 10th-century stone houses, all the modern-day luxuries are present including a beautiful swimming pool on the right as you enter and, on a lower terrace, tennis courts. Behind the main building is a separate stone house where you find a most appealing lounge with deep-green sofas and chairs grouped around a giant fireplace. Doors from the lounge lead into an intimate little bar and beyond to a dining room with honey-colored stone walls, beamed ceiling, and terracotta floors with tables dressed in the finest of linens. Marvelous meals are served, prepared almost totally from ingredients from the hotel's own farm, which is part of the property. The individually decorated bedrooms sport a rustic, yet elegant, ambiance. *Directions:* From Assisi follow signs toward Gualdo-Tadino and as you leave the town walls of Assisi, watch for and take the road to the right signposted Armenzano. From Armenzano, the hotel is well marked.

ROMANTIK HOTEL "LE SILVE DI ARMENZANO"
Owners: Marco Sirignani family
Localita: Armenzano
Armenzano, Assisi, (PG) 06081, Italy
Tel: (075) 80 19 000, Fax: (075) 80 19 005
20 Rooms, Double: €150–€185
Open: Mar to mid-Nov, Credit cards: all major
www.karenbrown.com/lesilvediarmenzano.html
HOTEL

A reader highly recommended La Fortezza, saying that it was a wonderful bargain and that he enjoyed the best meal of his entire trip there. We too were immediately captivated by this simple, charming place to stay in the center of Assisi. The restaurant seems to be the star attraction, with Guglielmo Chiocchetti in the kitchen cooking while his wife, Tina, takes care of the many dinner guests. Their two wonderful sons, Luca and Lorenzo, are also totally involved in this family operation, helping out wherever needed, assisted by Luca's pretty wife who was serving the day we stopped by. Without a doubt, it is the gentle, caring Chiocchetti family with their exceptional warmth that makes La Fortezza so special. Their restaurant's superior food features many Umbrian dishes, served in a cozy dining room with vaulted stone ceiling and wooden chairs painted a cheerful red. The guestrooms, which are an outstanding value, are located on two floors above the restaurant. Although not large, each is spotlessly clean and very tastefully decorated in a simple, country style. The choice bedroom even has its own little terrace. The hotel is hidden up a lane of stone steps at the northeast corner of the Piazza del Comune. There are lots of steps getting to the hotel, but then this is true throughout Assisi, which seems pasted to the side of the hillside. Just remember, bring a small suitcase. Closest parking: Piazza Matteotti.

LA FORTEZZA
Owners: Chiocchetti family
Above NE corner of Piazza del Comune
Assisi, (PG) 06081, Italy
Tel: (075) 81 24 18 or (075) 81 29 93
Fax: (075) 81 98 035
7 Rooms, Double: €65
Restaurant closed Thur
Closed: Feb, Credit cards: all major
www.karenbrown.com/lafortezza.html
B&B

The delightful Malvarina farm with its charming, country-style accommodations, excellent local cuisine, warm and congenial host family, and ideal location has been a long-time favorite of our readers. Just outside town, yet immersed in lush green vegetation at the foot of the Subasio Mountains, the property is comprised of the 15th-century stone farmhouse where the family lives and four independent cottages (converted barn and stalls) divided into bedrooms and suites with en suite bathrooms, plus three apartments with kitchenettes for two to four persons. Casa Angelo has several bedrooms plus a sweet breakfast room with a corner fireplace and cupboards filled with colorful Deruta ceramics. Great care has obviously been taken in the decor of rooms, using Mamma's family heirloom furniture. The old wine cellar has been cleverly converted into a cool and spacious taverna dining room with long wooden tables for dining en famille if not out on the veranda terrace. Cooking classes are very popular here. A collection of antique farm tools and brass pots cover walls near the enormous fireplace. Horses are available for three- to seven-day trekking trips into the scenic national park just beyond the house, led by gregarious host, Claudio. A welcome feature is a swimming pool. *Directions:* Exit at Rivotorto from the Perugia-Spello route 75. Turn right then left on Via Massera (Radio Subasio sign) and follow the road up to Malvarina.

MALVARINA
Hosts: Claudio Fabrizi family
Localita: Malvarina 32, Assisi, (PG) 06080, Italy
Tel & Fax: (075) 8064280
10 Rooms, Double: €93–€165
3 Apartments: €98 daily
Minimum Nights: 3
Open: all year, Credit cards: MC, VS
Other Languages: some English
www.karenbrown.com/malvarina.html
B&B, SELF CATERING

Il Palazzo, a three-star hotel in the heart of Assisi, offers surprisingly attractive accommodations for a modest price. Built in the 1500s as a palace for the prosperous Bindangoli-Bartocci family, its foundations date back even further. Amazingly, the hotel is still owned by Bartocci descendants. Indications of the palace's rich heritage can still be seen in the many important oil paintings and 18th-century tempera mythical scenes. As you enter off the street there is a simple reception area. Beyond is a large, beamed-ceilinged living room with comfortable sitting areas. The right wing of the palace has been turned into a restaurant serving local dishes. A buffet breakfast is served on the second floor. To reach the bedrooms, you walk out into a central courtyard and then up an exterior steel staircase. I assure you the climb is worthwhile because once you throw open the shutters of your bedroom, you are treated to a stunning panorama of the Umbrian countryside. Definitely splurge—request one of the superior bedrooms, all very spacious and attractively furnished with appealing antiques. One of my favorites, 204, has twin beds with pretty, painted iron headboards. Room 203, a corner room, is also a real winner with a canopy bed—it would be my first choice except that the bathroom is not very large. As with all the hotels in Assisi, take just a small overnight suitcase. Closest parking: Piazza San Francesco.

IL PALAZZO
Manager: Arianna Bartocci Fontana
Via San Francesco, 8
Assisi, (PG) 06081, Italy
Tel: (075) 81 68 41, Fax: (075) 81 23 70
12 Rooms, Double: €95–€150
Dinner by prior request
Closed: mid-Jan to mid-Mar, Credit cards: all major
www.karenbrown.com/palazzo.html
HOTEL

Fabrizio and Bianca, the Milanese hosts originally from this part of Umbria, restored their inherited La Fornace farmhouse, situated in the very desirable location just 2 km from Assisi, with their guests' comfort foremost in mind. With careful attention to detail, six comfortable apartments and two guestrooms were fashioned within the three stone houses. Each apartment has one or two bedrooms, bathroom, fully equipped kitchenette, and eating area. Interesting decorating touches such as parts of antique iron gates hung over beds, terra-cotta and white ceramic tiles in the immaculate bathrooms, and antique armoires give the accommodations a polished country flavor. Le Pannocchie includes a corner fireplace, while Papaveri looks out over the flat cornfields up to magnificent Assisi and the Subasio Mountains beyond. Anna and Franco look after guests when the owners are away. A small dining room has been created on the ground floor, next to the 18th-century wood oven, for morning breakfast. At guests' request guided tours are arranged to Umbria's top sights. Besides a lovely swimming pool for guests, a small gym, bikes, ping-pong, and games for children are on hand. *Directions:* From Perugia-Spoleto highway 75, exit at Ospedalicchio on route 147, turn left for Tordibetto after the bridge, then right for Assisi and follow signs for La Fornace.

PODERE LA FORNACE
Hosts: Bianca & Fabrizio Feliciani
Via Ombrosa 3, Tordibetto, Assisi, (PG) 06081, Italy
Tel: (075) 8019537, Fax: (075) 8019630
Cellphone: (338) 990-2903
2 Rooms, Double: €65–€90, Breakfast not included: €5
6 Apartments: €55–€270 daily
Minimum Nights: 2, Closed: Jan & Feb,
Credit cards: MC, VS, Other Languages: good English
www.karenbrown.com/lafornace.html
B&B, SELF CATERING

Assisi is one of our favorite places to stay and our guide can never recommend enough hotels here, so we were delighted to find the Residenza d'Epoca San Crispino, a fabulous, enchanting new hotel. Dating back to the 14th century when it was a religious site for the order of San Crispino, the hotel has been tenderly restored to maintain its rich heritage while adding every comfort for the 21st century. Almost all of the furnishings are beautiful antiques previously used in a nunnery. Throughout this tiny inn you find simple, uncluttered, tasteful decor with white walls, stone floors, crisp white embroidered curtains, bouquets of fresh flowers, and handsome antiques. The mood is set us you enter through very old double doors into a courtyard, bound on one side by the small, 5th-century church of San Biagio. From the courtyard, steps lead up to the foyer where the reception desk is an antique confessional. Accommodations are all suites, varying in size from a studio to a two-bedroom, two-bath apartment. Every room has an armoire, which conceals a small refrigerator, minibar, espresso machine, hot plate, dishes, and utensils for preparing light snacks. Laundry service is available upon request. Each room is a dream, but my very favorite is The Moon and The Stars, which not only has a lovely view, but also its own huge private garden. This small hotel is really special and a marvelous value.

RESIDENZA D'EPOCA SAN CRISPINO
Manager: Isabella Fischi
Via San Agnese, 11
Assisi, (PG) 06081, Italy
Tel: (075) 81 55 124
Fax: (075) 81 55 124 (9 am to 6 pm)
7 Rooms, Double: €130–€290
Open: all year, Credit cards: all major
www.karenbrown.com/sancrispino.html
HOTEL

For a moderately priced place to stay in the heart of Assisi, the Hotel Umbra is an unbeatable choice. The hotel is located just a few steps down a narrow little alley that leads off the Piazza del Comune, one of the central plazas in town. The entrance is through wrought-iron gates that open to a tiny patio where you are treated to an idyllic oasis with tables set under a trellis covered by vines creating a lacy pattern of shadows. There is a lovely view from this intimate terrace. After passing through the patio, you enter into a lounge/reception area with doors opening into the dining room where very good meals are served. The public rooms have accents of antiques, but have a homey rather than grand ambiance. Steps lead to the simple bedrooms, which are individually decorated and very pleasant. Splurge and ask for a room (such as 34) with a panoramic vista of the Umbrian valley. However, do not be disappointed if one is not available — the rooms (such as 35) overlooking the jumble of tiled roofs are also very nice. If you like small, family-run hotels that are not decorator-perfect in every detail, but offer great heart and hospitality, the Hotel Umbra is an excellent choice. The delightful Alberto Laudenzi family oversees every detail of this small inn and makes guests feel at home. The staff too is extremely gracious and accommodating. The location is absolutely perfect.

HOTEL UMBRA
Owners: Alberto Laudenzi family
Via Degli Archi, 6-Piazza del Comune
Assisi, (PG) 06081, Italy
Tel: (075) 81 22 40, Fax: (075) 81 36 53
26 Rooms, Double: €100–€123
Restaurant closed Sun
Closed: mid-Jan to mid-Mar
Credit cards: all major
www.karenbrown.com/hotelumbra.html
HOTEL

The expansive Pomurlo farm, home to the congenial Minghelli family, covers 370 acres of hills, woods, and open fields and is an excellent base for touring Umbria. A winding dirt road leads to the typical stone house, which contains a restaurant featuring organically grown, farm-fresh specialties. An antique cupboard and old farm implements on the walls enhance the rustic setting. A nearby converted stall houses two adorable independent rooms looking out over the lake. Other guestrooms and apartments with kitchens are found in two large hilltop homes commanding a breathtaking view of the entire valley with its grazing herds of longhorn cattle. The main house, a 12th-century tower fortress where the inn's personable hostess Daniela resides, accommodates guests in three additional suites of rooms. Breakfast fixings are provided in rooms. The acquisition of the neighboring property has resulted in a center (Le Casette) offering more service—two stone farmhouses containing several other rooms and a restaurant around a large swimming pool. Comfortable and cheerful, all rooms are decorated with wrought-iron beds, colorful bedspreads, and typical regional country antiques. Enjoy the pool and activities such as tennis, soccer, and mountain biking. *Directions:* The farm is located near the Rome-Florence autostrada. Take the Orvieto exit from the A1 and follow signs for Todi, not for Baschi. On route S.S.448 turn right at the sign for Pomurlo.

POMURLO VECCHIO
Hosts: Lazzaro Minghelli & family
Localita: Lago di Corbara, Baschi, (TR) 05023, Italy
Tel: (0744) 950190 or 957645, Fax: (0744) 950500
35 Rooms, Double: €55–€95
Minimum Nights: 3, 7 in July & Aug
Open: all year, Credit cards: MC, VS
Other Languages: some English, French
www.karenbrown.com/pomurlovecchio.html
B&B, SELF CATERING

The vast Torre Burchio property is immersed in 1,500 acres of wooded wildlife preserve where wild boar, deer, hare, and pheasant abound. Seemingly far away from "civilization," this Italian version of a ranch offers a relaxing holiday in close touch with nature, while still being in reach of Umbria's top sights. The reception, restaurant, and six guest bedrooms are within the main 18th-century farmhouse, which maintains the ambiance of the original hunting lodge with hunting trophies on the walls, large open fireplace, cozy living room, and library. The upstairs breakfast room, from which the bedrooms lead, is lined with colorful Deruta ceramics. An additional ten bedrooms are found in a single-story house just across from the lodge, while the very comfortable apartments with kitchenettes are in a beautifully restored 230-year-old stone house with inner courtyard 4 kilometers down the road. The rooms and apartments are very nicely appointed with antiques, pretty fabrics, paintings, and large bathrooms, and have telephones and televisions. Guests gather in the busy restaurant in the evening for a hearty meal based on organic products from the farm. Many activities such as cooking classes, horseback-riding weeks, and sports are available. *Directions:* 20 km from either Perugia or Assisi. From the center of Bettona, follow signs for 5 Cerri-Torre Burchio and follow the dirt road through the woods for 5 km to the main house/reception.

TORRE BURCHIO
Host: Alvaro Sfascia
Bettona, (PG) 06084, Italy
Tel: (075) 9885017, Fax: (075) 987150
Cellphone: (347) 8460995
16 Rooms, Double: €77–€104
13 Apartments: €672–€878 weekly
Minimum Nights: 3, 7 in high season
Closed: Jan, Credit cards: all major, Good English
www.karenbrown.com/burchio.html
B&B, SELF CATERING

L'Orto degli Angeli is a rare jewel. Located in the historic center of Bevagna (a small, picture-perfect walled village of Roman origin), this intimate inn exudes the genuine warmth of a private home, yet offers the comfort and sophistication of a fine hotel. The handsome stone house has been in the family of your gracious host, Francesco Antonini, since 1788. He and his sweet wife, Tiziana, welcome guests with such a gentle kindness that you will be immediately captivated by their charm. An impressive staircase leads up to the guest lounge, which has a stunning frescoed ceiling and comfortable sofa and chairs grouped around an immense stone fireplace. Main meals are served in the Redibis restaurant set in a well-preserved part of the ambulatory of the ancient Roman theater built in the 1st century A.D. All of the individually decorated guestrooms have pretty, tiled bathrooms, some antique furnishings, fireplaces, and color-coordinating fabrics on the bedspreads and curtains. Many of the rooms overlook a central garden, built upon the old Roman theatre. Bevagna is rich in historical importance—don't miss the stunning little 19th-century opera house, the well-preserved mosaics in the Roman baths, and the picturesque churches. *Directions:* From Perugia take 75 to Assisi-Foligno. Exit to the 316 to Bevagna and look for L'Orto degli Angeli signs.

L'ORTO DEGLI ANGELI
Owners: Tiziana & Francesco Antonini
Via Dante Alighieri, 1, Bevagna, (PG) 06031, Italy
Tel: (0742) 36 01 30, Fax: (0742) 36 17 56
14 Rooms, Double: €200–€350
Restaurant closed Tue
Closed: Jan to Feb, Credit cards: all major
Abitare la Storia
www.karenbrown.com/lortodegliangeli.html
HOTEL

The quaint medieval village of Calvi is just on the border between Lazio and Umbria and conveniently located at 15 kilometers from the autostrada and 80 kilometers from Rome. Louise, from Sweden, divides her time between Rome and the countryside where the farm's activities include production of wine and olive oil, and horse breeding on the 150-acre property. The fascinating family residence in town is a historic 15th-century palazzo filled with period furniture, paintings, and frescoed ceilings. Hospitality is offered in the ochre-colored farmhouse within four comfortable apartments, each with private garden area. Accommodations on the first and second floors are a combination of one or two bedrooms, living room with fireplace, fully equipped kitchen, bathroom, and outdoor barbecue. The house has been restored with new bathrooms and tiled floors, while maintaining original beamed ceilings and a country flavor in antique furnishings. Besides wandering around the many surrounding villages, you can visit Rome, Viterbo, and Orvieto, within one hour by car, or relax by the swimming pool. A children's playground and an exercise course are available. *Directions:* Leave the Rome-Florence autostrada A1 at Magliano Sabina. After Magliano turn left for Calvi. Just before Calvi you see signs for San Martino on the right.

CASALE SAN MARTINO
Host: Louise Calza Bini
Colle San Martino
Calvi dell'Umbria, (TR) 05032, Italy
Tel: (328) 1659514, Fax: (0744) 710644
4 Apartments: €60–€150 daily
Minimum Nights: 2, 7 in Jul & Aug
Open: all year, Credit cards: none
Other Languages: good English, French, German
www.karenbrown.com/casalesanmartino.html
SELF CATERING

Relais Il Canalicchio is snuggled within a medieval village on a hilltop overlooking a breathtaking vista of vineyards, olive groves, tiny villages, and forested hills that melt into the horizon. Because the hotel occupies almost the entire romantic village, it has secret little terraces and enchanting nooks to explore. The castle dates back to the 13th century and in its excellent restoration great care was taken to preserve its original architectural features such as terracotta floor tiles, beamed ceilings, thick stone walls, massive fireplaces, and arched brick doorways. The ancient Roman fortified walls of the village are incorporated into one side of the hotel and allow for a romantic lush garden that stretches to the edge of the wall and, on a lower terrace, a splendid swimming pool and a panoramic restaurant. Giant terracotta pots filled with brilliant red geraniums add color to the immaculately tended grounds. Inside, everything is decorator-perfect with a homelike, comfortable ambiance created by the use of fine antiques and lovely fabrics. The spacious bedrooms have the feel of an English country manor, with pretty floral fabrics, coordinating wallpapers, and accents of antiques. A footbridge takes you to an adjacent building with 16 new country suites, all with private entrances. *Directions:* From Perugia go south on E45 in the direction of Roma/Terni, exit at Ripabianca-Foligno, and follow signs to the hotel.

RELAIS IL CANALICCHIO
Manager: Federico Pittaluga
Via della Piazza, 4
Canalicchio di Collazzone, (PG) 06050, Italy
Tel: (075) 87 07 325, Fax: (075) 87 07 296
49 Rooms, Double: €149–€253
Open: Mar thru Nov & New Years
Credit cards: all major
www.karenbrown.com/relaiscanalicchio.html
HOTEL

A stay at the Villa Aureli with Count di Serego Alighieri (descendant of Dante) can only be memorable. With its back to the town and looking out over the Italian Renaissance garden and surrounding countryside, the imposing brick villa has been standing for the past 300 years. When it was bought by the di Serego family in the 18th century, it was meticulously restored and embellished with plasterwork, decorative painted ceilings, richly painted fabrics on walls, ornately framed paintings and prints, colorful tiles from Naples, and Umbrian antiques. Left intentionally intact by the Count, who disdains overly restored historical homes, the elegant apartments for guests maintain their original ambiance. They can accommodate from four to six persons and are spacious, having numerous sitting rooms with fireplaces; although don't expect updated bathrooms or kitchens. A small swimming pool set against the villa's stone walls is a refreshing spot for dreaming. The villa serves as an ideal base from which to explore Umbria and parts of Tuscany, as well as special local itineraries prepared for guests by the Count. *Directions:* Exit from the Perugia highway at Madonna Alta and follow route 220 for Citta della Pieve. After 6 km, turn left for Castel del Piano Umbro.

VILLA AURELI
Hosts: Sperello di Serego Alighieri family
Via Cirenei 70
Castel del Piano, (PG) 06071, Italy
Tel: (340) 6459061, Fax: (075) 514 9408
2 Apartments: €950–€1,200 weekly
Open: all year, Credit cards: MC, VS
Other Languages: good English, French, German
www.karenbrown.com/villaaureli.html
SELF CATERING

In the hills between Tuscany and Umbria, overlooking the Tiber and Chiana valleys, you find the Nannotti family's typical farm property. Renato and Maria Teresa used to run a restaurant nearby before deciding to open a bed and breakfast and serve delicious Tuscan-Umbrian recipes at home. The three adjacent red-stone houses include eight guestrooms, two apartments, and the family's private quarters. Rooms, many with terrace or garden space, are all decorated in a simple, pleasant country style with a mix of reproduction armoires, wrought-iron beds, and some modern pieces. Renato specializes in organic produce and makes his own honey, jams, grappa, D.O.C. red wine (Colli del Trasimeno), and extra-virgin olive oil, which are brought directly to their restaurant next door with large panoramic terrace, Le Due Valli, for Maria Teresa to use in her authentic homemade cooking. She creates an easy, informal ambiance and young daughter Aureliana and son Ernesto both help out. Being close to the charming, historical village and having easy access to the autostrada make this a super touring location. There are also bikes, a swimming pool, hiking trails, a special spa package at nearby thermal waters, a park for children, many farm animals, a fitness track, and horses to ride. *Directions:* Exit at Chiusi from the north or Fabro from the south and follow signs for Citta della Pieve. In town follow signs for Ponticelli, the bed and breakfast is signposted.

MADONNA DELLE GRAZIE
Hosts: Renato Nannotti family
Citta della Pieve, (PG) 06062, Italy
Tel: (0578) 299822, Fax: (0578) 297749
Cellphone: (340) 8210564
8 Rooms, Double: €90–€130
2 Apartments: €600–€1,000 weekly
Minimum Nights: 7 in Jul & Aug, Open: all year
Other Languages: some English, French, German
www.karenbrown.com/madonna.html
B&B, SELF CATERING

Just on the border between Umbria and Tuscany and conveniently close to the walled town of Citta della Pieve, the Relais dei Magi is an excellent choice for accommodations in this enchanting part of Italy. A quiet, tree-lined lane leads up to the handsome 18th-century yellow villa with symmetrical windows accented by green shutters and roof adorned by rustic tile. The setting is utterly tranquil, with idyllic views in every direction—over 160 acres of woodlands, olive groves, and meadows stretch out as far as the eye can see. To the right of the villa, perfectly positioned to capture the view, is a stunning swimming pool romantically nestled on a grassy terrace amongst beds of flowers and towering cypresses. In the villa there are five deluxe suites, two with stunning view terraces and all with fireplaces and Jacuzzi tubs. Also in the villa are comfortable lounges and a beautiful dining room where a set-menu dinner is offered. A homelike ambiance prevails, with comfortable yet decorator-perfect furnishings throughout. Additional suites are found in a wing of rooms near the pool, while for longer stays or for families/friends there are apartments for two to six persons with kitchens complete with dishwashers and every modern amenity. Spa facilities include a fitness center, sauna, Turkish bath, and small heated pool. *Directions:* From Citta della Pieve take N220 toward Perugia. The hotel is on the left side of the road.

RELAIS DEI MAGI
Owner: Paolo De Marchis
Localita Le Selve Nuove, 45,
Citta delle Pieve, (PG) 06062, Italy
Tel: (0578) 29 81 33, Fax: (0578) 29 88 58
11 Rooms, Double: €160–€320
Closed: Jan & Feb, Credit cards: all major
www.karenbrown.com/relaismagi.html
HOTEL, SELF CATERING

Leaving behind the road from Perugia with its developing industries, a country gravel road takes you up to the splendid 17th-century Villa di Montesolare overlooking in all directions its hilly estate of olive groves and vineyards. A wide, gray-stone staircase leads up to an elegant salon with marble fireplace and crystal chandelier off which are eight lovely guestrooms and two suites on two floors. They are individually appointed with authentic period antiques, which harmonize perfectly with the original features of the villa left intact. Seven newer suites and nine bedrooms are located within two 350-year-old farmhouses just down the road, offering magnificent views and utter tranquillity. A separate breakfast room is inside one of these two houses. Back at the main house, guests enjoy a drink at the bar before dinner served in one of the two intimate, frescoed dining rooms where varied Umbrian cuisine is presented along with a selection of 350 Umbrian wines. Summer concerts are held in a chapel in the formal Italian garden. Enjoy activities such as swimming in one of two hillside pools, tennis, theme menus, and the on site spa and beauty farm. Gracious and warm hosts Filippo and Rosemarie do an absolutely superb job of making guests feel totally pampered at their romantic retreat. *Directions:* From Perugia take S.S. 220 toward Citta di Pieve. After Fontignano (3 km), turn right at Colle Sao Paolo to the villa (4 km).

❄ ☕ 🏌 ♨ 💳 ☎ 🏠 � P 🍴 ❀ 🏊 🏃 🖼 🚶 👫 🏇 🍇

ROMANTIK HOTEL VILLA DI MONTESOLARE
Owners: Rosemarie & Filippo Strunk Iannarone
Panicale
Colle San Paolo, (PG) 06064, Italy
Tel: (075) 83 23 76, Fax: (075) 83 55 462
28 Rooms, Double: €180–€240
Open: all year
Credit cards: all major
www.karenbrown.com/villadimontesolare.html
HOTEL

The Antica Fattoria came highly recommended by several readers who stayed there in the first year it opened. It is indeed a delightful combination of pretty countryside, strategic touring position, comfortable rooms, excellent meals, and warm hospitality. Following the increasingly popular lifestyle trend of abandoning the city for a rural pace, Roman couple Alessandro and Anna left their offices to become, essentially, farmers. They bought and restored two connected stone farmhouses and incorporated a combination of seven rooms and two apartments, decorated pleasantly with a characteristic country flavor, for guests. While Alessandro tends to the crops and farm animals, Anna lives out her passion for cooking, much to guests' delight. Meals are served either outside at one long table or in the transformed cow stalls below with cozy sitting area and fireplace. At times the allegria and good food keep guests at the table until the wee hours. A lovely swimming pool looks over the wooded hills to the valley. The busy hosts take time to assist guests with the many local itineraries and organize a wide variety of games. Perfect for families and a great base for exploring Umbria. The town of Deruta is world famous for its painted ceramic pottery and filled with workshops and stores. *Directions:* From Perugia (18 km), exit from E45 at Casalina. Take the first right and follow signs to the Santuario Madonna dei Bagni and then to the Fattoria.

ANTICA FATTORIA DEL COLLE
Hosts: Anna & Alessandro Coluccelli
Strada Colle delle Forche 6, Deruta, (PG) 06053, Italy
Tel & Fax: (075) 972201, Cellphone: (329) 9897272
7 Rooms, Double: €76–€106
2 Apartments: €780–€1,035
Minimum Nights: 2, 7 in Aug
Open: Easter to Jan 10, Credit cards: none
Other Languages: good English
www.karenbrown.com/anticafattoriadelcolle.html
B&B, SELF CATERING

L'Antico Forziere in the capable hands of Daniela and her industrious family, formerly the manager of another hotel, is a pleasant and strategic place from which to tour the highlights of Umbria. The ancient stone fortress building on the Tiber river, is located just off the main road which leads to Deruta, one of Italy's most famous ceramic centers. The views from the house and swimming pool over the valley are quite lovely. Attention has been given to the preservation of the centuries-old building, with exposed stone walls, handmade brickwork, wood beamed ceilings. Accommodation within 3 suites with independent garden entrance or 6 double room are appointed in typical Umbrian style with iron wrought beds, hand-woven local fabrics and simple country furniture and many amenities. High emphasis has been given to the restaurant where sons, Stefano and Andrea continue to work wonders, serving excellent local fare including fish and meat specialities within the vaulted brick and stone dining room where many come for a specially-prepared regional meal. Daniela's husband and third son, Samuele, take care of the general property and serve in the restaurant. Perugia, Assisi, Todi, Orvieto and Spoleto are all within 30 minutes of this base. Excellent value and hospitality.
Directions: From Perugia, exit at Casalina just after Deruta and follow signs to the hotel for 1 km.

❄ ☕ ✂ 💳 🛏 ⌂ 🐕 ⛱ P 🍴 🏊 🖼 ⚘ ⚓ 🏌 👫 🏇 🏄

L'ANTICO FORZIERE   *New*
Owners: Daniela Taddia & Alessandro Rodella family
Via Rocca, 2–Località Casalina
Deruta, (PG) 06051, Italy
Tel: (075) 9724314, Fax: (075) 9729392
9 Rooms, Double: €85–€150
Restaurant closed Mondays
Open: all year, Credit cards: all major
www.karenbrown.com/anticoforziere.html
HOTEL

Best friends Luciano and Tommaso, refugees from city life, have over the past dozen or so years transformed the 1,000-acre property, La Casella, made up of woods, rivers, and valleys, into a veritable countryside haven for vacationers. Foremost attention has been given to the 32 rooms, which are divided between three separate stone houses. The Noci house contains seven doubles upstairs appointed with country antiques, and a large vaulted room downstairs used for small meetings or dining. La Terrazza, originally a hunting lodge, has nine rooms, one with namesake terrace looking over the poplar woods. On the highest point sits San Gregorio, with small chapel, where guests revel in the utter silence and a spectacular 360-degree view over the entire property. The lively dining room offers delectable cuisine, with ingredients direct from the farm. The many sports facilities include a beautiful big swimming pool, tennis, and an equestrian center where numerous special outings and events are organized. There is also a spa program with natural treatments. Well-marked trails lead the rider, biker, or hiker to such marvels as Todi, Orvieto, or even Perugia. *Directions:* Exit at Fabro from the Rome-Florence A1 autostrada. Follow signs for Parrano (7 km), turning right at the Casella sign, and continue for another 7 km on a rough gravel road.

LA CASELLA
Hosts: Luciano Nenna & Tommaso Campolmi
Localita: La Casella, Ficulle, (TR) 05016, Italy
Tel: (0763) 86588 or (0763) 86684
Fax: (0763) 86684 or (0763) 86075
32 Rooms, Double: €90–€100
Apartment €90–€115
Open: all year, Credit cards: all major
Other Languages: fluent English
www.karenbrown.com/lacasella.html
B&B

Gubbio is one of Umbria's many jewels: a small, wonderfully intact medieval town that presses against the wooded hillside. A not-to-be-missed sight in Gubbio is the Piazza Grande, considered to be one of the boldest examples of medieval town planning, and facing onto this awesome masterpiece is the Relais Ducale. Gazing from the square, you would hardly know that a hotel is secreted within the building, but you will notice a large, open, stone passageway. Enter here and climb up the stairs through a tunnel-like corridor where you will emerge into a little lane. Continue on until you come to a hotel sign by the gate on a stone wall. Ring the bell for entrance and suddenly the hotel reveals itself with a charming inner garden courtyard off which you find the discreet reception office. The hotel, once the guest quarters for the Ducale Palace, has been sleekly renovated, but impressive features of its past are seen throughout with massive thick walls, high vaulted ceilings, and stone archways. On the fourth level of the hotel there is a romantic garden with one side enclosed by a carved stone balustrade, where you can gaze out to a beautiful panoramic view. Fine antique furniture is used for accent, handsome oil paints adorn the walls, and Oriental carpets brighten the floors. The pretty guestrooms have a sedate, refined decor, showing an effort to preserve the aristocratic aura of the hotel's heritage.

RELAIS DUCALE
Owner: Rodolfo Mencarelli
Via Ducale, 2
Gubbio, (PG) 06024, Italy
Tel: (075) 92 20 157, Fax: (075) 92 20 159
32 Rooms, Double: €150–€267
Open: all year, Credit cards: all major
www.karenbrown.com/relaisducale.html
HOTEL

When Lois Martin, a retired teacher, spotted the lovely restored farmhouse at San Martino, she knew it literally had her name on it and immediately purchased it. The house is completely open to guests, from the upstairs cozy living room with large stone fireplace to the downstairs country kitchen and large family room. Ingredients for a full country breakfast await you in the kitchen with its impressive display of Deruta ceramics. One bedroom with king bed is joined by a bathroom to a small room with twin beds, ideal for a family. Each of the other two doubles has a bathroom, with one being en suite. Besides a swimming pool overlooking the wooded hills and valley, other extras are satellite TV, a travel library, American washer and dryer, bikes, guest bathrobes, and dinner upon request. Casa San Martino also offers onsite cooking, painting, art history, and writing classes with a visiting professional teacher in off-season. Being right on the border of Umbria and Tuscany, Lake Trasimeno and towns such as Gubbio, Perugia, Cortona, Assisi, and Deruta are all easily accessible. The entire house can also be rented weekly for a group of up to eight persons. *Directions:* From Lisciano square, pass the bar and turn left for San Martino. Continue for 2 km and take a right up the hill at the sign for San Martino for just over 1.5 km to the house.

CASA SAN MARTINO
Host: Lois Martin
Localita: San Martino 19
Lisciano Niccone, (PG) 06060, Italy
Tel: (075) 844288, Fax: (075) 844422
4 Rooms, Double: €140–€150
1 House: €2,000–€3,000 weekly
Minimum Nights: 3, Open: all year, Credit cards: none
Other Languages: fluent English, German, Spanish
www.karenbrown.com/casasanmartino.html
B&B, SELF CATERING

Still another undiscovered area is the peaceful countryside northeast of Todi, where you find the Castello di Loreto. After having meticulously restored part of this medieval fortress castle as a country home, Nino Segurini now coordinates restoration work on ancient buildings, besides continuing his own business as a consultant to antiques dealers. Nino is very knowledgeable on many subjects, and delights in introducing guests to the undiscovered treasures he has found in the immediate area. Nino and Francesca's home is a veritable museum, with collections of ancient artifacts naturally inhabiting the historical building. Within the base of the thick-walled fortress you find the main living room, two small bedrooms (one twin, one double) connected by a sitting area, and three bathrooms. The kitchen leads outside to the spacious patio with grape pergola overlooking the landscaped garden and swimming pool. The preferred and largest bedroom, arranged as a suite with its own sitting room, is reached by two flights of stairs past another living room with fireplace, appointed with antique armor and weaponry and an enclosed loggia. A fourth guestroom features a 16th-century carved, gilded bed of a noble Venetian family who once had Napoleon as a houseguest. *Directions:* Leave highway E45 at Todi/Orvieto, heading for Pian di Porto, then San Terenziano. After 2 km, fork right towards Loreto for another 4 km. The entrance gate is opposite the church.

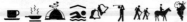

CASTELLO DI LORETO
Hosts: Nino & Francesca Segurini
Loreto-Todi, (PG) 06059, Italy
Tel & Fax: (075) 8852501, Cellphone: (335) 6249734
4 Rooms, Double: €110–€130
Minimum Nights: 2
Open: all year, Credit cards: none
Other Languages: good English, Spanish, French
www.karenbrown.com/loreto.html
B&B

The simple and economical Oasi Verde "green oasis" is just that: a convenient roadside stop for those traveling between Umbria and the Marches region. Carla and Andrea Rossi inherited the sprawling 200-year-old stone farmhouse and surrounding land, ideally located midway between Perugia and Gubbio (a not-to-be-missed medieval stone village set high up in the hillside), and decided to convert it to a bed and breakfast and restaurant. The eight rooms in the main house, each with its own bathroom, have been decorated like model room number 3, with its original beamed ceiling and country-antique bed and armoire. White-tiled floors may be out of character, but give a sense of cleanliness nonetheless. Another wing of the complex houses three simply furnished suites (two bedrooms and a bathroom) for longer stays, perfect for a family of four. Additional rooms, each with separate ground-floor entrance, are found in a wing renovated within the last few years. The windows at the back of the house open out to green hills with alternating patches of woods and sunflower fields. Facilities tempting you to linger for a while include a swimming pool and bikes available for rent. *Directions:* Traveling from Perugia on route 298, after 25 km you find the bed and breakfast on the left-hand side, at Mengara, 10 km before Gubbio.

OASI VERDE MENGARA
Hosts: Andrea & Carla Rossi
Localita: Mengara 1, Mengara, (PG) 06020, Italy
Tel: (075) 9227004, Fax: (075) 920049
Cellphone: (335) 1225738
19 Rooms, Double: €60–€76
Minimum Nights: 3 in high season
Open: Mar to Dec, Credit cards: MC, VS
Other Languages: some English
www.karenbrown.com/oasiverde.html
B&B

The scenic approach to the Fattoria di Vibio passes through lush green hills, by picturesque farms, and is highlighted by a romantic view of the quaint town of Todi, 20 kilometers away. Two handsome brothers from Rome run this top-drawer bed and breakfast consisting of several recently restored stone houses. The houses sit side by side and share between them 14 double rooms with private baths. Common areas for guests include a cozy, country-style living room with fireplace, games room, and country kitchen. The accommodations are enhanced by preserved architectural features such as terra-cotta floors and exposed-beam ceilings, and typical Umbrian handicrafts such as wrought-iron beds, renovated antiques, and Deruta ceramics. On the assumption that guests may find it difficult to leave this haven, the hosts offer half board plus lunch and snacks, along with spa facilities (massages and Turkish bath) indoor and outdoor heated swimming pools, tennis, hiking, horseback riding, fishing, and biking. Signora Gabriella, with a passion for cooking, gets all the richly deserved credit for the marvelous meals served either poolside or on the panoramic terrace. Four houses are also available for rent. *Directions:* From either Todi or Orvieto follow route S448 until the turnoff for Vibio at the sign for Prodo-Quadro and follow the well-marked dirt road for 10 km up to the farmhouse.

FATTORIA DI VIBIO
Hosts: Giuseppe & Filippo Saladini
Montecastello di Vibio, (PG) 06057, Italy
Tel: (075) 8749607, Fax: (075) 8780014
Cellphone: (335) 6594076
14 Rooms, Double: €100–€200
4 Villas: €800–€1,900 weekly
Minimum Nights: 7 in villas, Open: all year
Credit cards: all major, Other Languages: good English
www.karenbrown.com/fattoriadivibio.html
B&B, SELF CATERING

The hilltop home of the Lacetera family is equidistant to both Perugia and Lake Trasimeno with its small islands. The characteristic stone farmhouse is large enough to accommodate guests within six bedrooms and includes upstairs and downstairs living rooms with fireplace, a large dining room, and the family's private quarters. There are two regular doubles with en suite bathrooms (one in a separate little house just in front) plus two sets of two rooms with one bathroom making a perfect setup for families or two couples. Luminous, comfortable rooms are warmly decorated in peach and soft-yellow tones with traditional country furniture. Excellent light evening meals are prepared by Francesca's mother, Renata, and served in the attractive rustic dining room or out on the patio overlooking the scenic wooded hills. Beautiful views are captured as well from the stone-bordered swimming pool overlooking the valley and castle in Montemelino. Activities include biking, hiking, or horseback riding in the immediate area and you are close to the highlights of both Umbria and Tuscany. Guests easily become friends in the informal and very convivial atmosphere here. *Directions:* From Perugia (12 km) take the highway towards Lake Trasimeno and exit at Corciano. Follow signs for Montemelino and from there continue up through woods on a dirt road for 2 km to the house.

LA LOCANDA DELLE FONTANELLE
Hosts: Angelo & Francesca Lacetera
Vocabolo Fontanelle 25
Montemelino, (PG) 06063, Italy
Tel: (075) 8472674, Fax: (075) 8478287
6 Rooms, Double: €90–€94
Open: all year, Credit cards: all major
Other Languages: good English
www.karenbrown.com/locandafontanelle.html
B&B

La Locanda del Capitano is a tiny inn romantically tucked in the historic center of a medieval, picture-perfect walled village perched on a hilltop overlooking a serene, gentle, Umbrian landscape. The hotel is at heart a restaurant, which has quickly gained well-deserved publicity for the outstanding quality of the kitchen but, luckily for guests, there are also a few bedrooms. The guestrooms are small, but sweetly decorated in an appropriately simple, country style. All have pretty wrought-iron headboards with floral paintings hand-done by a local woman. The choice guestrooms are the two with a small terrace tucked up amongst the ancient tiled rooftops. At the time of our visit, there were eight guestrooms, but plans were under way to add two more suites in the adjacent stone house. La Locanda is the creation of your charming hosts, Carmen and Giancarlo Polito, who decided at the tender ages of 26 and 27 to begin their life together in the countryside and discovered in a newspaper ad the perfect site for their inn, a centuries-old stone house in the idyllic town of Montone. As soon as they saw the house, their hearts were won. Carmen and Giancarlo are wonderful with their guests, and even organize tours for a minimum of seven people into the countryside for truffle hunting during the season. *Directions:* Heading north from Perugia on the E45, take the Montone exit. The hotel is just a block from the town square.

LA LOCANDA DEL CAPITANO
Owners: Carmen & Giancarlo Polito
Via Roma, 7
Montone, (PG) 06014, Italy
Tel: (075) 93 06 521, Fax: (075) 93 06 455
8 Rooms, Double: €120
Closed: Jan & Feb, Credit cards: all major
www.karenbrown.com/capitano.html
HOTEL

In a small pocket of land in the southernmost point of Umbria is the Podere Costa Romana property, immersed in the green hillsides south of ancient Narni. Dynamic hostess Anna Maria left her native Naples for the peace and quiet of the Umbrian hills and meticulously restored the stone 18th-century farmhouse where she now hosts guests within six well-appointed apartments. Rooms have been thoughtfully decorated with antique country furnishings, which harmonize perfectly with the rustic quality of the original farmhouse. Each individual apartment (named for women) can accommodate from two (Giovanna is an adorable love nest) to five guests (Paola has two bedrooms) and is equipped with a kitchenette. Soft-peach and pale-yellow walls highlight exposed stones, beamed ceilings, and brick floors. The large main living room with fireplace and double arches opens out to the surrounding garden and swimming pool overlooking the hills. Travelers can easily reach many lesser-known Umbrian villages as well as the cities and from Orte frequent trains depart for either Rome or Florence. *Directions:* Exit the A1 autostrada at Magliano Sabina and turn right for Otricoli. 8 km after Otricoli turn right at the Narni-Testaccio-Itieli sign and then right again for the Podere Costa Romana.

PODERE COSTA ROMANA
Host: Anna Maria Giordano
S.S. Flaminia, Strada per Itieli
Narni, (TR) 05035, Italy
Tel: (0744) 722495, Fax: (0823) 797118
6 Apartments: €550–€750 weekly, €118–€136 daily
Minimum Nights: 2
Open: all year, Credit cards: none
Other Languages: some English
www.karenbrown.com/romana.html
SELF CATERING

The town of Orvieto, just off the main expressway between Rome and Florence, is one of the most picturesque of all the Umbrian hilltowns. This small city is perched on the top of a hill—an intriguing sight that can be viewed from many kilometers away. Less than a ten-minute drive south of Orvieto is a 12th-century Gothic abbey that has been converted into a hotel where you can stay surrounded by the romantic ruins of yesteryear. Although there is a commercial air to La Badia, the reception is caring and friendly. The manager, Ettore Pelletti, has been with the hotel for over 20 years, as has the chef, so, as you can see, there is a real continuity of management. Although this is not a cozy, small hotel, you are bound to enjoy the setting, the pool, the old-world ambiance, and the food. The dining room is one of the most attractive rooms in the hotel. It has an enormous, high-vaulted stone ceiling, wrought-iron fixtures, heavy wooden beams, eye-catching copper accents, and, at one end, a cavernous fireplace complete with a roasting spit. The standard bedrooms, although not large or with inspired decor, are comfortable and many have a stunning view up to the town of Orvieto. If you want to splurge, ask for one of the romantic suites, which have much prettier furnishings. In the meadows behind the monastery there is a lovely pool. *Directions:* From Orvieto, follow signs for Viterbo. The hotel is 4 km south of Orvieto.

LA BADIA
Owner: Contessa Luisa Fiumi
Manager: Ettore Pelletti
Orvieto, (TR) 05019, Italy
Tel: (0763) 30 19 59, Fax: (0763) 30 53 96
28 Rooms, Double: €190–€250
Restaurant closed Wednesdays
Closed: Jan & Feb, Credit cards: all major
www.karenbrown.com/badia.html
HOTEL

A very high rating goes to the Locanda Rosati on the border of Umbria and Lazio, and just steps away from Tuscany. Giampiero and sister, Alba, with their respective spouses, Luisa and Paolo, sold their cheese production business in Lucca and returned to Orvieto to transform the family farmhouse into a bed and breakfast. The results are splendid and guests, taking priority over the agricultural activity in this instance, are treated with extra-special care. The downstairs common areas include two cozy living rooms with fireplace and a large stone-walled dining room divided by a brick archway leading down to the "tufo" stone cellar. Seven bedrooms upstairs (one with access and bathroom for the handicapped) have been decorated with an animal theme evident in the carvings on bedboards and lamps. Three more bedrooms were added for guests on the top floor with mansard ceilings, leaving the entire home to the bed and breakfast business. Although the house is right on the road, most rooms face the countryside to the back where a large open lawn space leads to the inviting swimming pool. Paolo produces appetizing pastas, soups, and other specialties all written up in a recipe book for guests. *Directions:* Exit from the A1 autostrada at Orvieto and follow signs for Viterbo-Bolsena. Skirt town and continue towards Bolsena for about 8 km on route 71. After a series of sharp curves, the locanda comes up on the right.

LOCANDA ROSATI
Hosts: Rosati family
Localita: Buonviaggio 22
Orvieto, (TR) 05018, Italy
Tel & Fax: (0763) 217314
10 Rooms, Double: €110–€130
Closed: Jan & Feb, Credit cards: MC, VS
Other Languages: good English
www.karenbrown.com/locandarosati.html
B&B

With a rich history dating back to the 16th century, the Hotel Palazzo Piccolomini in the historic center of Orvieto, an incredible, walled city perched atop a high hill, was once home to the wealthy Piccolomini family. At the end of the 1980s the palace was rescued from neglect and after many years of restoration, opened in 1999 as a hotel. In the entrance some of the original architectural features remain, accented by a few pieces of antique furniture, but overall the mood is contemporary. From the reception hall, a flight of steps leads up to a large lounge where the frescoed ceiling again attests to the hotel's glamorous past. However, the room that most portrays the age of the building is the breakfast room in the cellar. It has a giant stone pillar supporting a coved ceiling, an ancient well tucked in a corner, and a carefully preserved medieval stone staircase leading to secret places far below. The standard bedrooms are moderate in size and well equipped in the style of a modern hotel with good lighting, writing desks, satellite TVs, mini-bars, air conditioning, and hairdryers. The hotel sits on a corner facing the small Piazza Ranieri and from here it is a delightful stroll through picturesque little squares to Orvieto's crown jewel, the stunning, not-to-be-missed cathedral. *Directions:* From the A1, exit at Orvieto and follow signs to the center. When the road splits, take the road to the right. Follow signs to the hotel.

HOTEL PALAZZO PICCOLOMINI
Manager: Roberto Mazzolai
Piazza Ranieri, 36
Orvieto, (TR) 05018, Italy
Tel: (0763) 34 17 43 or (0763) 39 10 14
Fax: (0763) 39 10 46
29 Rooms, Double: €120–€138
Open: all year, Credit cards: all major
www.karenbrown.com/piccolomini.html
HOTEL

A convenient stopover while heading either north or south along the main artery—the A1 autostrada—is the Villa Ciconia inn. Located below the historical center of Orvieto, in the newer commercial outskirts, the property maintains its tranquil setting thanks to the fortress of trees protecting the 16th-century stone villa. The first floor includes reception area, breakfast room, and two large high-ceilinged dining rooms. These latter, with their somber gray-stone fireplaces, tapestries, heavy dark-wood beams, and subdued-color frescoes depicting allegorical motifs and landscapes, give the place a medieval castle's air. The 12 air-conditioned bedrooms on the second floor are appointed either in appropriate style, with antique chests and wrought-iron beds, or with more contemporary furnishings (lower rates) and all the amenities of the four-star hotel that this is. Most rooms are quiet and look out onto the 8 acres of woods behind the villa. There are also two enormous beamed sitting rooms on this floor for guests and a beautiful new swimming pool. The restaurant has a solid reputation for creating excellent Umbrian specialties. Manager Anna Glena Petrangeli is always on hand to assist guests. *Directions:* Exiting from the autostrada, turn right towards Orvieto and right again where marked Arezzo, Perugia, passing under the tollway. The Ciconia is just after the river on the left-hand side of the road.

❄ ☕ ⚒ 📇 ☎ ⛾ P ⑂ ≈ 🖼 ⌂ 🚶 🏇 🍇

VILLA CICONIA   New
Owners: Petrangeli family
Via dei Tigli 69
Orvieto, (TR) 05019, Italy
Tel: (0763) 305582, Fax: (0763) 302077
12 Rooms, Double: €130–€155
Restaurant closed Mondays
Open: all year, Credit cards: all major
www.karenbrown.com/villaciconia.html
HOTEL

Claudia Spatola does a great job of single-handedly running a bed and breakfast in the complex of stone houses known as Borgo Spante, which dates back to the 15th century and has been in her family since 1752. Consisting of a main villa, connecting farmers' houses, chapel, barns, swimming pool, and garden, it is isolated in 500 acres of woods and hills, yet is located only 16 kilometers from Orvieto and not far from Assisi, Todi, and Perugia. Guests stay in a combination of rooms or apartments in the former farmers' quarters with their irregular-sized rooms, sloping worn-brick floors, and rustic country furnishings—very charming in its way. Authentic Umbrian meals, prepared by local women, are served in the dining room with long wooden tables and fireplace. A larger dining area has been added in the former barn, along with four additional mini-apartments, simply and characteristically decorated. Memorable evenings are spent in the garden or poolside conversing with other guests or listening to an impromptu concert or lecture. *Directions:* From the A1 autostrada exit at Orvieto and follow signs for Arezzo on route 71. After 7 km, turn right at Morrano and proceed for 12 km to the sign for Spante. Turn left and continue for 2 km.

BORGO SPANTE
Host: Claudia Spatola
Ospedaletto, (TR) 05010, Italy
Tel: (075) 8709134, Fax: (075) 8709201
Cellphone: (347) 0023581
5 Rooms, Double: €130 includes breakfast & dinner
8 Apartments: €365 (2 people)
Minimum Nights: 3, Open: all year, Credit cards: none
Other Languages: some English, French
www.karenbrown.com/borgospante.html
B&B, SELF CATERING

With her children grown and traveling around the world, Christine, an expatriate from England, decided to offer hospitality to travelers in her country home. Situated an hour north of Rome by train or car, the pretty countryside home made of typical local tufo brick is a short distance from the ancient village of Otricoli with its ancient Roman origins. It is one of many villages centered in the Tiber river valley, historically an important area for trade and commerce with Rome. A long wing off the main house, reserved for guests, offers three beamed bedrooms decorated with country furniture and overlooking the garden and hills. An order-as-you-like breakfast is served either in the kitchen or out on the patio. The cozy living room with open fireplace invites guests to relax after a day in the city. Being at the edge of Umbria and Lazio, she can suggest a myriad of local itineraries and destinations, known and not so well known, as well as town festivals throughout the region and concentrated in the months of May and June. This is a very informal, at-home accommodation just 7 kilometers from the main Rome-Florence autostrada. *Directions:* Exit at Magliano Sabina and turn left for Otricoli-Terni. Turn off for Otricoli and take the first road to the right—Strada Crepafico. Gates to Casa Spence are on the corner.

CASA SPENCE
Host: Christine Spence
Strada Crepafico 29, Otricoli, (TR) 05030, Italy
Tel & Fax: (0744) 719758
Cellphone: (329) 0832886
3 Rooms, Double: €75–€80
Open: all year, Credit cards: none
Other Languages: fluent English
www.karenbrown.com/casaspence.html
B&B

A truly classic hotel with old-world charm, the 120-year-old Brufani Palace was once two hotels sitting back to back in the main piazza of Perugia's historic center. Joined together like Siamese twins, the hotel has been recently restored to its original splendor with, of course, double of everything, including many spacious sitting rooms, two bars, a restaurant, and enormous formal breakfast room. Unlike many newly restored accommodation, obvious effort has been made to retain its old-fashioned flavor while updating amenities and maintaining a five-star level. Carpeted bedrooms are spacious and elegantly appointed with antiques, gilded mirrors, and marble bathrooms, most with lovely views over historic Perugia or the Umbrian countryside. Guests can choose from standard doubles, suites and junior suites with high ceilings, or cozy beamed mansard rooms. All guests can enjoy the full 360-degree views from the highest point in the city, the Brufani's rooftop terrace. Another unique feature of this hotel is the swimming pool down in the original cantinas with brick vaulted ceilings. Etruscan relics were found while digging and now the glass-bottom pool proudly displays this discovery! Step out of the hotel and you are right on the main street of charming Perugia, filled with shops, restaurants, and medieval monuments. *Directions:* Follow hotel signs up to the historic center to the Piazza Italia. Hotel staff will take care of parking.

HOTEL BRUFANI PALACE
Manager: Vittorio Morelli
Piazza Italia, 12, Perugia, (PG) 06100, Italy
Tel: (075) 57 32 541, Fax: (075) 57 20 210
94 Rooms, Double: €320–€850*
*Breakfast not included: €23, 10% tax not included
Open: all year, Credit cards: all major
www.karenbrown.com/brufani.html
HOTEL

Just north of Spoleto is the tiny 14th-century village of Poreta and farther up on the hillside are the remains of the walls of the castle that once dominated the valley. It is here that a group of friends, Luca, Bianca, and American Pam being the omnipresent, genial hosts, restored what was left of the ancient castle and transformed it into a country bed and breakfast. Their idea was to provide not only accommodation but also a special place offering a variety of cultural events such as classical concerts, art shows, poetry reading, and dinners with particular local food themes. The cluster of stone houses where the eight bedrooms are located includes a church restored in the baroque period with original frescoes and faux-marble borders. The small restaurant is made up of two cozy rooms with beamed ceilings, fireplace, and cheery yellow walls. A clean and pleasant country style pervades the bedrooms with their soothingly soft beige tones and occasional country antiques. They need no elaborate paintings for decoration as the views out the windows suffice. The buildings are united by an expansive brick terrace overlooking olive groves and sweeping views of the valley—a wonderful spot for watching the spectacular sunsets while enjoying a pre-dinner drink. *Directions:* From the N3 Spoleto-Perugia road turn right after 8 km at Poreta and follow signs up to the castle.

IL CASTELLO DI PORETA
Host: Luca Saint Amour di Chanaz
Pam Moskow & Bianca Lauteri
Localita: Poreta, Poreta–Spoleto, (PG) 06049, Italy
Tel: (0743) 275810, Fax: (0743) 270175
8 Rooms, Double: €100–€115
Open: all year, Credit cards: all major
Other Languages: good English
www.karenbrown.com/poreta.html
B&B

Sarah Townsend, artist, painter, decorator, landscape designer, and overall connoisseur of life's best offerings, can only be described as the Renaissance woman. She has astounded everyone with the magnificent restoration project of Palazzo Terranova, her greatest challenge after selling her previous bed and breakfast, Il Bacchino. Accessed by a steep, winding road, the 18th-century rectangular palazzo, which dominates the northern Tiber valley and seemingly all of Umbria, is softened by surrounding terraced gardens filled with roses, lavender, cascading geraniums, and magnolia trees. The stylish home is a showplace for the family's own precious heirlooms and paintings brought over from England, combined with the best artisans' creations that Umbria has to offer. Each masterpiece of a bedroom, with its stenciled and painted designs, holds some enchanting feature and, just as in the creation of a painting, utmost attention has been given to color scheme, composition, and lighting. The palatial Traviata suite, on a floor of its own, off one of the many sitting rooms open to guests, has it all—a king-sized wrought-iron poster bed, custom lace linens, solid marble bath, and stunning views. Delightful staff is on hand to satisfy any whim. If you cannot get a room, do reserve a meal prepared by Honor Townsend, their excellent chef. *Directions:* Ask the hotel to send you detailed directions.

PALAZZO TERRANOVA
Owners: Sarah & Johnny Townsend
Localita: Ronti nr Citta di Castello
Morra, Ronti, (PG) 06010, Italy
Tel: (075) 85 70 083, Fax: (075) 85 70 014
12 Rooms, Double: €350–€795
Open: all year, Credit cards: all major
www.karenbrown.com/terranova.html
HOTEL

The sleepy village of Solomeo, located between Perugia and Lake Trasimeno, had been almost completely abandoned until a well-known cashmere company bought and restored most of the town to its original charm, using the individual houses and apartments for offices and workshops. Pier Luigi Cavicchi, an import/export consultant, and his friendly wife Donatella (who runs the family's not-so-distant farm) inherited a turn-of-the-last-century villa, located right in the heart of town. Pier Luigi (who had spent many happy summers at the villa) and his wife thoroughly renovated the property and opened it as an inn. Their wish was to maintain the original character of the beloved residence while adding all possible amenities (including air conditioning). The result is a compact and quaint hotel that has it all. The 12 English-style country bedrooms are named after flowers and this theme is followed through in stenciled borders, bedspread fabrics, and bathrooms. Preserved stencil work on walls and ceilings in the entrance, tea room, and upstairs sitting room were done by the same artist who decorated the town's church across the street. The bright breakfast room downstairs has stone walls and beams and leads to terraces overlooking the countryside where a garden, swimming pool, exercise room with sauna and solarium, meeting room, and four garden bedrooms are situated. In the immediate area are a golf club and horseback-riding facilities.

LOCANDA SOLOMEO
Owners: Pier Luigi & Donatella Cavicchi
Piazza Carlo Alberto dalla Chiesa, 1
Solomeo, (PG) 06070, Italy
Tel: (075) 52 93 119, Fax: (075) 52 94 090
12 Rooms, Double: €100–€125
Restaurant by reservation only
Open: all year, Credit cards: all major
www.karenbrown.com/locandasolomeo.html
HOTEL

As you twist up the steep, narrow road from Spoleto toward Monteluco, you will see on your left an appealing, ochre-colored villa. The setting looks so fabulous that you will hope this is your hotel. It is, and you won't be disappointed. The Eremo delle Grazie is an astounding property—truly a living museum, with history simply oozing from every nook and cranny. The property has been the home of the Lalli family for many years, but its roots hark back to the 5th century when a small grotto where religious hermits came to live occupied the site. The grotto still exists, but now serves as a wine cellar behind the bar. From its humble beginnings the importance of this grotto grew, becoming so well known that one of Italy's important cardinals, Camillo Cybo, lived here (his bedroom is now one of the guestrooms). The cardinal enjoyed his comfort so instead of residing in the small damp grotto, he slept in a lovely bedroom, which he had painted to look like a cave. One of my favorite places in Eremo delle Grazie is the tiny, incredibly beautiful, vaulted chapel with beautifully preserved 15th-century paintings of the life of Mary. Another favorite is the splendid terrace with a sweeping view of the glorious Umbrian landscape. According to Signor Lalli, Michelangelo was once a guest here. In his letter to Vasari, Michelangelo wrote that he left part of his heart at Eremo delle Grazie—as you will, too.

EREMO DELLE GRAZIE
Owner: Professor Pio Lalli
Spoleto, Monteluco, (PG) 06049, Italy
Tel: (0743) 49 624, Fax: (0743) 49 650
11 Rooms, Double: €207–€362
Restaurant and Bar open daily during high season
Open: all year, Credit cards: all major
www.karenbrown.com/eremodellegrazie.html
HOTEL

The walled hill town of Spoleto is a must on any trip to Umbria. What Spoleto has that is so outstanding is its Bridge of Towers (Ponte delle Torri), an absolutely awesome feat of engineering. Built in the 13th century on the foundations of an old Roman aqueduct, this bridge, spanning a vast crevasse, is supported by ten Gothic arches that soar into the sky. The Hotel Gattapone (a mustard-yellow building with dark-green shutters) is built into the hillside and provides a box-seat location to admire this architectural masterpiece. As you enter, there is a cozy reception area. To the left is a bright, sunny lounge with modern black-leather sofas, a long black-leather bar, very pretty deep-blue walls, large pots of green plants, an antique grandfather clock, and, best of all, an entire wall of glass which provides a bird's-eye view of the bridge. To the right of the reception area, steps sweep down to another bar and lounge where breakfast is served. This room is even more starkly modern, with deep-red wall coverings. The newer wing of the hotel houses the superior-category bedrooms, each with a sitting area and large view windows. In the original section of the hotel the bedrooms are smaller, but also very attractive and every one has a view. Although most of the hotels in this guide have more of an antique ambiance, the Gattapone is highly recommended—a special hotel offering great warmth of welcome and superb vistas.

HOTEL GATTAPONE
Owner: Dr. Pier Hanke Giulio
Via del Ponte, 6
Spoleto, (PG) 06049, Italy
Tel: (0743) 22 34 47, Fax: (0743) 22 34 48
15 Rooms, Double: €140–€230
Open: all year
Credit cards: all major
www.karenbrown.com/hotelgattapone.html
HOTEL

Le Logge di Silvignano, a stunning castle of creamy-beige stone, embraces one side of a tiny 12th-century village with a population of about 85 people tucked high in the hills north of Spoleto. It is not surprising to learn the building was originally a strategic lookout to guard against enemy attack since the setting is breathtaking, with a sweeping view of the narrow valley far below. Although termed a "castle" the structure is not in the least foreboding, but rather a splendid edifice with a handsome, open, arched gallery supported by ornately carved, octagonal pillars stretching across the front. There are six beautiful, individually decorated suites, all extremely attractive with medieval stone floors accenting handsome furniture which is either antique or handcrafted locally of wood or wrought iron. The fine bed linens and fabrics are woven locally from the Montefalco looms. A huge terrace, magically transformed into a romantic, manicured garden enhanced by fragrant, colorful roses, spreads in front of the castle to the edge of the bluff. Although Le Logge would be a winner by any standards, it is the genuine warmth and charm of your lovely hosts that make a stay here so outstanding. For dinner, guests can prepare a light meal in their own kitchenette or dine in a local restaurant. The hotel has a beautiful pool with views of the valley and a club house where guests can relax. *Directions:* Ask for detailed driving instructions when you make reservations.

LE LOGGE DI SILVIGNANO
Owners: Diana & Alberto Araimo
Frazione Silvignano, 14, Spoleto, (PG) 06049, Italy
Tel: (0743) 27 40 98, Fax: (0473) 27 05 18
Cellphone: (347) 2221869
6 Rooms, Double: €180–€250
Closed: Nov 10 to Mar 31, Credit cards: all major
Abitare la Storia
www.karenbrown.com/silvignano.html
HOTEL

The town of Spoleto has gained international fame thanks to the July Due Mondi festival, a month-long series of cultural events including ballet, theater, opera, and concerts with renowned artists, which attracts a worldwide audience. Accommodations are reserved from one year to the next. For the rest of the year, however, Spoleto holds its own along with nearby Assisi, Spello, Todi, and Perugia as an enchanting medieval stone town, rich in its historical past. The 14th-century Palazzo Dragoni, situated on a quiet little street in the heart of the town near the famous cathedral, was completely renovated by the Diotallevi family and offers charming accommodation within 15 bedrooms. Son Roberto manages the bed and breakfast while his parents reside in a section of the palazzo. The spacious bedrooms (larger ones are considered suites) are spread out among the three floors, reached by elevator, and have new bathrooms and many modern amenities including air conditioning. Everything possible has been done to maintain the original architecture and ambiance of a private home, with vaulted and frescoed high ceilings, antique furnishings, Oriental carpets, and Murano chandeliers. The real treat is breakfast served in the glassed-in loggia, taking in splendid views of the tiled rooftops and bell tower of the Duomo. *Directions:* Follow signs for the center of Spoleto, by way of Via P. Bunilli, passing the football field (campo sportivo). Follow white signs for the hotel.

PALAZZO DRAGONI
Hosts: Roberto Diotallevi family
Via del Duomo 13
Spoleto, (PG) 06049, Italy
Tel: (0743) 222220, Fax: (0743) 222225
15 Rooms, Double: €119–€145
Open: all year, Credit cards: MC, VS
Other Languages: some English
www.karenbrown.com/dragoni.html
HOTEL

Spoleto is always a favorite with tourists, not only during the music festival (end of June until mid-July), but throughout the year. Due to its popularity, there used to be a shortage of charming places to stay within the walled city but happily that problem was solved with the opening of the Hotel San Luca in 1995. The family-owned San Luca is a splendid small hotel—very polished, very sophisticated, yet exuding great personal warmth and friendliness. Built within a 19th-century tannery, the hotel (which is painted yellow and has a traditional red-tiled roof) only hints at its past. The renovation has been so extensive that much of what you see today is of new construction, but the ambiance is old world. From the moment you enter, there is a fresh, luminous atmosphere with pastel walls reflecting light streaming in through large arched windows opening onto a central courtyard. The reception lounge is especially appealing, with comfortable chairs upholstered in cheerful peach fabric grouped around a large fireplace and a few choice antiques adding greatly to the homelike feeling. A pair of canaries in an antique birdcage repeats the color scheme. The spacious, pastel-colored, completely soundproofed guestrooms are all equally attractive and well equipped with lots of closets, excellent lighting, and large, exceptionally modern bathrooms. And the surprise is that the price for such high quality is amazingly low.

HOTEL SAN LUCA
Manager: Daniela Zuccari
Via Interna delle Mura, 21
Spoleto, (PG) 06049, Italy
Tel: (0743) 22 33 99, Fax: (0743) 22 38 00
35 Rooms, Double: €150–€300
Open: all year
Credit cards: all major
www.karenbrown.com/hotelsanluca.html
HOTEL

Italy abounds with romantic places to stay, but none can surpass the outstanding beauty of the Villa Milani. This stunning property, on a hill overlooking Spoleto, just about has it all: enchanting architecture, breathtaking 360-degree view, splendid decor, gorgeous antiques, and owners who shower their guests with kindness. The villa was built in 1880 by one of Rome's most famous architects, Giovanni Battista Milani, the great-grandfather of your hostess Giovanna Milani Capobianchi. Milani obviously poured both his talent and heart into his countryside retreat, embellishing his home with splendid ceilings, fireplaces, columns, marble statues, romantic gardens, and ancient Roman artifacts. The result is splendid. The current owners lived for many years in Rome then changed their lifestyle completely and moved to Spoleto, where they tenderly restored the home to its original splendor, adding beautiful bathrooms to each bedroom and a fantastic pool, perched on a terrace looking out to the soft wooded hills of Umbria. Giovanna must have inherited some of her grandfather's talent, for she has decorated each room to perfection. The smallest room is also the most romantic, located in the tower with windows on four sides. *Directions:* Coming from the north on S.S.3, turn right at the second exit after the Spoleto tunnel (opposite the Monteluco road). At the first intersection turn left and go uphill following signs to the villa.

VILLA MILANI
Owners: Giovanna & Luigi Capobianchi
Localita Colle Attivoli, 4
Spoleto, (PG) 06049, Italy
Tel: (0743) 22 50 56, Fax: (0743) 49 824
11 Rooms, Double: €190–€640
Meals for hotel guests
Open: all year, Credit cards: all major
www.karenbrown.com/villamilani.html
HOTEL

The well-preserved medieval village of Stroncone sits on the southernmost edge of Umbria bordering Lazio, 7 kilometers from Terni. It is here that Cristiana from Genoa and her husband, Massimiliano, whose parents were originally from this area, bought and restored an ancient building in the stone village and opened a charming bed and breakfast. The eight bedrooms are divided among the top three floors of the medieval building, which centuries ago was once the police station. The old wooden doors of the cells remain intact and are part of the small reception and breakfast room where a buffet table holds breads and cakes each morning. Each bedroom is unique in size and pastel color scheme, with stenciled borders, new bathrooms, and variations according to the original architecture, with either brick-vaulted or wood-beamed ceilings. A mansard bedroom on the top floor offers privacy and rooftop views over the village, besides being the only bedroom with air conditioning (the others remain naturally cool with the thick stone walls). The hosts organize a week-long painting course with daily excursions taking advantage of the scenic surrounding landscapes and villages. The Brunellis have just opened an agritourism business with apartments near Orvieto. *Directions:* Stroncone is 9 km directly south of Terni. The bed and breakfast is on Via del Sacramento, the main street of the village.

LA PORTA DEL TEMPO
Hosts: Cristiana & Massimiliano Brunelli
Via del Sacramento 2, Stroncone, (TR) 05039, Italy
Tel: (0744) 608190, Fax: (0744) 609034
Cellphone: (333) 3742957
8 Rooms, Double: €83–€125
Apartments: €78–€105 daily
Minimum Nights: 2, Open: all year
Credit cards: all major, Good English
www.karenbrown.com/portadeltempo.html
B&B, SELF CATERING

In order to stand out among the crowd of recently opened bed and breakfasts in Italy, many hosts have begun to specialize according to their own personal interests. This is true for enthusiastic and friendly hosts, Alberto and his Brazilian wife Luzia, who opened a gourmet vegetarian bed and breakfast on their isolated 27-acre farm up on a mountain ridge between Perugia and Lake Trasimeno, the first of its kind in Umbria. A 4-kilometer gravel road ends at the panoramic property with its main house, two stone guesthouses, and cultural center where courses on yoga and meditation and ethnic music concerts are held. An informal ambiance prevails and the total respect for nature and tranquillity is evident among guests who take hikes in the surrounding woods or read poolside, enjoying both sunrise and sunset over the opposite valleys. The ten neat rooms with independent outside entrances are comfortably decorated with teakwood beds and armoires and the paintings of a reputed artist. The sun-filled dining room is where guests convene for Luzia's and Alberto's famed fare based on strictly organic produce from the farm. So unique is this bed and breakfast that the BBC did a special documentary on it, and it received the Best Hotel Award 2002. *Directions:* From Perugia follow route 220 for approximately 22 km and turn right before Tavernelle at Colle San Paolo.

COUNTRY HOUSE MONTALI
Hosts: Luzia & Alberto Musacchio
Via Montali 23
Tavernelle di Panicale, (PG) 06068, Italy
Tel: (075) 8350680, Fax: (075) 8350144
10 Rooms, Double: €170–€200*
*Includes breakfast & dinner
Minimum Nights: 3, Open: Mar to Oct
Credit cards: MC, VS, Other Languages: good English
www.karenbrown.com/montali.html
B&B

Since 1830, the remote 12th-century castle and 4,000-acre farm of Titignano have belonged to the noble Corsini family who now offer travelers 15 guestrooms in the main house, a swimming pool, and three apartments in what was originally the farmer's quarters. They are pleasantly decorated with scattered country antiques. Management is in the hands of Monica and Francesca, delightful hostesses who take care of everything from looking after guests to cooking and serving. Meals are shared at a long table in one of the castle's graciously neglected rooms with an enormous gray-stone fireplace sporting the family coat of arms, and lofty ceilings made of the stamped terra-cotta blocks typical of Umbria. Off the dining hall are the spacious bedrooms, each with modernized pink travertine bathrooms and decorated eclectically with unrefined antiques and wrought-iron beds. They have a worn charm about them. Common areas include a living room with bright floral sofas around a fireplace, a game and TV room for children, and a large terrace with a breathtaking, sweeping view covering three regions. Bikes are available for touring the regional park of the River Tiber (part of the property). *Directions:* Leave the Roma-Florence A1 autostrada at Orvieto. Follow signs for Arezzo, turning on route 79 for Prodo. Follow the long winding road for 26 km past Prodo to Titignano. (30 km from Orvieto.)

FATTORIA TITIGNANO
Hosts: Monica Gori & Francesca Marchetti
Localita: Titignano 7
Titignano, (TR) 05010, Italy
Tel: (0763) 308000 or 308022, Fax: (0763) 308002
15 Rooms, Double: €90
Minimum Nights: 2
Open: all year, Credit cards: MC, VS
Other Languages: some English, French
www.karenbrown.com/titignano.html
B&B

Crowning the top of a small hill near the enchanting walled village of Todi (which you can see in the distance), the Relais Todini has a breathtaking, 360-degree view of wooded hills, soft valleys, manicured fields, vineyards, and tiny villages. You will be captivated at first sight of this charming, 14th-century stone hotel with architectural roots going back to the Etruscan-Roman period. Although built of rustic, tan-colored stone, there is nothing rustic about this hotel. From the moment you walk through the manicured gardens and into the beautiful frescoed lobby, you are surrounded by elegance and luxury. You register at an intimate table rather than a hotel-like counter before being shown to your room. All the guestrooms are beautifully decorated and the suites are especially opulent, with fine antique furniture and lush fabrics. The public rooms are also handsomely furnished, particularly the dining room with its tall-back chairs upholstered in tapestry and charming chandeliers embellished with clusters of grapes. One wall has windows of glass that open out to a terrace and beyond to a large swimming pool. On the estate tennis, biking, walking, swimming and a gorgeous health and body center with Turkish baths are just a few of the options available to guests. *Directions:* From Rome, take the A1 north, exit at Orte. Follow E45 toward Perugia. Exit at Casigliano-Collevalenza and follow signs toward Todi. Turn left Rosceto Scalo to the hotel.

RELAIS TODINI
Manager: Clementi Paolo
Collevalenza, Todi, (PG) 06050, Italy
Tel: (075) 88 75 21, Fax: (075) 88 71 82
12 Rooms, Double: €175–€240
Restaurant open Thu to Sun
Open: all year, Credit cards: all major
www.karenbrown.com/todini.html
HOTEL

Fortunate guests at the fascinating Tenuta di Canonica are assured of an unforgettable stay. Maria and Daniele, with son Michelangelo, have transformed a massive stone tower with foundation dating to the ancient Roman period and adjoining century-old house into a bed and breakfast of dreams. The spacious living room with stone fireplace and vaulted ceiling is reached down a few stairs from the entryway and looks out over the stunning valley down to Lake Corbara. Outstanding medieval architectural features such as stone walls, brick floors, and high, beamed ceilings have been enhanced by Provence-inspired colors. Stairs lead up to the library and bedrooms are divided between the three-story tower and house, respecting the epoch of each: bathrooms in the medieval quarters have gray stone tiles and travertine, while the others have white tile alternating with terra-cotta pieces. Each tastefully decorated, antique-filled room has some attractive feature, whether it be the more suite-like arrangements with sitting area or the smaller corner rooms with head-spinning views over hills and up to Todi. Common areas include a dining room and large swimming pool with 360-degree views. Cooking classes with a Cordon Bleu cook are also arranged. *Directions:* From Todi take the road for Orvieto, turning right at the sign for Prado/Titignano. After 2 km turn left for Cordigliano and follow the signpost for Tenuta di Canonica to the end of the road (1 km).

TENUTA DI CANONICA
Hosts: Maria & Daniele Fano
Localita: Canonica, Todi, (PG) 06059, Italy
Tel: (075) 8947545, Fax: (075) 8947581
Cellphone: (335) 369492
11 Rooms, Double: €130–€220
2 Apartments €800– €950 weekly
Closed: Dec 1 to Mar 1, Credit cards: MC, VS
Other Languages: good English
www.karenbrown.com/canonicatodi.html
B&B, SELF CATERING

The elegant Le Tre Vaselle is located in Torgiano, a small wine village not far from Assisi. The interior reflects the ambiance of a graceful country manor with sophisticated furnishings and exquisite taste displayed in every detail. The hotel belongs to the Lungarotti family who are famous for their production of superb wines and who own all of the vineyards surrounding Torgiano for as far as the eye can see. Excellent meals, accompanied by fine Lungarotti wines, are served in the beautiful dining room. The guestrooms are attractively decorated and offer every amenity of a deluxe hotel. Le Tre Vaselle also has outstanding conference rooms furnished in antiques with adjacent dining rooms. The Lungarotti family has thought of everything—to keep the wives happy while their husbands are in meetings, cooking classes are sometimes offered. Other diversions include an outdoor swimming pool, an indoor pool with whirlpool and jet-tech swimming, a sauna, a gym, and even a small outdoor amphitheater. The Lungarottis also have a private wine museum that would be a masterpiece anywhere in the world. Not only do they have an incredible and comprehensive collection of anything pertaining to wine throughout the ages, but the display is a work of art. If you are interested in the production of wine, the museum alone would be worth a detour to Le Tre Vaselle. *Directions:* The hotel is well marked in the center of town.

LE TRE VASELLE
Owners: Lungarotti family
Via Garibaldi, 48
Torgiano, (PG) 06089, Italy
Tel: (075) 98 80 447, Fax: (075) 98 80 214
61 Rooms, Double: €200–€270
Open: all year
Credit cards: all major
www.karenbrown.com/letrevaselle.html
HOTEL

Just off the busy road that connects the major towns of Umbria—Perugia, Assisi, Spoleto, and Todi—is the elegant country house Giulia, which has been in the Petrucci family since its 14th-century origins. Later additions were built on to the main stone villa, one of which Signora Caterina has opened up to guests. Time seems to have stood still in the six bedrooms, all but one with en suite bathroom, and filled with lovely antique wrought-iron beds, armoires, and period paintings. They are divided among two floors, accessed by a steep stone staircase, the largest having a ceiling fresco depicting the local landscape. Another room with handicapped facilities has been added on the ground floor. Breakfast is served either in the chandeliered dining room upstairs, with Oriental carpets, lace curtains, and a large fireplace, or under the oak trees in the front garden during the warmer months. Part of the barn has been converted into two independent units for up to four persons, including a fully equipped kitchenette. Although the large swimming pool overlooks a rather barren field and the distant main road, it is a welcome respite after a full day of touring, which guests do a lot of from this strategically convenient location. *Directions:* Just off the Perugia-Spoleto route 75 between Trevi and Campello.

CASA GIULIA
Host: Caterina Alessandrini Petrucci
Via Corciano, 1, Trevi, (PG) 06039, Italy
Tel: (0742) 78257, Fax: (0742) 381632
Cellphone: (348) 360 4619
7 Rooms, Double: €80–€101
2 Apartments: €52–€104 daily
Minimum Nights: 3 in Jul & Aug, Open: all year
Credit cards: all major, Some English, French
www.karenbrown.com/casagiulia.html
B&B, SELF CATERING

When the Marti family from Rome came across the abandoned castle of Montegualandro 20 years ago, it was love at first sight—only pure passion could have driven them to tackle such an overwhelming project as the entire restoration of the property following original plans. A winding dirt road (1.5 kilometers) leads up to the gates of the walled 9th-century castle. As you enter into the courtyard, the main building and family residence lies to the left and immediately to the right is a cluster of stone dwellings, originally farmers' quarters, with small tower, stable, pottery kiln, dove house, and private chapel. There are four rustic guest apartments, cleverly incorporating all original architectural features. All different, each has a living area with fireplace, very basic kitchen facilities, and bathroom, and is furnished with country-style antiques. A walk up in the turreted walls gives a glimpse of the spectacular view out over olive groves to the lake. An internet point has been set up in the newly restored library. The Martis take special interest in guests' needs, providing a breakfast basket upon arrival, and can also suggest easy day trips. Cortona is just 10 kilometers away. *Directions:* Montegualandro is marked on most maps. Leave the A1-Perugia highway at Tuoro. Take the road 75 bis towards Cortona and Arezzo. After 3 km, at km sign 44,700, follow the signs up to the castle or call from town.

CASTELLO DI MONTEGUALANDRO
Hosts: Franca & Claudio Marti
Via di Montegualandro 1
Tuoro Sul Trasimeno, (PG) 06069, Italy
Tel & Fax: (075) 8230267
Cellphone: (335) 6579378
4 Apartments: €600–€700 weekly
Minimum Nights: 3, Open: all year, Credit cards: none
Other Languages: good English
www.karenbrown.com/castellodimontegualandro.html
SELF CATERING

The Villa di Piazzano is a enchanting inn with all the ingredients to make it very special: an historic villa, a lovely landscape, a convenient location, beautiful decor, pretty antiques, and, best of all, the heart-felt hospitality of the Wimpole family who pamper guests and welcome them like friends. As their surname suggests, your hosts are not all Italian-born. Damien Wimpole, an Australian, met his Italian wife, Adriana, in Rome. After their marriage, they traveled extensively throughout the world and, as a result, their charming daughter, Alessandra, is fluent in several languages. When searching for a perfect property to convert to a small hotel, they discovered the stunning but long-neglected Villa di Piazzano, one of the oldest villas in Umbria. The task to bring the property back to its original splendor was awesome, but well worth the effort. Today the delightful villa, set amidst romantic gardens, is a jewel—the interior decorator-perfect with handsome fabrics and many antiques. Everything has been thought of to make a stay here special, including a large swimming pool tucked in the garden. The villa is officially in Umbria, but part of the property is in Tuscany, making it a great choice for those who want a base for exploring both areas. *Directions:* Totally ignore the name of the town, Tuoro Sul Trasimeno—although it is the official address, it is at least 20 km away. In reality the villa is 5 km southeast of Cortona. Ask for detailed driving instructions.

VILLA DI PIAZZANO
Owners: Wimpole family
Località: Piazzano, Cortona
Tuoro Sul Trasimeno, (PG) 06069, Italy
Tel: (075) 82 62 26, Fax: (075) 82 63 36
17 Rooms, Double: €185–€275
Closed: Dec to Mar, Credit cards: all major
Abitare la Storia
www.karenbrown.com/villapiazzano.html
HOTEL

Index

KAREN BROWN wrote her first travel guide in 1976. Her personalized travel series has grown to 17 titles, which Karen and her small staff work diligently to keep updated. Karen, lives in Moss Beach, a small town on the coast south of San Francisco. Karen, and her husband Rick, settled here in 1991 when they opened Seal Cove Inn.

JUNE EVELEIGH BROWN hails from Sheffield, England and lived in Zambia and Canada before moving to northern California where she lives in San Mateo with her husband, Tony, their daughter Clare, their two German Shepherds, and a Siamese cat.

NICOLE FRANCHINI was born in Chicago and raised in a bilingual family, her father being Italian. She received a B.A. degree in languages from William Smith College and the Sorbonne, Paris, and has been residing in Italy for many years. Currently living in the countryside of Sabina near Rome with husband, Carlo, and daughters, Livia and Sabina, she runs her own travel consulting business, Hidden Treasures of Italy, which organizes personalized group and individual itineraries. *www.htitaly.com*

CLARE BROWN was a travel consultant for many years. The focus of her job remains unchanged, but now her expertise is available to a larger audience—the readers of her daughter Karen's travel guides. When Clare and her husband, Bill, are not traveling, they live either in Hillsborough, California, or at their home in Vail, Colorado.

ELISABETTA FRANCHINI, the artist responsible for many of the illustrations in this guide lives in Chicago with her husband, Chris, and their two young children, where she paints predominantly European landscapes and architectural scenes. A Smith College graduate in Art History and French Literature, Elisabetta has exhibited extensively in the past 20 years. *www.elisabettafranchini.com.*

BARBARA MACLURCAN TAPP, the talented artist who produces all of the hotel sketches and delightful illustrations in this guide, was raised in Sydney, Australia where she studied interior design. Although Barbara continues with architectural rendering and watercolor painting, she devotes much of her time to illustrating the Karen Brown guides. Barbara lives in Kensington, California, with her husband, Richard, and is Mum to Jono, Alex and Georgia.

JANN POLLARD, the artist of the cover painting has studied art since childhood, and is well known for her outstanding impressionistic-style watercolors. Jann's original paintings are represented through The Gallery, Burlingame, CA, *www.thegalleryart.net* or 650-347-9392. Fine-art giclée prints her paintings are also available at *www.karenbrown.com.*

Watch for a New Thriller Series
Featuring "Karen Brown"
As Travel Writer & Undercover Sleuth

Author M. Diane Vogt, the creator of the critically acclaimed and popular Judge Wilhelmina Carson legal suspense novels, is writing a new series featuring the exploits of "Karen Brown".

Combine the heroic salvage consultant Travis McGee – from John D. MacDonald's hugely successful Ft. Lauderdale mystery/thriller series – with *Under the Tuscan Sun's* Frances Mayes, and that's Karen Brown, clandestine recovery specialist and world renowned travel writer.

Based on actual places and destinations as featured in Karen Brown's guides, join Karen in her travels as by day she inspects charming hotels, and by night she dabbles in intrigue and defeats the world of killers, scoundrels, and scam artists.

To learn more, visit **www.karenbrown.com/thriller/**